HEART HEALTHY COOKBOOK FOR BEGINNERS 2023

The Easiest Guide for Heart Health with 2000 Days of Low-Sodium, Low-Fat Recipes with 30 Days Meal Plan | Heart Healthy Recipes, Low Cholesterol Cookbook, Low Carb Cookbook

SCOTT CURREY

Introduction

In today's fast-paced world, it's easy to neglect our heart health amidst the chaos of daily life. But fear not! The Heart Healthy Cookbook for Beginners 2023 is here to guide you on a transformative journey toward a healthier heart and a more vibrant life.

Imagine a life where you effortlessly create meals that not only tantalize your palate but also promote optimal heart health. Say goodbye to the confusion and frustration of not knowing what to cook or how to make your meals both nutritious and delicious. This book is your roadmap to a heart-healthy kitchen, where you'll find practical solutions to your culinary dilemmas.

Authored by a renowned expert in heart health, this book is your trusted companion on your wellness journey. With years of experience and a passion for empowering individuals to take charge of their heart health, the author brings invaluable expertise to every page. You can rest assured that you are in capable hands, receiving guidance from someone who truly understands your challenges.

So, let's embark on this culinary adventure together! In Chapter 1, we will dive deep into the fundamentals of heart-healthy cooking, equipping you with essential knowledge and techniques to make informed choices in the kitchen. Get ready to explore a world of flavorful ingredients, nourishing recipes, and a newfound understanding of how your diet impacts your heart health.

Get ready to take the first step towards a healthier heart and a happier you. Turn the page, and let the transformation begin.

Table of Contents

Chapter 1

The Basic Principles of the Heart-Healthy Diet

Section 1:

What is Meant by Eating Healthy and Caring for the Heart?

Eating for Heart Health:

A heart-healthy diet emphasizes consuming nutrient-dense foods such as fruits, vegetables, whole grains, lean proteins, and healthy fats.

These foods provide essential vitamins, minerals, and antioxidants that support optimal heart function and reduce the risk of cardiovascular diseases.

Understanding the Role of Nutrition:

Omega-3 fatty acids, found in fatty fish and certain plant-based sources, help lower blood pressure and reduce the risk of heart disease.

Fiber-rich foods like whole grains, fruits, and vegetables help maintain healthy cholesterol levels and promote healthy digestion.

Plant sterols in certain nuts, seeds, and legumes can help lower LDL cholesterol levels.

Section 2: Alcohol and Its Impact on Heart Health

The Relationship Between Alcohol and Heart Health:

Moderate alcohol consumption, defined as up to one drink per day for women and up to two drinks per day for men, may have cardiovascular benefits, such as increasing HDL (good) cholesterol levels.

Excessive alcohol consumption can lead to high blood pressure, irregular heart rhythms, and an increased risk of heart disease.

Making Responsible Choices:

Set limits and adhere to the guidelines for moderate alcohol consumption to reduce the risk of negative health effects.

Understand standard drink sizes and be mindful of the alcohol content in different beverages.

Consider non-alcoholic alternatives or creative mocktail recipes to enjoy social gatherings without the potential risks associated with alcohol.

Section 3:

Understanding Excess Calories and Their Impact on Heart Health

The Importance of Caloric Balance:

Consuming more calories than your body needs can lead to weight gain, obesity, and an increased risk of heart disease.

Balancing calorie intake with physical activity is crucial for maintaining a healthy weight and promoting heart health.

Gradually Reducing Excess Calories:

Portion control is essential for managing calorie intake. Use smaller plates, bowls, and utensils to help control portion sizes.

Practicing mindful eating, such as attention to hunger and fullness cues, can prevent overeating and promote healthier food choices.

Gradually reducing calorie intake by making small changes to your diet, such as swapping sugary beverages for water or incorporating more fruits and vegetables into your meals, can lead to long-term success.

Chapter 2:

Benefits of a Heart-Healthy Diet

Section 1:

Reduced Risk of Heart Disease:

A heart-healthy diet can significantly lower the risk of developing heart disease, including coronary artery disease, heart attacks, and strokes.

By following a diet rich in fruits, vegetables, whole grains, lean proteins, and healthy fats, you can help protect your heart and maintain optimal cardiovascular health.

Lower Blood Pressure:

Consuming a heart-healthy diet has been shown to help lower high blood pressure, a major risk factor for heart disease.

By incorporating nutrient-dense foods and reducing sodium intake, you can help maintain healthy blood pressure levels and support a healthy heart.

Improved Cholesterol Levels:

A heart-healthy diet can help improve cholesterol levels by reducing LDL (bad) cholesterol and increasing HDL (good) cholesterol.

Foods rich in soluble fiber, omega-3 fatty acids, and plant sterols can help lower LDL cholesterol levels and promote a healthier lipid profile.

Weight Management:

Adopting a heart-healthy diet can contribute to achieving and maintaining a healthy weight.

By focusing on whole, unprocessed foods and practicing portion control, you can effectively manage your weight, which is essential for reducing the risk of heart disease.

Section 2:

Overcoming Disadvantages and Challenges

Overcoming Common Challenges:

The transition to a heart-healthy diet may come with its challenges, such as adjusting to new tastes, meal planning, and navigating social situations.

We provide practical tips, strategies, and delicious recipes to help you overcome these challenges and successfully embrace a heart-healthy lifestyle.

Long-Term Health and Well-Being:

Beyond the immediate benefits, a heart-healthy diet can improve your long-term health and overall well-being.

By prioritizing nutritious foods, you can reduce the risk of other chronic conditions like type 2 diabetes, certain cancers, and obesity.

Chapter 3:

What Are the Risk Factors for Heart Disease?

Section 1:

Common Risk Factors for Heart Disease

High Blood Pressure:

High blood pressure, or hypertension, is a leading risk factor for heart disease.

To manage blood pressure, limit sodium intake by avoiding processed foods and incorporating more potassium-rich foods like bananas, spinach, and sweet potatoes.

High Cholesterol Levels:

Elevated cholesterol levels, especially high LDL (bad) cholesterol, contribute to the development of heart disease.

Reduce cholesterol intake by choosing lean proteins, such as skinless poultry and fish, and incorporating more soluble fiber-rich foods like oats, beans, and fruits into your meals.

Obesity and Excess Weight:

Obesity and excess weight strain the heart and increase the risk of heart disease.

Maintain a healthy weight by focusing on portion control, eating balanced meals, and incorporating regular physical activity into your routine.

Diabetes:

Diabetes significantly raises the risk of heart disease.

Control blood sugar levels by consuming a balanced diet that includes whole grains, lean proteins, non-starchy vegetables, and healthy fats while limiting added sugars and refined carbohydrates.

Section 2:

The Role of Nutrition in Reducing Heart Disease Risk

Heart-Healthy Eating Patterns:

Embrace heart-healthy eating patterns, such as the Mediterranean or DASH diet, which emphasizes whole foods, fruits, vegetables, whole grains, lean proteins, and healthy fats.

Incorporate these eating patterns into your meals by enjoying meals centered around plant-based foods and incorporating moderate amounts of lean meats and seafood.

Nutrients for Heart Health:

Include heart-healthy nutrients in your diet, such as omega-3 fatty acids in fatty fish like salmon, walnuts, and flaxseeds, which can help reduce inflammation and support heart health.

Antioxidant-rich foods like berries, dark leafy greens, and nuts protect against oxidative stress, a contributing factor to heart disease.

Balancing Macronutrients:

Strive for a balanced intake of macronutrients by including a variety of complex carbohydrates, lean proteins, and healthy fats in your meals.

Opt for whole grains, legumes, skinless poultry, fish, nuts, seeds, and avocados to ensure a balanced and heart-healthy macronutrient profile.

Chapter 4:

Foods to Eat, Limit, and Avoid

Section 1:

Foods to Include for Heart Health

Fruits and Vegetables:

Include a variety of colorful fruits and vegetables in your diet, such as berries, citrus fruits, leafy greens, and cruciferous vegetables.

These nutrient-rich foods contain antioxidants, fiber, vitamins, and minerals that promote heart health.

Whole Grains:

Opt for whole grains like brown rice, quinoa, whole wheat bread, and oats.

Whole grains provide fiber, B vitamins, and minerals that can help lower the risk of heart disease and regulate blood sugar levels.

Lean Proteins:

Choose lean protein sources like skinless poultry, fish, legumes, and tofu.

These protein sources are low in saturated fat and provide essential amino acids without compromising heart health.

Healthy Fats:

Include sources of healthy fats in your diet, such as avocados, nuts, seeds, and olive oil.

These fats contain monounsaturated and polyunsaturated fats, which can help reduce LDL cholesterol levels and lower the risk of heart disease.

Section 2:

Foods to Limit for Heart Health

Sodium:

Limit the intake of high-sodium foods like processed meats, canned soups, and packaged snacks.

Excessive sodium consumption can contribute to high blood pressure and increase the risk of heart disease.

Added Sugars:

Minimize the consumption of foods and beverages with added sugars, such as sugary drinks, desserts, and processed snacks.

High sugar intake can lead to weight gain, diabetes, and cardiovascular complications.

Saturated and Trans Fats:

Limit foods high in saturated fats, including fatty meats, full-fat dairy products, and tropical oils.

Avoid trans fats found in fried foods, baked goods, and processed snacks, as they can raise LDL cholesterol and increase the risk of heart disease.

Section 3:

Foods to Avoid for Heart Health

Processed Foods:

Avoid highly processed foods like fast food, packaged meals, and sugary cereals.

These foods often contain unhealthy fats, added sugars, and high sodium levels, which can harm heart health.

Chapter 5: Breakfast

Berry Yogurt Parfait

Total Servings: 1 serving
Preparation Time: 10 minutes
Cooking Time: (No cooking required)

- Ingredients:
- 1/2 cup low-fat Greek yogurt
- 1/4 cup fresh mixed berries (such as strawberries,
- blueberries, raspberries)
- 2 tablespoons granola (preferably low-sugar)
- 1 tablespoon honey (optional)
- Fresh mint leaves for garnish (optional)

Instructions:

1. Start by layering half of the Greek yogurt in a glass or a bowl.

2. Add a layer of half of the mixed berries on top of the yogurt.

3. Sprinkle half of the granola over the berries.

4. Repeat the layers with the remaining Greek yogurt, mixed berries, and granola.

5. Drizzle honey over the top layer if desired for added sweetness.

6. Garnish with fresh mint leaves for a refreshing touch.

7. Serve immediately and enjoy!

Nutritional value (1 serving):

Calories: 220 Protein: 16g Fat: 4 Salt: 40mg

Veggie Omelet

Total Servings: 1 serving
Preparation Time: 10 minutes
Cooking Time: 10 minutes

Ingredients:

- 2 large eggs
- 1/4 cup diced bell peppers (any color)
- 1/4 cup diced onions
- 1/4 cup sliced mushrooms
- 1/4 cup baby spinach leaves
- 1 tablespoon olive oil
- Salt and pepper to taste

- Fresh herbs for garnish (such as parsley or chives)

Instructions:

1. In a bowl, whisk the eggs until well beaten. Set aside.

2. Heat olive oil in a non-stick skillet over medium heat.

3. Add the diced bell peppers and onions to the skillet and sauté for 2 minutes until slightly softened.

4. Add the mushrooms and baby spinach to the skillet and cook for another 2 minutes until the vegetables are tender.

5. Season the vegetables with salt and pepper to taste.

6. Pour the beaten eggs into the skillet, evenly covering the vegetables.

7. Cook for 3-4 minutes or until the edges of the omelet are set.

8. Carefully flip the omelet using a spatula and cook for 2-3 minutes until fully cooked.

9. Transfer the omelet to a plate and garnish with fresh herbs.

10. Serve hot, and enjoy!

Nutritional value (1 serving):

Calories: 250 Protein: 17g Fat: 18g Salt: 400mg

Overnight Chia Pudding

Total Servings: 1 serving
Preparation Time: 5 minutes
Time to Set: Overnight (at least 6 hours)

Ingredients:

- 2 tablespoons chia seeds
- 1/2 cup unsweetened almond milk (or any other plant-based milk)
- 1/4 teaspoon vanilla extract
- 1 teaspoon maple syrup or honey (optional)
- Fresh fruits and nuts for topping (e.g., sliced berries, chopped almonds)

Instructions:

1. In a small bowl or jar, combine chia seeds, almond milk, vanilla extract, and sweetener (if using).

2. Stir the mixture well to ensure that the chia seeds are evenly distributed.

3. Cover the bowl or jar and refrigerate overnight or for at least 6 hours to allow the chia seeds to absorb the liquid and thicken into a pudding-like consistency.

4. Once set, give the pudding a good stir to break up any clumps that may have formed.

5. Transfer the chia pudding to a serving bowl or glass.

6. Top with your favorite fresh fruits and nuts for added texture and flavor.

7. Serve chilled, and enjoy!

Nutritional value (1 serving):

Calories: 180 Protein: 6g Fat: 10g Salt: 0mg

Avocado Toast

Total Servings: 1 serving
Preparation Time: 5 minutes
Time to Cook: 5 minutes

Ingredients:

- 1 slice of whole-grain bread
- 1/2 ripe avocado
- 1 small tomato, sliced
- 1 teaspoon lemon juice
- Pinch of salt and black pepper
- Optional toppings: sliced radishes, sprouts, or a sprinkle of chili flakes

Instructions:

1. Toast the slice of whole-grain bread until golden and crispy.

2. Mash the ripe avocado with lemon juice, salt, and black pepper in a small bowl.

3. Spread the mashed avocado evenly onto the toasted bread.

4. Top the avocado toast with sliced tomatoes and any additional toppings you choose.

5. Sprinkle with a pinch of salt and black pepper for extra flavor.

6. Serve immediately and enjoy!

Nutritional value (1 serving):

Calories: 200 Protein: 5g Fat: 13g Salt: 150mg

Green Smoothie Bowl

Total Servings: 1 serving
Preparation Time: 10 minutes
Time to Cook: N/A (No cooking required)

Ingredients:

- 1 ripe banana
- 1 cup spinach leaves
- 1/2 cup chopped kale leaves

- 1/2 cup unsweetened almond milk (or any other plant-based milk)
- 1/4 avocado
- 1 tablespoon chia seeds
- 1 tablespoon unsweetened shredded coconut
- Fresh fruits and nuts for topping (e.g., sliced kiwi, blueberries, almonds)

Instructions:

1. Combine the ripe banana, spinach, kale, almond milk, and avocado in a blender.

2. Blend on high speed until the mixture is smooth and creamy.

3. Pour the green smoothie into a bowl.

4. Sprinkle the chia seeds and unsweetened shredded coconut on top.

5. Arrange your favorite fresh fruits and nuts as toppings.

6. Serve immediately and enjoy!

Nutritional value (1 serving):

Calories: 280 Protein: 7g Fat: 14g Salt: 80mg

Quinoa Breakfast Bowl

Total Servings: 1 serving
Preparation Time: 5 minutes
Time to Cook: 15-20 minutes

Ingredients:

- 1/2 cup cooked quinoa
- 1/2 cup unsweetened almond milk (or any other plant based milk)
- 1/4 teaspoon cinnamon
- 1/4 teaspoon vanilla extract
- 1 tablespoon chopped nuts (such as walnuts or almonds)
- 1 tablespoon seeds (such as chia seeds or flaxseeds)
- Fresh fruits for topping (e.g., sliced banana, berries)

Instructions:

1. Heat the cooked quinoa and almond milk in a small saucepan over medium heat.

2. Stir in the cinnamon and vanilla extract.

3. Cook for 5-7 minutes, stirring occasionally, until the mixture thickens and reaches your desired consistency.

4. Once cooked, transfer the quinoa mixture to a bowl.

5. Top with chopped nuts and seeds.

6. Add your favorite fresh fruits as toppings.

7. Serve warm, and enjoy!

Nutritional value (1 serving):

Calories: 320 Protein: 11g Fat: 12g Salt: 60mg

Egg White Scramble

Total Servings: 1 serving
Preparation Time: 5 minutes
Time to Cook: 10 minutes

Ingredients:

- 4 egg whites
- 1/4 cup diced bell peppers (any color)
- 1/4 cup diced onions
- 1/4 cup sliced mushrooms
- 1/4 cup baby spinach leaves
- 1 teaspoon olive oil
- Salt and pepper to taste
- Fresh herbs for garnish (such as parsley or chives)

Instructions:

1. In a bowl, whisk the egg whites until frothy.

2. Heat olive oil in a non-stick skillet over medium heat.

3. Add the diced bell peppers and onions to the skillet and sauté for 2 minutes until slightly softened.

4. Add the mushrooms and baby spinach to the skillet and cook for another 2 minutes until the vegetables are tender.

5. Season the vegetables with salt and pepper to taste.

6. Pour the whisked egg whites into the skillet, covering the sautéed vegetables.

7. Cook for 3-4 minutes, stirring occasionally, until the egg whites are fully cooked and scrambled.

8. Transfer the egg white scramble to a plate.

9. Garnish with fresh herbs for added flavor and presentation.

10. Serve hot, and enjoy!

Nutritional value (1 serving):

Calories: 120 Protein: 25g Fat: 0g Salt: 200mg

Banana Pancakes

Total Servings: 1 serving (2 small pancakes)
Preparation Time: 10 minutes
Time to Cook: 10 minutes

Ingredients:

- 1 ripe banana

- 1/4 cup whole wheat flour
- 1/4 cup unsweetened almond milk (or any other plant-based milk)
- 1/2 teaspoon baking powder
- 1/4 teaspoon vanilla extract
- Pinch of cinnamon (optional)
- Fresh fruits and a drizzle of honey (optional) for topping

Instructions:

1. In a mixing bowl, mash the ripe banana until smooth.

2. Add the whole wheat flour, almond milk, baking powder, vanilla extract, and cinnamon (if using). Stir until well combined.

3. Heat a non-stick skillet or griddle over medium heat.

4. Pour small amounts of the pancake batter onto the skillet, forming small pancakes.

5. Cook for 2-3 minutes on one side until small bubbles appear on the surface.

6. Flip the pancakes and cook for 2-3 minutes until golden brown.

7. Repeat with the remaining batter until all pancakes are cooked.

8. Transfer the pancakes to a plate.

9. Top with fresh fruits and a drizzle of honey if desired.

10. Serve warm, and enjoy!

Nutritional value (1 serving - 2 small pancakes):

Calories: 230 Protein: 7g Fat: 2g Salt: 150mg

Spinach Feta Frittata

Total Servings: 1 serving
Preparation Time: 10 minutes
Time to Cook: 20 minutes

Ingredients:

- 2 large eggs
- 2 egg whites
- 1/4 cup chopped spinach
- 1/4 cup crumbled feta cheese
- 1/4 cup diced tomatoes
- 1/4 cup diced onions
- 1/2 teaspoon olive oil
- Salt and pepper to taste
- Fresh herbs for garnish (such as parsley or basil)

Instructions:

1. Preheat the oven to 350°F (175°C).

2. Whisk the eggs and egg whites until well combined in a mixing bowl.

3. Heat olive oil in an oven-safe skillet over medium heat.

4. Add the diced onions to the skillet and sauté for 2 minutes until slightly softened.

5. Add the chopped spinach and diced tomatoes to the skillet and cook for another 2 minutes until the vegetables are wilted.

6. Season the vegetables with salt and pepper to taste.

7. Pour the whisked eggs over the cooked vegetables in the skillet.

8. Sprinkle the crumbled feta cheese evenly over the egg mixture.

9. Place the skillet in the oven and bake for 15-18 minutes until the frittata is set and slightly golden.

10. Remove from the oven and let it cool for a few minutes.

11. Garnish with fresh herbs for added flavor and presentation.

12. Serve warm or at room temperature, and enjoy!

Nutritional value (1 serving):

Calories: 280 Protein: 26g Fat: 15g Salt: 350mg

Almond Butter Toast

Total Servings: 1 serving
Preparation Time: 5 minutes
Time to Cook: N/A (No cooking required)

Ingredients:

- 1 slice of whole-grain bread
- 1 tablespoon almond butter
- 1/2 medium banana, sliced
- 1 teaspoon honey (optional)
- Pinch of cinnamon (optional)

Instructions:

1. Toast the slice of whole-grain bread until golden and crispy.

2. Spread the almond butter evenly on the toasted bread.

3. Arrange the banana slices on top of the almond butter.

4. Drizzle with honey and sprinkle a pinch of cinnamon if desired.

5. Serve immediately and enjoy!

Nutritional value (1 serving):

Calories: 250 Protein: 7g Fat: 12g Salt: 150mg

Greek Yogurt Bowl

Total Servings: 1 serving
Preparation Time: 5 minutes
Time to Cook: N/A (No cooking required)

Ingredients:

- 1 cup plain Greek yogurt
- 1/4 cup mixed berries (such as blueberries, strawberries, and raspberries)
- 1 tablespoon honey or maple syrup
- 1 tablespoon chopped nuts (such as almonds or walnuts)
- 1 tablespoon unsweetened shredded coconut
- Optional toppings: chia seeds, flaxseeds, or granola

Instructions:

1. Spoon the Greek yogurt as the base of the bowl in a bowl.

2. Top the yogurt with mixed berries, spreading them evenly over the surface.

3. Drizzle honey or maple syrup over the berries for added sweetness.

4. Sprinkle chopped nuts and unsweetened shredded coconut on top.

5. Add any optional toppings, such as chia seeds, flaxseeds, or granola, for added texture and nutrition.

6. Serve immediately and enjoy!

Nutritional value (1 serving):

Calories: 250 Protein: 20g Fat: 10g Salt: 80mg

Sweet Potato Hash

Total Servings: 1 serving
Preparation Time: 10 minutes
Time to Cook: 15-20 minutes

Ingredients:

- 1 small sweet potato, peeled and diced
- 1/4 cup diced bell peppers (any color)
- 1/4 cup diced onions
- 1/4 cup diced zucchini
- 1/2 teaspoon olive oil
- Salt and pepper to taste
- Fresh herbs for garnish (such as parsley or cilantro)

Instructions:

1. Heat olive oil in a non-stick skillet over medium heat.

2. Add the diced sweet potato to the skillet and sauté for 5-7 minutes until slightly softened.

3. Add the diced bell peppers, onions, and zucchini to the skillet and cook for another 5-7 minutes until the vegetables are tender.

4. Season the hash with salt and pepper to taste.

5. Cook for 2-3 minutes until the sweet potatoes are golden brown and cooked.

6. Remove from heat and transfer the sweet potato hash to a plate.

7. Garnish with fresh herbs for added flavor and presentation.

8. Serve hot, and enjoy!

Nutritional value (1 serving):

Calories: 220 Protein: 4g Fat: 4g Salt: 150mg

Blueberry Protein Shake

Total Servings: 1 serving
Preparation Time: 5 minutes
Time to Cook: N/A (No cooking required)

Ingredients:

- 1 cup unsweetened almond milk (or any other plant-based milk)
- 1/2 cup frozen blueberries
- 1/2 ripe banana
- 1 scoop of vanilla protein powder
- 1 tablespoon almond butter (or any other nut butter)
- 1 teaspoon honey or maple syrup (optional)
- Ice cubes (optional)

Instructions:

1. Combine the almond milk, frozen blueberries, ripe banana, vanilla protein powder, and almond butter in a blender.

2. Blend quickly until all the ingredients are well combined and the shake is smooth.

3. Taste and add honey or maple syrup if desired for added sweetness.

4. Add a few ice cubes to make the shake colder and more refreshing if expected.

5. Blend for 10-20 seconds until the ice cubes are fully incorporated.

6. Pour the blueberry protein shake into a glass.

7. Serve immediately and enjoy!

Nutritional value (1 serving):

Calories: 280 Protein: 25g Fat: 10g Salt: 150mg

Oatmeal with Berries

Total Servings: 1 serving
Preparation Time: 5 minutes
Time to Cook: 10 minutes

Ingredients:

- 1/2 cup rolled oats
- 1 cup unsweetened almond milk (or any other plant-based milk)
- 1/2 cup mixed berries (such as blueberries, strawberries, and raspberries)
- 1 tablespoon chia seeds
- 1 tablespoon chopped nuts (such as almonds or walnuts)
- 1 teaspoon honey or maple syrup (optional)
- Pinch of cinnamon (optional)

Instructions:

1. In a saucepan, combine the rolled oats and almond milk.

2. Bring the mixture to a boil over medium heat.

3. Reduce the heat to low and simmer for 5-7 minutes, stirring occasionally, until the oats are cooked and have absorbed most of the liquid.

4. Remove from heat and let it rest for a minute.

5. Stir in the mixed berries, chia seeds, and chopped nuts.

6. If desired, add honey or maple syrup for added sweetness and a pinch of cinnamon for extra flavor.

7. Mix well until all the ingredients are combined.

8. Transfer the oatmeal to a bowl.

9. Serve hot, and enjoy!

Nutritional value (1 serving):

Calories: 300 Protein: 10g Fat: 10g Salt: 100mg

Smoked Salmon Wrap

Total Servings: 1 serving
Preparation Time: 10 minutes
Time to Cook: N/A (No cooking required)

Ingredients:

- 1 whole wheat tortilla or wrap
- 2 ounces of smoked salmon

- 2 tablespoons plain Greek yogurt or low-fat sour cream
- 1/4 cup sliced cucumber
- 1/4 cup shredded lettuce or spinach leaves
- 1 tablespoon chopped fresh dill (optional)
- Freshly ground black pepper to taste

Instructions:

1. Lay the whole wheat tortilla or wrap it flat on a clean surface.

2. Spread the plain Greek yogurt or low-fat sour cream evenly over the tortilla.

3. Arrange the smoked salmon slices on top of the yogurt or sour cream.

4. Add the sliced cucumber and shredded lettuce or spinach leaves on top of the salmon.

5. Sprinkle the chopped fresh dill, if using, over the vegetables.

6. Season with freshly ground black pepper to taste.

7. Fold the sides of the tortilla inward and roll it up tightly into a wrap.

8. Slice the wrap in half if desired.

9. Serve immediately or wrap it up for later consumption.

10. Enjoy this delicious and heart-healthy smoked salmon wrap!

Nutritional value (1 serving):

Calories: 250 Protein: 20g Fat: 10g Salt: 500mg

Peanut Butter Banana Smoothie

Total Servings: 1 serving
Preparation Time: 5 minutes
Time to Cook: N/A (No cooking required)

Ingredients:

- 1 ripe banana
- 1 cup unsweetened almond milk (or any other plant-based milk)
- 2 tablespoons natural peanut butter
- 1 tablespoon honey or maple syrup (optional)
- 1/2 cup ice cubes

Instructions:

1. Combine the ripe banana, almond milk, natural peanut butter, honey, maple syrup (if desired), and ice cubes in a blender.

2. Blend on high speed until all the ingredients are well combined, and the smoothie is creamy.

3. Taste and adjust the sweetness by adding more honey or maple syrup if desired.

4. If the smoothie is too thick, add more almond milk and blend again.

5. Pour the peanut butter banana smoothie into a glass.

6. Serve immediately and enjoy!

Nutritional value (1 serving):

Calories: 320 Protein: 9g Fat: 15g Salt: 100mg

Veggie Breakfast Burrito

Total Servings: 1 serving
Preparation Time: 10 minutes
Time to Cook: 10 minutes

Ingredients:

- 1 whole wheat tortilla or wrap
- 1/4 cup egg whites
- 1/4 cup diced bell peppers (any color)
- 1/4 cup diced onions
- 1/4 cup diced tomatoes
- 1/4 cup sliced mushrooms
- 1/4 cup baby spinach leaves
- 1 tablespoon olive oil
- Salt and pepper to taste
- Optional toppings: salsa, avocado slices, or Greek yogurt

Instructions:

1. Heat olive oil in a non-stick skillet over medium heat.

2. Add the diced bell peppers, onions, tomatoes, and mushrooms to the skillet.

3. Sauté the vegetables for 3-4 minutes until they start to soften.

4. Add the baby spinach leaves to the skillet and cook for another 1-2 minutes until wilted.

5. Season the vegetables with salt and pepper to taste.

6. Push the vegetables to one side of the skillet and add the egg whites to the other side.

7. Scramble the egg whites until fully cooked and combine them with the sautéed vegetables.

8. Warm the whole wheat tortilla or wrap it in a separate skillet or microwave for a few seconds to make it pliable.

9. Place the scrambled egg whites and vegetable mixture in the center of the tortilla or wrap.

10. Optional: Add salsa, avocado slices, or Greek yogurt as toppings for added flavor and creaminess.

11. Roll the tortilla or wrap it tightly to form a burrito.

12. Serve immediately or wrap it up for later consumption.

13. Enjoy this nutritious and heart-healthy veggie breakfast burrito!

Nutritional value (1 serving):

Calories: 250 Protein: 12g Fat: 8g Salt: 300mg

Quinoa Fruit Salad

Total Servings: 1 serving
Preparation Time: 10 minutes
Time to Cook: 15 minutes

Ingredients:

- 1/4 cup cooked quinoa
- 1/2 cup mixed fresh fruits (such as berries, diced apples, diced pears, or sliced bananas)
- 1 tablespoon chopped nuts (such as almonds or walnuts)
- 1 tablespoon dried cranberries or raisins
- 1 tablespoon fresh lemon or lime juice
- 1 teaspoon honey or maple syrup (optional)
- Fresh mint leaves for garnish (optional)

Instructions:

1. Combine the cooked quinoa, mixed fresh fruits, chopped nuts, and dried cranberries or raisins in a bowl.

2. Drizzle fresh lemon or lime juice over the salad for a refreshing tang.

3. If desired, add honey or maple syrup for added sweetness.

4. Gently toss all the ingredients until well combined.

5. Transfer the quinoa fruit salad to a serving dish or bowl.

6. Optional: Garnish with fresh mint leaves for a pop of color and added freshness.

7. Serve immediately or refrigerate for later consumption.

8. Enjoy this delicious and heart-healthy quinoa fruit salad!

Nutritional value (1 serving):

Calories: 200 Protein: 6g Fat: 5g Salt: 20mg

Spinach Mushroom Omelet

Total Servings: 1 serving
Preparation Time: 10 minutes
Time to Cook: 10 minutes

Ingredients:

- 2 large eggs
- 1/4 cup sliced mushrooms
- 1/4 cup baby spinach leaves
- 1/4 cup diced onions
- 1/4 cup diced tomatoes
- 1 teaspoon olive oil
- Salt and pepper to taste
- Optional toppings: chopped fresh herbs (such as parsley or chives)

Instructions:

1. In a bowl, beat the eggs until well-mixed. Season with salt and pepper to taste.

2. Heat olive oil in a non-stick skillet over medium heat.

3. Add the diced onions and sliced mushrooms to the skillet and sauté for 2-3 minutes until they soften.

4. Add the baby spinach leaves and diced tomatoes to the skillet and cook for another 1-2 minutes until the spinach wilts.

5. Season the vegetable mixture with salt and pepper to taste.

6. Push the vegetables to one side of the skillet and pour the beaten eggs into the other.

7. Allow the eggs to cook for a minute until the edges start to set.

8. Gently fold the cooked vegetables over the eggs.

9. Continue cooking the omelet for another 2-3 minutes until the eggs are fully cooked and set.

10. Carefully transfer the omelet to a plate and fold it in half.

11. Optional: Garnish with chopped fresh herbs for added flavor and presentation.

12. Serve immediately and enjoy this heart-healthy spinach mushroom omelet!

Nutritional value (1 serving):

Calories: 200 Protein: 15g Fat: 12g Salt: 300mg

Apple Cinnamon Overnight Oats

Total Servings: 1 serving
Preparation Time: 5 minutes
Time to Cook: Overnight (6-8 hours)

Ingredients:

- 1/2 cup rolled oats
- 1/2 cup unsweetened almond milk (or any other plant-based milk)

- 1/2 medium-sized apple, diced
- 1 tablespoon chia seeds
- 1 tablespoon chopped nuts (such as almonds or walnuts)
- 1 teaspoon honey or maple syrup (optional)
- 1/2 teaspoon ground cinnamon

Instructions:

1. Combine the rolled oats, almond milk, diced apple, chia seeds, chopped nuts, honey, or maple syrup (if desired), and ground cinnamon in a mason jar or container with a lid.

2. Stir all the ingredients until well combined.

3. Close the lid tightly and refrigerate the mixture overnight for 6-8 hours.

4. In the morning, give the overnight oats a good stir.

5. If desired, add additional almond milk to achieve the desired consistency.

6. Transfer the apple cinnamon overnight oats to a serving bowl.

7. Optional: Top with an additional diced apple and a sprinkle of cinnamon for extra flavor and texture.

8. Serve chilled, and enjoy this healthy and heart-healthy breakfast!

Nutritional value (1 serving):

Calories: 300 Protein: 8g Fat: 10g Salt: 100mg

Mediterranean Egg Muffins

Total Servings: 1 serving
Preparation Time: 10 minutes
Time to Cook: 20 minutes

Ingredients:

- 2 large eggs
- 1/4 cup diced bell peppers (any color)
- 1/4 cup diced onions
- 1/4 cup diced tomatoes
- 1/4 cup chopped spinach
- 2 tablespoons crumbled feta cheese
- 1 tablespoon chopped black olives
- 1 teaspoon olive oil
- Salt and pepper to taste
- Optional toppings: chopped fresh herbs (such as parsley or dill)

Instructions:

1. Preheat the oven to 350°F (175°C) and grease a muffin tin with olive oil or use silicone cups.

2. In a bowl, beat the eggs until well-mixed. Season with salt and pepper to taste.

3. Heat olive oil in a skillet over medium heat.

4. Add the diced bell peppers and onions to the skillet and sauté for 2-3 minutes until they soften.

5. Add the diced tomatoes and chopped spinach to the skillet and cook for another 1-2 minutes until the spinach wilts.

6. Season the vegetable mixture with salt and pepper to taste.

7. In the greased muffin tin, evenly distribute the sautéed vegetables.

8. Sprinkle crumbled feta cheese and chopped black olives over the vegetables.

9. Pour the beaten eggs over the vegetable mixture in each muffin cup, filling them about 3/4 full.

10. Optional: Sprinkle chopped fresh herbs over the egg muffins for added flavor and presentation.

11. Bake in the oven for 15-20 minutes or until the egg muffins are set and slightly golden.

12. Carefully remove the egg muffins from the tin and let them cool slightly.

13. Serve warm or at room temperature, and enjoy these heart-healthy Mediterranean egg muffins!

Nutritional value (1 serving):

Calories: 250 Protein: 18g Fat: 16g Salt: 400mg

Almond Flour Pancakes

Total Servings: 1 serving
Preparation Time: 5 minutes
Time to Cook: 10 minutes

Ingredients:

- 1/4 cup almond flour
- 1 large egg
- 2 tablespoons unsweetened almond milk (or any other plant-based milk)
- 1/2 teaspoon baking powder
- 1/2 teaspoon vanilla extract
- Pinch of salt
- Optional toppings: fresh berries, sliced bananas, or a drizzle of honey or maple syrup

Instructions:

1. Whisk together the almond flour, egg, almond milk, baking powder, vanilla extract, and salt until well combined.

2. Heat a non-stick skillet or griddle over medium heat.

3. Lightly grease the skillet with cooking spray or a small amount of oil.

4. Pour about 1/4 cup of the pancake batter onto the skillet, spreading it slightly to form a circular shape.

5. Cook the pancake for 2-3 minutes on one side until bubbles form on the surface.

6. Flip the pancake and cook for another 1-2 minutes on the other side until it is cooked through and lightly golden.

7. Repeat steps 4-6 with the remaining pancake batter to make additional pancakes.

8. Transfer the almond flour pancakes to a serving plate.

9. Optional: Top the pancakes with fresh berries, sliced bananas, or a drizzle of honey or maple syrup for added sweetness and flavor.

10. Serve immediately and enjoy these delicious and heart-healthy almond flour pancakes!

Nutritional value (1 serving):

Calories: 280 Protein: 12g Fat: 21g Salt: 150mg

Green Detox Smoothie

Total Servings: 1 serving
Preparation Time: 5 minutes
Time to Cook: N/A

Ingredients:

- 1 cup fresh spinach leaves
- 1 small cucumber, peeled and chopped
- 1 green apple, cored and chopped
- 1/2 ripe avocado
- 1/2 lemon, juiced
- 1/2 cup unsweetened almond milk (or any other plant-based milk)
- Optional: 1 tablespoon of chia seeds or flaxseeds

Instructions:

1. Combine the fresh spinach leaves, chopped cucumber, chopped green apple, ripe avocado, lemon juice, and unsweetened almond milk in a blender.

2. Blend on high speed until the ingredients are well combined, achieving a smooth and creamy consistency.

3. If desired, add chia seeds or flaxseeds to the blender and blend for a few more seconds to incorporate.

4. Pour the green detox smoothie into a glass.

5. Optional: Garnish with a slice of lemon or a sprinkle of chia seeds for presentation.

6. Serve immediately and enjoy this refreshing and nutritious green detox smoothie!

Nutritional value (1 serving):

Calories: 220 Protein: 6g Fat: 12g Salt: 120mg

Tofu Scramble

Total Servings: 1 serving
Preparation Time: 10 minutes
Time to Cook: 10 minutes

Ingredients:

- 1/2 block of firm tofu, drained and crumbled
- 1/4 small onion, finely chopped
- 1/4 bell pepper, finely chopped
- 1/4 cup sliced mushrooms
- 1/2 teaspoon turmeric powder
- 1/2 teaspoon garlic powder
- 1/4 teaspoon ground cumin
- Salt and pepper to taste
- 1 teaspoon olive oil
- Optional: Fresh herbs (such as parsley or chives) for garnish

Instructions:

1. Heat olive oil in a skillet over medium heat.

2. Add the chopped onion, bell pepper, and sliced mushrooms to the skillet.

3. Sauté the vegetables for 3-4 minutes until they begin to soften.

4. Add the crumbled tofu to the skillet and stir to combine with the vegetables.

5. Sprinkle turmeric powder, garlic powder, ground cumin, salt, and pepper over the tofu and vegetables.

6. Cook for another 5-6 minutes, stirring occasionally, until the tofu is heated and lightly golden.

7. Optional: Garnish with fresh herbs, such as parsley or chives, for added freshness.

8. Remove from heat and transfer the tofu scramble to a plate.

9. Serve hot, and enjoy this hearty and protein-rich tofu scramble!

Nutritional value (1 serving):

Calories: 180 Protein: 15g Fat: 10g Salt: 350mg

Walnut Banana Bread

Total Servings: 1 loaf (about 10 slices)
Preparation Time: 15 minutes
Time to Cook: 50-60 minutes

Ingredients:

- 2 ripe bananas
- 1/4 cup honey or maple syrup
- 1/4 cup unsweetened applesauce
- 1/4 cup plain Greek yogurt
- 1/4 cup unsweetened almond milk (or any other plant-based milk)
- 2 tablespoons coconut oil, melted
- 1 teaspoon vanilla extract
- 1 1/2 cups whole wheat flour
- 1 teaspoon baking powder
- 1/2 teaspoon baking soda
- 1/2 teaspoon ground cinnamon
- 1/4 teaspoon salt
- 1/2 cup chopped walnuts

Instructions:

1. Preheat the oven to 350°F (175°C) and grease a loaf pan with non-stick cooking spray.

2. Mash the ripe bananas with a fork until smooth in a large mixing bowl.

3. Add honey or maple syrup, unsweetened applesauce, Greek yogurt, almond milk, melted coconut oil, and vanilla extract to the mashed bananas. Mix well to combine.

4. Whisk together the whole wheat flour, baking powder, baking soda, ground cinnamon, and salt in a separate bowl.

5. Gradually add the dry ingredients to the wet ingredients and stir until combined. Avoid overmixing.

6. Fold the chopped walnuts into the batter.

7. Pour the batter into the greased loaf pan and spread it evenly.

8. Bake in the oven for 50-60 minutes or until a toothpick inserted into the center comes clean.

9. Remove the banana bread from the oven and let it cool in the pan for 10 minutes.

10. Transfer the bread to a wire rack to cool completely before slicing.

11. Once cooled, slice into 10 pieces and serve. Enjoy this delicious and heart-healthy walnut banana bread!

Nutritional value (1 serving - 1 slice):

Calories: 190 Protein: 4g Fat: 7g Salt: 100mg

Quinoa Breakfast Cookies

Total Servings: 12 cookies
Preparation Time: 15 minutes
Time to Cook: 20 minutes

Ingredients:

- 1 cup cooked quinoa
- 1/4 cup almond butter
- 2 tablespoons honey or maple syrup
- 1/2 teaspoon vanilla extract
- 1/4 teaspoon ground cinnamon
- 1/4 cup dried cranberries or raisins
- 1/4 cup chopped nuts (e.g., almonds, walnuts)
- 2 tablespoons ground flaxseeds
- 2 tablespoons unsweetened shredded coconut (optional)

Instructions:

1. Preheat the oven to 350°F (175°C) and line a baking sheet with parchment paper.

2. Combine cooked quinoa, almond butter, honey or maple syrup, vanilla extract, and ground cinnamon in a mixing bowl. Mix well until all the ingredients are thoroughly combined.

3. Add dried cranberries or raisins, chopped nuts, ground flaxseeds, and unsweetened shredded coconut (if using) to the quinoa mixture. Stir until all the ingredients are evenly incorporated.

4. Scoop approximately 2 tablespoons of the cookie mixture and form it into a ball using your hands. Place it on the lined baking sheet and flatten it slightly to create a cookie shape. Repeat with the remaining mixture to make 12 cookies.

5. Bake in the oven for 18-20 minutes or until the cookies are golden brown around the edges.

6. Remove from the oven and allow the cookies to cool on the baking sheet for 5 minutes. Then transfer them to a wire rack to cool completely before serving.

Nutritional value (1 serving - 1 cookie):

Calories: 110 Protein: 3g Fat: 5g Salt: 10mg

Spinach and Tomato Wrap

Total servings: 1 serving
Preparation time: 10 minutes
Time to cook: 5 minutes

Ingredients:

- 1 whole wheat or whole grain tortilla wrap
- 1 cup fresh spinach leaves
- 1/2 cup cherry tomatoes, halved
- 2 tablespoons hummus (low-fat or homemade)
- 1/4 red onion, thinly sliced
- 1/4 avocado, sliced
- 1/2 teaspoon olive oil
- Salt and pepper to taste

Instructions:

1. Heat a non-stick pan over medium heat. Add the olive oil.

2. Add the spinach leaves to the pan and sauté for 1-2 minutes until wilted. Remove from heat and set aside.

3. Warm the tortilla wrap in a microwave for a few seconds or on a stovetop pan for 30 seconds on each side.

4. Spread the hummus evenly over the tortilla wrap.

5. Arrange the sautéed spinach, cherry tomatoes, red onion, and avocado slices on the hummus.

6. Season with salt and pepper to taste.

7. Gently fold the sides of the tortilla wrap over the filling and roll it tightly from one end to the other to create a wrap.

Nutritional value (1 serving):

Calories: 280 Protein: 9g Fat: 12g Salt: 400mg

Raspberry Chia Pudding

Total servings: 2 servings
Preparation time: 10 minutes
Time to cook: 0 minutes

Ingredients:

- 1 cup unsweetened almond milk (or any plant-based milk)
- 1/4 cup chia seeds
- 1 tablespoon maple syrup or honey (optional)
- 1/2 teaspoon vanilla extract
- 1/2 cup fresh raspberries (or any other berries)

Instructions:

1. Combine the almond milk, chia seeds, maple syrup (or honey), and vanilla extract in a bowl. Stir well until all the ingredients are thoroughly combined.

2. Let the mixture sit for 5 minutes, then stir again to prevent the chia seeds from clumping together.

3. Cover the bowl with plastic wrap or a lid and refrigerate overnight or for at least 4 hours, allowing the chia seeds to absorb the liquid and create a pudding-like consistency.

4. Before serving, give the chia pudding a good stir to break up any clumps that may have formed.

5. Divide the pudding into two serving glasses or bowls.

6. Top the pudding with fresh raspberries (or other berries) and serve chilled.

Nutritional value (1 serving):

Calories: 150 Protein: 5g Fat: 9g Salt: 40mg

Greek Yogurt Parfait

Total servings: 1 serving
Preparation time: 5 minutes
Time to assemble: 5 minutes

Ingredients:

- 1/2 cup non-fat Greek yogurt
- 1/4 cup fresh berries (strawberries, blueberries, or raspberries)
- 2 tablespoons granola (low-sugar or homemade)
- 1 tablespoon chopped nuts (almonds, walnuts, or pistachios)
- 1 teaspoon honey (optional)

Instructions:

1. Layer half of the Greek yogurt in a glass or bowl at the bottom.

2. Add half of the berries on top of the yogurt.

3. Sprinkle half of the granola and chopped nuts over the berries.

4. Repeat the layering process with the remaining Greek yogurt, berries, granola, and nuts.

5. Drizzle honey on top for added sweetness, if desired.

6. Serve immediately and enjoy!

Nutritional value (1 serving):

Calories: 220 Protein: 17g Fat: 8g Salt: 70mg

Veggie Frittata Muffins

Total servings: 6 muffins
Preparation time: 10 minutes
Time to cook: 20 minutes

Ingredients:

- 6 large eggs
- 1/4 cup milk (low-fat or plant-based)
- 1/4 teaspoon salt
- 1/4 teaspoon black pepper
- 1/2 cup diced bell peppers (red, green, or yellow)
- 1/2 cup chopped spinach
- 1/4 cup diced onion
- 1/4 cup diced tomatoes
- 1/4 cup shredded low-fat cheese (cheddar or mozzarella)

Instructions:

1. Preheat the oven to 350°F (175°C). Grease a muffin tin or line it with paper liners.

2. Whisk the eggs, milk, salt, and black pepper in a bowl until well combined.

3. Stir in the diced bell peppers, chopped spinach, onion, tomatoes, and shredded cheese.

4. Pour the egg and vegetable mixture evenly into the prepared muffin tin, filling each cup about 3/4 full.

5. Bake in the oven for 18-20 minutes or until the frittata muffins are set and slightly golden on top.

6. Remove from the oven and let them cool for a few minutes before serving.

7. Store any leftovers in an airtight container in the refrigerator for up to 3 days. Reheat in the microwave before serving, if desired.

Nutritional value (1 serving - 1 muffin):

Calories: 90 Protein: 7g Fat: 5g Salt: 180mg

Peanut Butter Protein Balls

Total servings: 12 balls
Preparation time: 15 minutes
Time to chill: 30 minutes

Ingredients:

- 1 cup of old-fashioned oats
- 1/2 cup natural peanut butter (no added sugar or oil)
- 1/4 cup honey or maple syrup
- 1/4 cup ground flaxseed
- 1/4 cup unsweetened shredded coconut
- 1/4 cup mini dark chocolate chips
- 1/2 teaspoon vanilla extract
- Pinch of salt

Instructions:

1. Combine oats, peanut butter, honey (or maple syrup), ground flaxseed, shredded coconut, dark chocolate chips, vanilla extract, and salt in a large bowl.

2. Mix well until all the ingredients are evenly combined.

3. Place the mixture in the refrigerator for 15-20 minutes to make it easier to handle.

4. Once chilled, remove the mixture from the refrigerator and roll it into small balls about 1 inch in diameter.

5. Place the peanut butter protein balls on a baking sheet lined with parchment paper.

6. Return the balls to the refrigerator and let them chill for 15-30 minutes to firm up.

7. Store the protein balls in an airtight container in the refrigerator for up to 1 week.

Nutritional value (1 serving - 1 ball):

Calories: 120 Protein: 4g Fat: 7g Salt: 35mg

Egg White Wrap

Total servings: 1 serving
Preparation time: 5 minutes
Time to cook: 5 minutes

Ingredients:

- 3 egg whites
- 1 whole wheat or whole grain tortilla wrap
- 1/4 cup chopped vegetables (bell peppers, onions, spinach, etc.)
- Salt and pepper to taste
- Cooking spray (optional)

Instructions:

1. In a small bowl, whisk the egg whites until frothy—season with salt and pepper.

2. Heat a non-stick skillet over medium heat. If needed, lightly coat the skillet with cooking spray to prevent sticking.

3. Pour the whisked egg whites into the skillet and spread them evenly to cover the surface.

4. Cook the egg whites for 2-3 minutes until they start to set.

5. Carefully flip the egg whites using a spatula and cook for 1-2 minutes until fully cooked.

6. Remove the cooked egg whites from the skillet and place them on a tortilla wrap.

7. Top the egg whites with chopped vegetables.

8. Gently fold the sides of the tortilla wrap over the filling and roll it tightly from one end to the other to create a wrap.

Nutritional value (1 serving):

Calories: 170 Protein: 14g Fat: 3g Salt: 250mg

Buckwheat Pancakes

Total servings: 2 pancakes
Preparation time: 10 minutes
Time to cook: 10 minutes

Ingredients:

- 1/2 cup buckwheat flour
- 1/2 teaspoon baking powder
- 1/4 teaspoon salt
- 1/2 cup unsweetened almond milk (or any plant-based milk)
- 1 tablespoon honey or maple syrup
- 1/2 teaspoon vanilla extract
- Cooking spray or a small amount of oil for greasing the pan
- Optional toppings: fresh berries, sliced banana, chopped nuts

Instructions:

1. Whisk together the buckwheat flour, baking powder, and salt in a bowl.

2. Add the almond milk, honey (or maple syrup), and vanilla extract to the dry ingredients. Stir well until a smooth batter forms.

3. Let the batter sit for a few minutes to thicken.

4. Heat a non-stick skillet or griddle over medium heat. Lightly grease the surface with cooking spray or a small amount of oil.

5. Pour about 1/4 cup of the batter onto the heated skillet, using a spoon or measuring cup, to form a round pancake.

6. Cook the pancake for 2-3 minutes until bubbles form on the surface. Flip the pancake and cook for 1-2 minutes until golden brown.

7. Transfer the cooked pancake to a plate and repeat the process with the remaining batter.

8. Serve the buckwheat pancakes warm with your choice of toppings, such as fresh berries, sliced bananas, or chopped nuts.

Nutritional value (1 serving - 2 pancakes):

Calories: 250 Protein: 7g Fat: 2g Salt: 300mg

Mango Coconut Smoothie

Total servings: 1 serving
Preparation time: 5 minutes

Ingredients:

- 1 ripe mango, peeled and pitted
- 1/2 cup unsweetened coconut milk (or any plant-based milk)
- 1/2 cup plain low-fat yogurt (or dairy-free yogurt)
- 1 tablespoon honey or maple syrup
- 1/2 teaspoon vanilla extract
- Ice cubes (optional)

Instructions:

1. Combine the ripe mango, coconut milk, plain yogurt, honey (or maple syrup), and vanilla extract in a blender.

2. Blend on high speed until all the ingredients are well combined and smooth.

3. Add a few ice cubes to the blender and blend until the smoothie is chilled.

4. Pour the mango coconut smoothie into a glass and serve immediately.

Nutritional value (1 serving):

Calories: 250 Protein: 7g Fat: 4g Salt: 60mg

Sweet Potato Toast

Total servings: 1 serving
Preparation time: 5 minutes
Time to cook: 15-20 minutes

Ingredients:

- 1 small sweet potato
- Cooking spray or a small amount of oil for greasing
- Optional toppings: avocado slices, cherry tomatoes, cucumber slices, feta cheese, fresh herbs (e.g., parsley or cilantro), salt, and pepper

Instructions:

1. Preheat the oven to 400°F (200°C).

2. Wash the sweet potato thoroughly and pat it dry.

3. Slice the sweet potato lengthwise into 1/4-inch thick slices.

4. Lightly grease a baking sheet with cooking spray or a small amount of oil.

5. Place the sweet potato slices on the baking sheet in a single layer.

6. Bake in the oven for 15-20 minutes or until the slices are tender and lightly golden around the edges.

7. Remove the sweet potato slices from the oven and let them cool for a few minutes.

8. Top the sweet potato toast with toppings such as avocado, cherry tomatoes, cucumber, feta cheese, fresh herbs, salt, and pepper.

Nutritional value (1 serving):

Calories: 180 Protein: 3g Fat: 0.5g

Mixed Berry Quinoa Bowl

Total servings: 1 serving
Preparation time: 10 minutes
Time to cook: 15 minutes

Ingredients:

- 1/2 cup cooked quinoa
- 1/2 cup mixed berries (strawberries, blueberries, raspberries)
- 2 tablespoons unsweetened Greek yogurt
- 1 tablespoon chopped nuts (almonds, walnuts, or pistachios)
- 1 teaspoon honey or maple syrup
- Fresh mint leaves (optional)

Instructions:

1. In a bowl, combine the cooked quinoa and mixed berries.

2. Top the quinoa and berry mixture with unsweetened Greek yogurt.

3. Sprinkle the chopped nuts over the yogurt.

4. Drizzle honey or maple syrup on top for added sweetness.

5. Garnish with fresh mint leaves, if desired.

6. Serve the mixed berry quinoa bowl immediately.

Nutritional value (1 serving):

Calories: 250 Protein: 8g Fat: 6g Salt: 30mg

Broccoli and Cheese Omelet

Total servings: 1 serving
Preparation time: 10 minutes
Time to cook: 10 minutes

Ingredients:

- 2 large eggs
- 1/4 cup chopped broccoli florets
- 1/4 cup shredded low-fat cheddar cheese
- 1 tablespoon diced onion
- 1 tablespoon diced bell pepper
- Salt and pepper to taste
- Cooking spray or a small amount of oil for greasing

Instructions:

1. In a bowl, whisk the eggs until well beaten—season with salt and pepper.

2. Heat a non-stick skillet over medium heat. Lightly grease the skillet with cooking spray or a small amount of oil.

3. Add the diced onion and bell pepper to the skillet and sauté for 2-3 minutes until slightly softened.

4. Add the chopped broccoli to the skillet and cook for 2 minutes until tender-crisp.

5. Pour the beaten eggs over the cooked vegetables in the skillet, ensuring they spread evenly.

6. Cook the omelet for 3-4 minutes or until the edges are set.

7. Sprinkle the shredded cheddar cheese over one-half of the omelet.

8. Fold the other half of the omelet over the cheese and continue cooking for another 1-2 minutes until the cheese melts and the omelet is cooked.

9. Slide the omelet onto a plate and serve hot.

Nutritional value (1 serving):

Calories: 210 Protein: 18g Fat: 14g Salt: 350mg

Apple Cinnamon Protein Shake

Total servings: 1 serving
Preparation time: 5 minutes

Ingredients:

- 1 medium apple, cored and chopped
- 1 cup unsweetened almond milk (or any plant-based milk)

- 1 scoop vanilla protein powder
- 1/2 teaspoon ground cinnamon
- 1/4 teaspoon vanilla extract
- Ice cubes (optional)

Instructions:

1. Combine the chopped apple, almond milk, vanilla protein powder, ground cinnamon, and vanilla extract in a blender.

2. Blend quickly until all the ingredients are well combined and the shake is smooth.

3. Add a few ice cubes to the blender and blend until the shake is chilled.

4. Pour the apple cinnamon protein shake into a glass and serve immediately.

Nutritional value (1 serving):

Calories: 220 Protein: 25g Fat: 4g Salt: 200mg

Mushroom Breakfast Skillet

Total servings: 1 serving
Preparation time: 10 minutes
Time to cook: 10 minutes

Ingredients:

- 1 cup sliced mushrooms (such as button or cremini mushrooms)
- 1/4 cup diced onion
- 1/4 cup diced bell pepper
- 1 clove garlic, minced
- 2 teaspoons olive oil
- 2 large eggs
- Salt and pepper to taste
- Fresh parsley or chives for garnish (optional)

Instructions:

5. Heat a non-stick skillet over medium heat.

6. Add the olive oil to the skillet and swirl it around to coat the bottom.

7. Add the diced onion, bell pepper, and minced garlic to the skillet. Sauté for 2-3 minutes until the vegetables start to soften.

8. Add the sliced mushrooms to the skillet and continue cooking for another 5 minutes until the mushrooms are tender and lightly browned.

9. Create two small wells in the mushroom mixture and crack the eggs into each well.

10. Season the eggs with salt and pepper to taste.

11. Cover the skillet with a lid and cook for 3-4 minutes until the eggs are cooked to your desired doneness.

12. Remove the skillet from the heat and garnish with fresh parsley or chives.

13. Serve the mushroom breakfast skillet hot.

Nutritional value (1 serving):

Calories: 240 Protein: 13g Fat: 18g Salt: 350mg

Chocolate Protein Overnight Oats

Total servings: 1 serving
Preparation time: 5 minutes

Ingredients:

- 1/2 cup rolled oats
- 1 cup unsweetened almond milk (or any plant-based milk)
- 1 scoop of chocolate protein powder
- 1 tablespoon chia seeds
- 1 tablespoon unsweetened cocoa powder
- 1 tablespoon honey or maple syrup (optional)
- Toppings: sliced bananas, berries, chopped nuts (optional)

Instructions:

14. Combine the rolled oats, almond milk, chocolate protein powder, chia seeds, unsweetened cocoa powder, and honey (or maple syrup if desired) in a mason jar or container.

15. Stir well to combine all the ingredients.

16. Cover the jar or container and refrigerate overnight or for at least 4-6 hours.

17. In the morning, give the mixture a good stir. If the consistency is too thick, add more almond milk to reach the desired consistency.

18. Top the chocolate protein overnight oats with sliced bananas, berries, or chopped nuts if desired.

19. Enjoy the cold oats, or gently heat them in the microwave or stovetop if you prefer warm.

Nutritional value (1 serving):

Calories: 350 Protein: 25g Fat: 10g Salt: 200mg

Chapter 6: Sides

Roasted Garlic Asparagus

Total servings: 1 serving
Preparation time: 5 minutes
Time to cook: 15 minutes

Ingredients:

- 1/2 bunch asparagus, tough ends trimmed
- 1 tablespoon olive oil
- 2 cloves garlic, minced
- Salt and pepper to taste
- Lemon wedges for serving (optional)

Instructions:

1. Preheat the oven to 425°F (220°C).
2. Place the asparagus on a baking sheet.
3. Drizzle olive oil over the asparagus and sprinkle minced garlic evenly.
4. Season with salt and pepper to taste.
5. Toss the asparagus gently to coat them with oil, garlic, salt, and pepper.
6. Spread the asparagus in a single layer on the baking sheet.
7. Roast in the oven for 12-15 minutes until the asparagus is tender but crisp.
8. Remove from the oven and serve the roasted garlic asparagus hot, with lemon wedges on the side if desired.

Nutritional value (1 serving):

Calories: 70 Protein: 3g Fat: 4g Salt: 150mg

Lemon Herb Quinoa

Total servings: 1 serving
Preparation time: 5 minutes
Time to cook: 15-20 minutes

Ingredients:

- 1/2 cup cooked quinoa
- 1 tablespoon freshly squeezed lemon juice
- 1 tablespoon chopped fresh herbs (such as parsley, cilantro, or basil)
- 1/4 teaspoon lemon zest
- Salt and pepper to taste

Instructions:

1. Combine the cooked quinoa, lemon juice, chopped fresh herbs, lemon zest, salt, and pepper in a bowl.
2. Toss the quinoa mixture gently to distribute the flavors evenly.
3. Taste and adjust the seasoning if needed.
4. Serve the lemon herb quinoa as a side dish or as a base for other ingredients.

Nutritional value (1 serving):

Calories: 120 Protein: 4g Fat: 2g Salt: 200mg

Steamed Broccoli Florets

Total servings: 1 serving
Preparation time: 5 minutes
Time to cook: 5-7 minutes

Ingredients:

- 1 cup broccoli florets
- Water for steaming
- Salt and pepper to taste
- Lemon wedges for serving (optional)

Instructions:

1. Fill a pot with about an inch of water and place a steamer basket inside.
2. Bring the water to a boil over medium-high heat.
3. Add the broccoli florets to the steamer basket.
4. Cover the pot and steam the broccoli for 5-7 minutes until it becomes tender but crisp.
5. Check the broccoli for doneness by inserting a fork or knife into a floret. It should easily pierce through.
6. Season the steamed broccoli with salt and pepper to taste.
7. Transfer the broccoli to a serving plate.
8. Serve the steamed broccoli hot, optionally accompanied by lemon wedges for squeezing over the florets.

Nutritional value (1 serving):

Calories: 30 Protein: 3g Fat: 0.5g Salt: 150mg

Balsamic Roasted Brussels Sprouts

Total servings: 1 serving
Preparation time: 10 minutes
Time to cook: 25-30 minutes

Ingredients:

- 1 cup Brussels sprouts, trimmed and halved
- 1 tablespoon olive oil
- 1 tablespoon balsamic vinegar
- Salt and pepper to taste

Instructions:

1. Preheat the oven to 425°F (220°C).

2. Toss the Brussels sprouts in a bowl with olive oil, balsamic vinegar, salt, and pepper.

3. Ensure the Brussels sprouts are evenly coated with the oil and vinegar mixture.

4. Spread the Brussels sprouts in a single layer on a baking sheet.

5. Roast in the preheated oven for 25-30 minutes, stirring once halfway through, until the Brussels sprouts are browned and tender.

6. Remove from the oven and let them cool for a few minutes.

7. Serve the balsamic roasted Brussels sprouts warm.

Nutritional value (1 serving):

Calories: 80 Protein: 4g Fat: 4g Salt: 150mg

Cucumber Tomato Salad

Total servings: 1 serving
Preparation time: 10 minutes
Time to cook: No cooking required

Ingredients:

- 1 medium cucumber, sliced
- 1 medium tomato, diced
- 1/4 small red onion, thinly sliced
- 2 tablespoons chopped fresh parsley
- 1 tablespoon extra virgin olive oil
- 1 tablespoon fresh lemon juice
- Salt and pepper to taste

Instructions:

1. Combine the sliced cucumber, diced tomato, thinly sliced red onion, and chopped fresh parsley.

2. Whisk together the extra virgin olive oil and fresh lemon juice separately.

3. Pour the dressing over the cucumber-tomato mixture and toss gently to coat.

4. Season with salt and pepper to taste.

5. Let the salad sit for a few minutes to allow the flavors to blend.

6. Serve the cucumber tomato salad chilled or at room temperature.

Nutritional value (1 serving):

Calories: 70 Protein: 2g Fat: 5g Salt: 150mg

Grilled Zucchini Spears

Total servings: 1 serving
Preparation time: 10 minutes
Time to cook: 8-10 minutes

Ingredients:

- 1 medium zucchini, cut into spears
- 1 tablespoon olive oil
- 1/2 teaspoon dried herbs (such as oregano, basil, or thyme)
- Salt and pepper to taste

Instructions:

1. Preheat a grill or grill pan over medium-high heat.

2. Toss the zucchini spears in a bowl with olive oil, dried herbs, salt, and pepper.

3. Make sure the zucchini spears are evenly coated with the oil and herbs.

4. Place the zucchini spears on the preheated grill or grill pan.

5. Grill 4-5 minutes on each side until the zucchini is tender and slightly charred.

6. Remove from the grill and let them cool for a few minutes.

7. Serve the grilled zucchini spears warm.

Nutritional value (1 serving):

Calories: 60 Protein: 2g Fat: 5g Salt: 150mg

Roasted Cauliflower Bites

Total servings: 1 serving
Preparation time: 10 minutes
Time to cook: 25-30 minutes

Ingredients:

- 1 cup cauliflower florets

- 1 tablespoon olive oil
- 1/2 teaspoon smoked paprika
- 1/4 teaspoon garlic powder
- Salt and pepper to taste

Instructions:

1. Preheat the oven to 425°F (220°C).

2. Toss the cauliflower florets in a bowl with olive oil, smoked paprika, garlic powder, salt, and pepper.

3. Make sure the cauliflower florets are evenly coated with the oil and spices.

4. Spread the cauliflower in a single layer on a baking sheet.

5. Roast in the preheated oven for 25-30 minutes, stirring once halfway through, until the cauliflower is golden brown and tender.

6. Remove from the oven and let them cool for a few minutes.

7. Serve the roasted cauliflower bites warm.

Nutritional value (1 serving):

Calories: 70 Protein: 2g Fat: 5g Salt: 150mg

Garlic Parmesan Green Beans

Total servings: 1 serving
Preparation time: 10 minutes
Time to cook: 10-12 minutes

Ingredients:

- 1 cup green beans, trimmed
- 1 teaspoon olive oil
- 1 clove garlic, minced
- 1 tablespoon grated Parmesan cheese
- Salt and pepper to taste

Instructions:

1. Blanch the green beans in boiling water for 2-3 minutes until they turn bright green and slightly tender.

2. Drain the green beans and set aside.

3. In a skillet, heat olive oil over medium heat.

4. Add minced garlic to the skillet and sauté for 1-2 minutes until fragrant.

5. Add the blanched green beans to the skillet and sauté for 3-4 minutes until cooked to your desired tenderness.

6. Sprinkle grated Parmesan cheese over the green beans and toss to coat.

7. Season with salt and pepper to taste.

8. Remove from the heat and let them cool for a few minutes.

9. Serve the garlic Parmesan green beans warm.

Nutritional value (1 serving):

Calories: 80 Protein: 4g Fat: 4g Salt: 200mg

Sweet Potato Wedges

Total servings: 1 serving
Preparation time: 10 minutes
Time to cook: 25-30 minutes

Ingredients:

- 1 medium sweet potato
- 1 tablespoon olive oil
- 1/2 teaspoon paprika
- 1/4 teaspoon garlic powder
- Salt and pepper to taste

Instructions:

1. Preheat the oven to 425°F (220°C).

2. Wash the sweet potato thoroughly and pat it dry.

3. Cut the sweet potato into wedges, about 1/2 inch thick.

4. Toss the sweet potato wedges with olive oil, paprika, garlic powder, salt, and pepper in a bowl.

5. Ensure the sweet potato wedges are evenly coated with the oil and spices.

6. Spread the wedges in a single layer on a baking sheet.

7. Roast in the preheated oven for 25-30 minutes, flipping halfway through, until the sweet potato wedges are crispy and golden brown.

8. Remove from the oven and let them cool for a few minutes.

9. Serve the sweet potato wedges warm.

Nutritional value (1 serving):

Calories: 150 Protein: 2g Fat: 4g Salt: 150mg

Spinach Strawberry Salad

Total servings: 1 serving
Preparation time: 10 minutes
Time to cook: No cooking required

Ingredients:

- 2 cups fresh spinach leaves

- 1/2 cup sliced strawberries
- 2 tablespoons chopped walnuts
- 1 tablespoon crumbled feta cheese
- 1 tablespoon balsamic vinegar
- 1/2 tablespoon extra virgin olive oil
- Salt and pepper to taste

Instructions:

1. Combine the fresh spinach leaves, sliced strawberries, chopped walnuts, and crumbled feta cheese in a bowl.

2. Whisk together the balsamic vinegar, extra virgin olive oil, salt, and pepper in a small separate bowl.

3. Pour the dressing over the salad mixture and toss gently to coat.

4. Adjust the seasoning with salt and pepper if needed.

5. Let the salad sit for a few minutes to allow the flavors to meld.

6. Serve the spinach-strawberry salad immediately.

Nutritional value (1 serving):

Calories: 180 Protein: 4g Fat: 12g Salt: 250mg

Grilled Eggplant Slices

Total servings: 1 serving
Preparation time: 10 minutes
Time to cook: 8–10 minutes

Ingredients:

- 1 small eggplant
- 1 tablespoon olive oil
- 1/2 teaspoon dried oregano
- 1/4 teaspoon garlic powder
- Salt and pepper to taste

Instructions:

1. Preheat the grill or grill pan over medium-high heat.

2. Slice the eggplant into 1/2-inch thick rounds.

3. Combine the olive oil, dried oregano, garlic powder, salt, and pepper in a bowl.

4. Brush both sides of the eggplant slices with the oil and spice mixture.

5. Place the eggplant slices on the preheated grill or grill pan.

6. Grill 4–5 minutes on each side until the eggplant is tender and grill marks appear.

7. Remove from the grill and let them cool for a few minutes.

8. Serve the grilled eggplant slices warm.

Nutritional value (1 serving):

Calories: 120 Protein: 2g Fat: 8g Salt: 150mg

Mediterranean Quinoa Salad

Total servings: 1 serving
Preparation time: 10 minutes
Time to cook: 15–20 minutes

Ingredients:

- 1/2 cup cooked quinoa
- 1/4 cup diced cucumber
- 1/4 cup halved cherry tomatoes
- 2 tablespoons diced red onion
- 2 tablespoons chopped Kalamata olives
- 2 tablespoons crumbled feta cheese
- 1 tablespoon fresh lemon juice
- 1 tablespoon extra virgin olive oil
- 1/2 tablespoon chopped fresh parsley
- Salt and pepper to taste

Instructions:

1. Combine the cooked quinoa, diced cucumber, halved cherry tomatoes, red onion, chopped Kalamata olives, and crumbled feta cheese in a bowl.

2. Whisk together the fresh lemon juice, extra virgin olive oil, chopped fresh parsley, salt, and pepper in a small separate bowl.

3. Pour the dressing over the quinoa salad mixture and toss gently to coat.

4. Adjust the seasoning with salt and pepper if needed.

5. Let the salad sit for a few minutes to allow the flavors to meld.

6. Serve the Mediterranean quinoa salad chilled or at room temperature.

Nutritional value (1 serving):

Calories: 220 Protein: 8g Fat: 12g Salt: 400mg

Sesame Ginger Snap Peas

Total servings: 1 serving
Preparation time: 5 minutes
Time to cook: 5 minutes

Ingredients:

- 1 cup snap peas
- 1 teaspoon sesame oil
- 1/2 teaspoon grated ginger
- 1/2 teaspoon low-sodium soy sauce
- 1/2 teaspoon sesame seeds
- Salt to taste

Instructions:

1. Trim the ends of the snap peas and rinse them under cold water.

2. In a skillet or wok, heat the sesame oil over medium heat.

3. Add the snap peas to the skillet and stir-fry for 3-4 minutes until tender-crisp.

4. Mix the grated ginger, low-sodium soy sauce, sesame seeds, and a pinch of salt in a small bowl.

5. Pour the ginger sauce over the snap peas in the skillet and toss to coat evenly.

6. Cook for an additional minute, allowing the flavors to meld.

7. Remove from heat and transfer the sesame ginger snap peas to a serving dish.

8. Serve the snap peas warm or at room temperature.

Nutritional value (1 serving):

Calories: 60 Protein: 2g Fat: 3g Salt: 200mg

Caprese Skewers

Total servings: 1 serving
Preparation time: 10 minutes
Time to cook: No cooking required

Ingredients:

- 4 cherry tomatoes
- 4 small fresh mozzarella balls
- 4 fresh basil leaves
- 1 teaspoon extra virgin olive oil
- 1/2 teaspoon balsamic glaze
- Salt and pepper to taste

Instructions:

1. Rinse the cherry tomatoes and basil leaves under cold water.

2. Thread one cherry tomato, mozzarella ball, and basil leaf onto a skewer or toothpick.

3. Repeat the process for the remaining tomatoes, mozzarella, and basil, creating four skewers.

4. Place the skewers on a serving plate.

5. Drizzle the extra virgin olive oil and balsamic glaze over the skewers.

6. Sprinkle with salt and pepper to taste.

7. Let the caprese skewers sit for a few minutes to allow the flavors to meld.

8. Serve the skewers at room temperature.

Nutritional value (1 serving):

Calories: 120 Protein: 8g Fat: 8g Salt: 250mg

Roasted Beet Salad

Total servings: 1 serving
Preparation time: 10 minutes
Time to cook: 40 minutes

Ingredients:

- 1 small beet
- 2 cups mixed salad greens
- 1/4 cup crumbled goat cheese
- 2 tablespoons chopped walnuts
- 1 tablespoon balsamic vinegar
- 1 tablespoon extra virgin olive oil
- Salt and pepper to taste

Instructions:

1. Preheat the oven to 400°F (200°C).

2. Scrub the beet clean and trim off the ends. Wrap the beet in aluminum foil.

3. Place the wrapped beet on a baking sheet and roast in the oven for 40 minutes or until tender when pierced with a fork.

4. Remove the beet from the oven and let it cool. Once cool, peel off the skin and cut the beet into bite-sized cubes.

5. Combine the mixed salad greens, cubed beet, crumbled goat cheese, and chopped walnuts in a large bowl.

6. Whisk together the balsamic vinegar, extra virgin olive oil, salt, and pepper in a small separate bowl.

7. Pour the dressing over the salad mixture and toss gently to coat.

8. Adjust the seasoning with salt and pepper if needed.

9. Serve the roasted beet salad chilled or at room temperature.

Nutritional value (1 serving):

Calories: 250 Protein: 8g Fat: 16g Salt: 300mg

Grilled Portobello Mushrooms

Total servings: 1 serving
Preparation time: 5 minutes
Time to cook: 10 minutes

Ingredients:

- 1 large portobello mushroom cap
- 1 tablespoon balsamic vinegar
- 1 tablespoon extra virgin olive oil
- 1/2 teaspoon dried thyme
- Salt and pepper to taste

Instructions:

1. Preheat the grill or grill pan over medium-high heat.

2. Clean the portobello mushroom cap and remove the stem.

3. Whisk together the balsamic vinegar, extra virgin olive oil dried thyme, salt, and pepper in a small bowl.

4. Brush both sides of the portobello mushroom cap with the oil and spice mixture.

5. Place the mushroom cap on the preheated grill or grill pan, gill-side down.

6. Grill for about 5 minutes, then flip the mushroom cap and grill for 5 minutes until it is tender and juicy.

7. Remove from the grill and let it cool for a few minutes.

8. Slice the grilled portobello mushroom cap into strips or serve it whole.

9. Serve the grilled portobello mushrooms warm.

Nutritional value (1 serving):

Calories: 120 Protein: 6g Fat: 8g Salt: 200mg

Citrus Kale Salad

Total servings: 1 serving
Preparation time: 10 minutes
Time to cook: No cooking required

Ingredients:

- 2 cups kale leaves, stems removed and torn into bite-sized pieces
- 1 small orange, peeled and segmented
- 1/4 cup sliced almonds
- 1 tablespoon extra virgin olive oil
- 1 tablespoon freshly squeezed lemon juice
- 1/2 teaspoon honey or maple syrup (optional)
- Salt and pepper to taste

Instructions:

1. Combine the kale leaves, orange segments, and sliced almonds in a large bowl.

2. Whisk together the extra virgin olive oil, lemon juice, honey, or maple syrup (if using), salt, and pepper in a small separate bowl.

3. Pour the dressing over the kale mixture.

4. Using clean hands, gently massage the dressing into the kale leaves for a few minutes to help soften them.

5. Let the salad sit for 5 minutes to allow the flavors to meld.

6. Adjust the seasoning with salt and pepper if needed.

7. Serve the citrus kale salad as a refreshing side dish, or add grilled chicken or chickpeas for a complete meal.

Nutritional value (1 serving):

Calories: 220 Protein: 7g Fat: 15g Salt: 150mg

Ratatouille

Total servings: 1 serving
Preparation time: 15 minutes
Time to cook: 30 minutes

Ingredients:

- 1 small eggplant, diced
- 1 small zucchini, diced
- 1 small yellow squash, diced
- 1 small red bell pepper, diced
- 1 small onion, diced
- 2 cloves garlic, minced
- 1 cup diced tomatoes (fresh or canned)
- 1 tablespoon extra virgin olive oil
- 1/2 teaspoon dried thyme
- 1/2 teaspoon dried basil
- Salt and pepper to taste

Instructions:

1. Heat the extra virgin olive oil in a large skillet or pot over medium heat.

2. Add the diced eggplant, zucchini, yellow squash, red bell pepper, onion, and minced garlic to the skillet.

3. Sauté the vegetables for about 10 minutes, stirring occasionally, until they soften.

4. Add the diced tomatoes, dried thyme, basil, salt, and pepper to the skillet.

5. Stir well to combine all the ingredients.

6. Reduce the heat to low and let the ratatouille simmer

for about 20 minutes, allowing the flavors to meld and the vegetables to tender.

7. Adjust the seasoning with salt and pepper if needed.

8. Serve the ratatouille warm as a side dish or a main course with whole-grain bread or brown rice.

Nutritional value (1 serving):

Calories: 180 Protein: 5g Fat: 8g Salt: 250mg

Quinoa Stuffed Bell Peppers

Total servings: 1 serving
Preparation time: 15 minutes
Time to cook: 35 minutes

Ingredients:

- 1 bell pepper (any color), halved and seeds removed
- 1/4 cup quinoa, rinsed
- 1/2 cup vegetable broth
- 1/4 cup diced tomatoes (fresh or canned)
- 1/4 cup diced zucchini
- 1/4 cup diced yellow squash
- 2 tablespoons diced onion
- 2 cloves garlic, minced
- 1/2 teaspoon dried basil
- 1/2 teaspoon dried oregano
- Salt and pepper to taste
- 1 tablespoon grated Parmesan cheese (optional)

Instructions:

1. Preheat the oven to 375°F (190°C).

2. In a small saucepan, bring the vegetable broth to a boil. Add the quinoa, reduce the heat to low, cover, and simmer for 15 minutes or until the quinoa is cooked and the liquid is absorbed.

3. While the quinoa is cooking, prepare the bell pepper halves by placing them cut side up in a baking dish.

4. Combine the cooked quinoa, diced tomatoes, zucchini, yellow squash, onion, minced garlic, dried basil, dried oregano, salt, and pepper in a mixing bowl. Stir well to combine.

5. Spoon the quinoa mixture into the bell pepper halves, filling them generously.

6. Cover the baking dish with aluminum foil and bake for 20 minutes.

7. Remove the foil, sprinkle the stuffed bell peppers with grated Parmesan cheese (if using), and bake for 5 minutes or until the peppers are tender and the cheese is melted.

8. Serve the quinoa stuffed bell peppers as a satisfying and nutritious main course.

Nutritional value (1 serving):

Calories: 280 Protein: 12g Fat: 5g Salt: 650mg

Greek Cucumber Salad

Total servings: 1 serving
Preparation time: 10 minutes
Time to cook: No cooking required

Ingredients:

- 1 small cucumber, peeled and sliced
- 1/4 cup cherry tomatoes, halved
- 1/4 cup sliced Kalamata olives
- 2 tablespoons crumbled feta cheese
- 1 tablespoon extra virgin olive oil
- 1 tablespoon freshly squeezed lemon juice
- 1/2 teaspoon dried oregano
- Salt and pepper to taste

Instructions:

1. Combine the sliced cucumber, cherry tomatoes, Kalamata olives, and crumbled feta cheese in a bowl.

2. Whisk together the extra virgin olive oil, lemon juice, dried oregano, salt, and pepper in a small separate bowl.

3. Pour the dressing over the cucumber mixture and toss gently to coat all the ingredients.

4. Let the salad marinate for a few minutes to allow the flavors to blend.

5. Adjust the seasoning with salt and pepper if needed.

6. Serve the Greek cucumber salad as a refreshing, tangy side dish or a light lunch option.

Nutritional value (1 serving):

Calories: 170 Protein: 4g Fat: 13g Salt: 600mg

Steamed Asparagus Bundles

Total servings: 1 serving
Preparation time: 10 minutes
Time to cook: 10 minutes

Ingredients:

- 6-8 asparagus spears
- 1 teaspoon olive oil

- 1 clove garlic, minced
- Salt and pepper to taste
- Lemon wedges for serving

Instructions:

1. Trim the tough ends of the asparagus spears about 1-2 inches from the bottom.

2. Divide the asparagus spears into 2 bundles, then tie each with kitchen twine.

3. Fill a pot with about an inch of water and bring it to a boil.

4. Place the asparagus bundles in a steamer basket or a heatproof colander, ensuring they are elevated above the water level.

5. Carefully place the steamer basket or colander in the pot, cover, and steam for about 5-7 minutes or until the asparagus is tender yet still crisp.

6. While the asparagus is steaming, heat olive oil in a small skillet over medium heat. Add minced garlic and sauté for 1-2 minutes until fragrant. Remove from heat.

7. Once the asparagus is done steaming, transfer the bundles to a serving plate. Remove the twine.

8. Drizzle the garlic-infused olive oil over the asparagus and season with salt and pepper.

9. Serve the steamed asparagus bundles with lemon wedges on the side for squeezing over the asparagus.

Nutritional value (1 serving):

Calories: 50 Protein: 3g Fat: 2g Salt: 150mg

Lemon Garlic Roasted Potatoes

Total servings: 1 serving
Preparation time: 10 minutes
Time to cook: 30 minutes

Ingredients:

- 1 medium-sized potato cut into small wedges
- 1 teaspoon olive oil
- 1 clove garlic, minced
- 1 tablespoon freshly squeezed lemon juice
- 1/2 teaspoon dried thyme
- Salt and pepper to taste
- Chopped fresh parsley for garnish (optional)

Instructions:

1. Preheat the oven to 400°F (200°C).

2. Combine the potato wedges, olive oil, minced garlic, lemon juice, dried thyme, salt, and pepper in a mixing bowl. Toss well to coat the potatoes evenly.

3. Transfer the seasoned potato wedges to a baking sheet lined with parchment paper, spreading them out in a single layer.

4. Place the baking sheet in the preheated oven and roast for about 25-30 minutes or until the potatoes are golden brown and crispy on the outside and tender on the inside. Flip the wedges halfway through cooking for even browning.

5. Once done, remove the roasted potatoes from the oven and transfer them to a serving dish.

6. Garnish with chopped fresh parsley, if desired.

7. Serve the lemon garlic roasted potatoes as a delicious and satisfying side dish.

Nutritional value (1 serving):

Calories: 180 Protein: 3g Fat: 4g Salt: 200mg

Spicy Roasted Chickpeas

Total servings: 1 serving
Preparation time: 5 minutes
Time to cook: 25 minutes

Ingredients:

- 1 cup cooked chickpeas (canned or cooked from dry)
- 1 tablespoon olive oil
- 1/2 teaspoon ground cumin
- 1/2 teaspoon paprika
- 1/4 teaspoon cayenne pepper (adjust to taste)
- 1/4 teaspoon garlic powder
- Salt to taste

Instructions:

1. Preheat the oven to 400°F (200°C).

2. Rinse and drain the chickpeas, then pat them dry using a clean kitchen towel or paper towel.

3. Combine chickpeas, olive oil, ground cumin, paprika, cayenne pepper, garlic powder, and salt in a bowl. Toss well to coat the chickpeas with the spices and oil evenly.

4. Spread the seasoned chickpeas on a baking sheet lined with parchment paper, ensuring they are in a single layer.

5. Place the baking sheet in the preheated oven and roast for about 20-25 minutes or until the chickpeas are crispy and golden brown, stirring them halfway through to ensure even cooking.

6. Once done, remove the roasted chickpeas from the oven and let them cool slightly before serving.

Nutritional value (1 serving):

Calories: 220 Protein: 10g Fat: 7g Salt: 200mg

Grilled Corn on the Cob

Total servings: 1 serving
Preparation time: 5 minutes
Time to cook: 10-15 minutes

Ingredients:

- 1 ear of corn
- 1 teaspoon olive oil
- Salt and pepper to taste
- Fresh lime wedges for serving (optional)
- Chopped fresh herbs (such as cilantro or parsley) for garnish (optional)

Instructions:

1. Preheat the grill to medium-high heat.

2. Peel back the husks of the corn, leaving them attached at the base. Remove the silk strands and fold the husks back over the corn.

3. Mix the olive oil, salt, and pepper in a small bowl.

4. Brush the olive oil mixture onto the corn, ensuring it is evenly coated.

5. Place the corn on the grill and close the lid. Grill for 10-15 minutes, turning occasionally, until the corn is tender and lightly charred.

6. Once done, carefully remove the corn from the grill and let it cool for a few minutes.

7. Remove the husks and silk from the corn, or leave the husks partially attached for a rustic presentation.

8. Squeeze fresh lime juice over the grilled corn, and sprinkle with chopped fresh herbs for added flavor and garnish.

Nutritional value (1 serving):

Calories: 100 Protein: 3g Fat: 3g Salt: 150mg

Green Bean Almondine

Total servings: 1 serving
Preparation time: 10 minutes
Time to cook: 10 minutes

Ingredients:

- 1 cup green beans, trimmed
- 1 tablespoon sliced almonds
- 1 tablespoon olive oil

- 1 garlic clove, minced
- 1 teaspoon lemon juice
- Salt and pepper to taste

Instructions:

1. Bring a pot of salted water to a boil. Add the green beans and cook for 2-3 minutes until they are tender-crisp. Drain and set aside.

2. In a skillet, heat the olive oil over medium heat. Add the sliced almonds and toast until golden brown, stirring frequently to prevent burning.

3. Add the minced garlic to the skillet and sauté for 30 seconds until fragrant.

4. Add the cooked green beans to the skillet and toss them with the garlic and almonds.

5. Drizzle the lemon juice over the green beans and season with salt and pepper to taste. Toss well to combine.

6. Cook for another 1-2 minutes until the flavors are well incorporated.

7. Remove from heat and serve the green beans almondine as a side dish.

Nutritional value (1 serving):

Calories: 120 Protein: 4g Fat: 9g Salt: 150mg

Mediterranean Lentil Salad

Total servings: 1 serving
Preparation time: 10 minutes
Time to cook: 20 minutes

Ingredients:

- 1/2 cup cooked lentils
- 1/4 cup cherry tomatoes, halved
- 1/4 cup cucumber, diced
- 2 tablespoons red onion, finely chopped
- 1 tablespoon fresh parsley, chopped
- 1 tablespoon lemon juice
- 1 tablespoon extra-virgin olive oil
- Salt and pepper to taste

Instructions:

1. Combine the cooked lentils, cherry tomatoes, cucumber, red onion, and fresh parsley in a bowl.

2. Whisk the lemon juice and extra-virgin olive oil in a separate small bowl to make the dressing.

3. Pour the sauce over the lentil mixture and toss gently to coat all the ingredients.

4. Season with salt and pepper to taste.

5. Let the salad marinate for at least 10 minutes to allow the flavors to blend.

6. Serve the Mediterranean lentil salad as a refreshing and nutritious or light meal.

Nutritional value (1 serving):

Calories: 180 Protein: 8g Fat: 6g Salt: 200mg

Baked Sweet Potato Fries

Total servings: 1 serving
Preparation time: 10 minutes
Time to cook: 25 minutes

Ingredients:

- 1 medium sweet potato
- 1 tablespoon olive oil
- 1/2 teaspoon paprika
- 1/4 teaspoon garlic powder
- Salt and pepper to taste

Instructions:

1. Preheat the oven to 425°F (220°C) and line a baking sheet with parchment paper.

2. Wash and peel the sweet potato. Cut it into long, thin strips resembling fries.

3. Toss the sweet potato strips with olive oil, paprika, garlic powder, salt, and pepper in a bowl. Ensure the fries are evenly coated with the seasonings.

4. Arrange the seasoned sweet potato fries in a single layer on the prepared baking sheet.

5. Bake in the oven for approximately 20-25 minutes or until the fries are golden brown and crispy. Flip them halfway through the cooking time for even browning.

6. Once cooked, remove the sweet potato fries from the oven and let them cool for a few minutes before serving.

Nutritional value (1 serving):

Calories: 150 Protein: 2g Fat: 7g Salt: 200mg

Tomatoes and Mozzarella Salad

Total servings: 1 serving
Preparation time: 10 minutes

Ingredients:

- 1 medium tomato, sliced
- 2 ounces fresh mozzarella cheese, sliced

- Fresh basil leaves, torn
- 1 tablespoon balsamic vinegar
- 1 tablespoon extra-virgin olive oil
- Salt and pepper to taste

Instructions:

1. Arrange the tomato slices and mozzarella slices on a plate or platter.

2. Scatter torn basil leaves over the tomatoes and mozzarella.

3. Whisk the balsamic vinegar and extra-virgin olive oil in a small bowl to make the dressing.

4. Drizzle the sauce over the tomato and mozzarella slices.

5. Season with salt and pepper to taste.

6. Allow the flavors to meld together for a few minutes before serving.

7. Nutritional value (1 serving):

Calories: 220 Protein: 10g Fat: 16g Salt: 300mg

Herb Roasted Carrots

Total servings: 1 serving
Preparation time: 10 minutes
Time to cook: 25 minutes

Ingredients:

- 3 medium carrots, peeled and sliced into sticks
- 1 tablespoon olive oil
- 1/2 teaspoon dried thyme
- 1/2 teaspoon dried rosemary
- 1/4 teaspoon garlic powder
- Salt and pepper to taste

Instructions:

1. Preheat the oven to 400°F (200°C) and line a baking sheet with parchment paper.

2. Toss the carrot sticks with olive oil, dried thyme, rosemary, garlic powder, salt, and pepper in a bowl. Ensure the carrots are evenly coated with the herbs and seasonings.

3. Arrange the seasoned carrot sticks in a single layer on the prepared baking sheet.

4. Roast in the oven for approximately 20-25 minutes, or until the carrots are tender and slightly caramelized, stirring them halfway through for even cooking.

5. Once roasted, remove the carrots from the oven and let them cool for a few minutes before serving.

Nutritional value (1 serving):

Quinoa Cucumber Cups

Total servings: 1 serving
Preparation time: 15 minutes
Time to cook: 15 minutes

Ingredients:

- 1/4 cup quinoa
- 1/2 cup water
- 1 small cucumber
- 1/4 cup cherry tomatoes, halved
- 2 tablespoons chopped fresh parsley
- 1 tablespoon lemon juice
- 1 tablespoon extra-virgin olive oil
- Salt and pepper to taste

Instructions:

1. Rinse the quinoa under cold water and drain well.

2. In a small saucepan, bring the water to a boil. Add the quinoa, reduce the heat to low, cover, and simmer for 12-15 minutes, or until the water is absorbed and the quinoa is tender.

3. While the quinoa is cooking, slice the cucumber into 1-inch thick rounds. Using a melon baller or a small spoon, scoop out the center of each cucumber slice to create a small cup shape.

4. Combine the cooked quinoa, cherry tomatoes, chopped parsley, lemon juice, extra-virgin olive oil, salt, and pepper in a bowl. Mix well to combine.

5. Spoon the quinoa mixture into the cucumber cups, filling them evenly.

6. Serve the quinoa cucumber cups as a refreshing and nutritious appetizer or light meal.

Nutritional value (1 serving):

Calories: 180 Protein: 4g Fat: 8g Salt: 100mg

Roasted Red Pepper Hummus

Total servings: 1 serving
Preparation time: 10 minutes
Time to cook: 20 minutes

Ingredients:

- 1 can (15 ounces) chickpeas, drained and rinsed
- 1 roasted red pepper, peeled and deseeded
- 2 tablespoons tahini
- 2 tablespoons lemon juice
- 1 garlic clove, minced
- 1/2 teaspoon ground cumin
- 2 tablespoons extra-virgin olive oil
- Salt to taste

Instructions:

1. Combine chickpeas, roasted red pepper, tahini, lemon juice, garlic, cumin, and salt in a food processor. Process until smooth.

2. While the food processor is running, slowly drizzle in the olive oil and continue blending until well incorporated and the hummus has a creamy consistency.

3. Taste the hummus and adjust the seasoning if needed, adding more salt or lemon juice to your preference.

4. Transfer the hummus to a serving bowl and garnish with a drizzle of olive oil and a sprinkle of cumin, if desired.

5. Serve the roasted red pepper hummus with fresh-cut vegetables, whole-grain crackers, or pita bread.

Nutritional value (1 serving):

Calories: 180 Protein: 7g Fat: 10g Salt: 200mg

Steamed Artichoke with Lemon Aioli

Total servings: 1 serving
Preparation time: 10 minutes
Time to cook: 25 minutes

Ingredients:

- 1 medium-sized artichoke
- 1 lemon, halved
- Water for steaming
- For the Lemon Aioli:
- 2 tablespoons mayonnaise
- 1 tablespoon lemon juice
- 1 garlic clove, minced
- Salt and pepper to taste

Instructions:

1. Trim the stem of the artichoke, leaving about 1 inch attached. Remove any tough outer leaves.

2. Cut about 1/4 inch off the top of the artichoke to remove the prickly tips.

3. Rub the cut surfaces of the artichoke with half of a lemon to prevent browning.

4. Fill a pot with a few inches of water and squeeze in the juice of the remaining lemon. Place a steamer basket or colander over the pool.

5. Place the artichoke in the steamer basket, cover the pot, and bring the water to a boil. Reduce the heat to medium-low and steam the artichoke for about 20-25 minutes or until the outer leaves pull off easily.

6. While the artichoke is steaming, prepare the lemon aioli by combining mayonnaise, lemon juice, minced garlic, salt, and pepper in a small bowl. Mix well.

7. Once the artichoke is cooked, please remove it from the steamer and let it cool for a few minutes.

8. Serve the steamed artichoke with the lemon aioli as a dipping sauce. To eat, pull off the leaves one at a time, dipping the base of each leaf into the lemon aioli, and scrape off the tender portion with your teeth. Discard the remaining leaves and enjoy the artichoke heart.

Nutritional value (1 serving):

Calories: 220 Protein: 2g Fat: 17g Salt: 300mg

Watermelon Feta Salad

Total servings: 1 serving
Preparation time: 15 minutes
Time to cook: None (no cooking required)

Ingredients:

- 2 cups cubed watermelon
- 2 ounces of crumbled feta cheese
- 2 tablespoons fresh mint leaves, chopped
- 1 tablespoon extra-virgin olive oil
- 1 tablespoon balsamic vinegar
- Salt and pepper to taste

Instructions:

1. Combine the cubed watermelon, crumbled feta cheese, and chopped mint leaves in a large bowl.

2. Whisk the extra-virgin olive oil and balsamic vinegar in a small bowl to make the dressing.

3. Drizzle the dressing over the watermelon, feta, and mint mixture.

4. Gently toss the salad to coat the ingredients with the sauce.

5. Season with salt and pepper to taste.

6. Serve the watermelon feta salad immediately as a refreshing, light side dish or appetizer.

Nutritional value (1 serving):

Calories: 190 Protein: 6g Fat: 10g Salt: 300mg

Grilled Radicchio with Balsamic Glaze

Total servings: 1 serving
Preparation time: 5 minutes
Time to cook: 10 minutes

Ingredients:

- 1 head of radicchio, halved
- 1 tablespoon extra-virgin olive oil
- Salt and pepper to taste
- 1 tablespoon balsamic glaze

Instructions:

1. Preheat the grill to medium-high heat.

2. Drizzle the cut sides of the radicchio halves with extra-virgin olive oil.

3. Season with salt and pepper to taste.

4. Place the radicchio halves on the preheated grill, cut side down.

5. Grill for about 4-5 minutes or until charred and slightly wilted.

6. Flip the radicchio halves and grill on the other side for 4-5 minutes.

7. Remove the grilled radicchio from the heat and transfer it to a serving plate.

8. Drizzle the balsamic glaze over the grilled radicchio.

9. Serve the grilled radicchio with balsamic glaze as a flavorful and nutritious side dish or salad component.

Nutritional value (1 serving):

Calories: 90 Protein: 2g Fat: 6g Salt: 150mg

Spaghetti Squash with Marinara Sauce

Total servings: 1 serving
Preparation time: 10 minutes
Time to cook: 40 minutes

Ingredients:

- 1 small spaghetti squash
- 1 cup marinara sauce (store-bought or homemade)
- 1 tablespoon olive oil
- 2 cloves garlic, minced
- 1/4 teaspoon dried oregano

- Salt and pepper to taste
- Fresh basil leaves, chopped (for garnish)

Instructions:

1. Preheat the oven to 400°F (200°C).

2. Cut the spaghetti squash in half lengthwise. Scoop out the seeds and discard them.

3. Brush the cut sides of the squash with olive oil and season with salt and pepper.

4. Place the squash halves, cut side down, on a baking sheet lined with parchment paper.

5. Roast in the preheated oven for 35-40 minutes or until the flesh is tender and easily separates into spaghetti-like strands when scraped with a fork.

6. While the squash is roasting, prepare the marinara sauce. In a saucepan, heat olive oil over medium heat.

7. Add minced garlic and dried oregano. Sauté for about 1 minute until fragrant.

8. Pour the marinara sauce and simmer for 5-10 minutes, stirring occasionally—season with salt and pepper to taste.

9. Once the spaghetti squash is cooked, use a fork to scrape the flesh into strands, creating "spaghetti."

10. Serve the spaghetti squash with marinara sauce, spooning the sauce over the squash strands.

11. Garnish with fresh basil leaves.

12. Enjoy this healthy and flavorful alternative to traditional pasta!

Nutritional value (1 serving):

Calories: 250 Protein: 4g Fat: 10g Salt: 600mg

Greek Spinach Rice

Total servings: 1 serving
Preparation time: 10 minutes
Time to cook: 20 minutes

Ingredients:

- 1/2 cup brown rice
- 1 cup water
- 1 tablespoon olive oil
- 1 small onion, finely chopped
- 2 cloves garlic, minced
- 2 cups fresh spinach leaves
- 1/4 cup chopped fresh dill
- 1 tablespoon lemon juice
- Salt and pepper to taste

Instructions:

1. Rinse the brown rice under cold water until the water runs clear.

2. In a saucepan, combine the rinsed rice and water. Bring to a boil over medium heat.

3. Reduce the heat to low, cover the saucepan, and simmer for 45 minutes or until the rice is tender.

4. In a separate skillet, heat olive oil over medium heat.

5. Add chopped onion and minced garlic to the skillet. Sauté for 3-4 minutes until the onion becomes translucent.

6. Add the fresh spinach leaves to the skillet and cook until wilted.

7. Stir in the cooked brown rice, chopped dill, and lemon juice. Mix well.

8. Season with salt and pepper to taste.

9. Cook for 2-3 minutes to allow the flavors to meld together.

10. Serve the Greek spinach rice as a delicious and nutritious side dish.

Nutritional value (1 serving):

Calories: 300 Protein: 7g Fat: 8g Salt: 200mg

Orange Sesame Edamame

Total servings: 1 serving
Preparation time: 5 minutes
Time to cook: 10 minutes

Ingredients:

- 1 cup frozen edamame beans
- 1 tablespoon low-sodium soy sauce
- 1 tablespoon orange juice
- 1/2 teaspoon sesame oil
- 1/2 teaspoon sesame seeds
- 1 green onion, sliced (optional)

Instructions:

1. Cook the edamame beans according to the package instructions, usually boiling them for about 5 minutes or until tender.

2. Drain the cooked edamame beans and set them aside.

3. Whisk the low-sodium soy sauce, orange juice, and sesame oil in a small bowl.

4. Heat a skillet or non-stick pan over medium heat.

5. Add the cooked edamame beans to the pan and pour the sauce.

6. Stir-fry the edamame beans for 2-3 minutes, until they are well-coated with the sauce and heated.

7. Sprinkle sesame seeds over the edamame beans and toss them gently.

8. Remove from heat and transfer to a serving dish.

9. Garnish with sliced green onion, if desired.

10. Serve the orange sesame edamame as a healthy and flavorful appetizer or snack.

Nutritional value (1 serving):

Calories: 150 Protein: 13g Fat: 6g Salt: 300mg

Zucchini Noodles with Pesto

Total servings: 1 serving
Preparation time: 10 minutes
Time to cook: 5 minutes

Ingredients:

- 1 medium-sized zucchini
- 2 tablespoons homemade or store-bought pesto
- 1 tablespoon pine nuts
- Fresh basil leaves, chopped (for garnish)
- Salt and pepper to taste

Instructions:

1. Using a spiralizer or a julienne peeler, create zucchini noodles by thinly slicing the zucchini into long, noodle-like strands.

2. Heat a non-stick skillet over medium heat.

3. Add the zucchini noodles to the skillet and sauté for 2-3 minutes until they are slightly softened but still retain a crunch.

4. Remove the skillet from heat.

5. Add the pesto to the zucchini noodles and toss them gently until they are well-coated.

6. Season with salt and pepper to taste.

7. Toast the pine nuts in a dry skillet over medium heat for 1-2 minutes until lightly browned and fragrant. Be careful not to burn them.

8. Sprinkle the toasted pine nuts over the zucchini noodles.

9. Garnish with freshly chopped basil leaves.

10. Serve the zucchini noodles with pesto as a light, nutritious main course or side dish.

Nutritional value (1 serving):

Calories: 250 Protein: 8g Fat: 20g Salt: 400mg

Roasted Bell Pepper Quinoa

Total servings: 1 serving
Preparation time: 10 minutes
Time to cook: 25 minutes

Ingredients:

- 1 bell pepper (any color), halved and seeds removed
- 1/2 cup quinoa, rinsed
- 1 cup vegetable broth
- 1/4 cup diced tomatoes
- 2 tablespoons chopped fresh parsley
- 1 tablespoon lemon juice
- 1/2 tablespoon olive oil
- Salt and pepper to taste

Instructions:

1. Preheat the oven to 400°F (200°C).

2. Place the bell pepper halves on a baking sheet, cut side down.

3. Roast the bell peppers in the oven for 15-20 minutes or until the skin is slightly charred and softened.

4. While the bell peppers are roasting, prepare the quinoa. In a saucepan, combine the rinsed quinoa and vegetable broth.

5. Bring the quinoa to a boil over medium heat, then reduce the heat to low and cover the saucepan.

6. Simmer the quinoa for 15 minutes, or until all the liquid is absorbed and the quinoa is tender.

7. Once cooked, remove the quinoa from the heat and let it cool for a few minutes.

8. Combine the cooked quinoa, diced tomatoes, chopped parsley, lemon juice, olive oil, salt, and pepper in a bowl. Mix well.

9. Carefully peel off the charred skin once the roasted bell peppers have cooled slightly.

10. Fill each bell pepper half with the quinoa mixture, pressing it down gently.

11. Place the stuffed bell peppers on the baking sheet and bake for 5 minutes to warm through.

12. Serve the roasted bell pepper quinoa as a flavorful and nutritious meal.

Nutritional value (1 serving):

Calories: 320 Protein: 9g Fat: 7g Salt: 600mg

Caprese Zucchini Boats

Total servings: 1 serving
Preparation time: 10 minutes
Time to cook: 20 minutes

Ingredients:

- 1 medium-sized zucchini
- 1/2 cup cherry tomatoes, halved
- 1/4 cup fresh mozzarella, diced
- 2 tablespoons chopped fresh basil
- 1 tablespoon balsamic glaze
- Salt and pepper to taste

Instructions:

1. Preheat the oven to 375°F (190°C).

2. Slice the zucchini in half lengthwise and scoop out the center to create a hollow space for filling.

3. Combine the cherry tomatoes, fresh mozzarella, chopped basil, balsamic glaze, salt, and pepper in a bowl. Mix well.

4. Spoon the tomato and mozzarella mixture into the hollowed-out zucchini halves, dividing it evenly between them.

5. Place the filled zucchini boats on a baking sheet.

6. Bake in the oven for 15-20 minutes or until the zucchini is tender and the cheese has melted.

7. Remove from the oven and let the zucchini boats cool for a few minutes.

8. Garnish with additional fresh basil leaves if desired.

9. Serve the Caprese zucchini boats as a delicious and healthy main course or side dish.

Nutritional value (1 serving):

Calories: 180 Protein: 12g Fat: 9g Salt: 400mg

Steamed Kale with Lemon Tahini Dressing

Total servings: 1 serving
Preparation time: 5 minutes
Time to cook: 10 minutes

Ingredients:

- 1 bunch of kale, stems removed and leaves torn into bite-sized pieces
- 1 tablespoon tahini

- 1 tablespoon lemon juice
- 1 clove garlic, minced
- 1 tablespoon water
- Salt and pepper to taste

Instructions:

1. Fill a pot with a few inches of water and place a steamer basket inside.

2. Bring the water to a boil over medium heat.

3. Add the kale leaves to the steamer basket, cover the pot, and steam for about 5 minutes or until the kale is tender but still vibrant green.

4. While the kale is steaming, prepare the lemon tahini dressing. In a small bowl, whisk together the tahini, lemon juice, minced garlic, water, salt, and pepper until smooth and well combined.

5. Once the kale is steamed, transfer it to a serving plate or bowl.

6. Drizzle the lemon tahini dressing over the steamed kale.

7. Toss the kale gently to ensure the dressing is evenly distributed.

8. Serve the steamed kale with lemon tahini dressing as a nutritious, flavorful side dish or light meal.

Nutritional value (1 serving):

Calories: 120 Protein: 7g Fat: 6g Salt: 300mg

Roasted Parmesan Broccoli

Total servings: 1 serving
Preparation time: 5 minutes
Time to cook: 20 minutes

Ingredients:

- 1 cup broccoli florets
- 1 tablespoon olive oil
- 1 tablespoon grated Parmesan cheese
- 1/2 teaspoon garlic powder
- Salt and pepper to taste

Instructions:

1. Preheat the oven to 425°F (220°C).

2. Place the broccoli florets on a baking sheet.

3. Drizzle the olive oil over the broccoli and toss to coat evenly.

4. Sprinkle the grated Parmesan cheese, garlic powder, salt, and pepper over the broccoli.

5. Toss again to ensure the seasonings are well distributed.

6. Spread the broccoli out in a single layer on the baking sheet.

7. Roast in the oven for 15-20 minutes or until the broccoli is tender and the edges are slightly crispy.

8. Remove the roasted broccoli from the oven and let it cool for a few minutes.

9. Serve the roasted Parmesan broccoli as a delicious and nutritious side dish.

Nutritional value (1 serving):

Calories: 120 Protein: 8g Fat: 8g Salt: 300mg

Quinoa Stuffed Mushrooms

Total servings: 1 serving
Preparation time: 15 minutes
Time to cook: 25 minutes

Ingredients:

- 4 large button mushrooms
- 1/4 cup cooked quinoa
- 1/4 cup diced tomatoes
- 1/4 cup diced bell peppers (any color)
- 1/4 cup diced onion
- 1 garlic clove, minced
- 1 tablespoon olive oil
- 1/4 teaspoon dried oregano
- Salt and pepper to taste
- Fresh parsley, chopped (for garnish)

Instructions:

1. Preheat the oven to 375°F (190°C).

2. Clean the mushrooms by gently wiping them with a damp cloth. Remove the stems and set them aside.

3. In a skillet, heat the olive oil over medium heat.

4. Add the diced onion, bell peppers, and garlic to the skillet. Sauté for about 2-3 minutes until the vegetables are tender.

5. Add the diced tomatoes and cooked quinoa to the skillet. Stir well to combine.

6. Season the mixture with dried oregano, salt, and pepper. Cook for an additional 1-2 minutes.

7. Place the mushroom caps on a baking sheet, cavity side up.

8. Spoon the quinoa mixture into each mushroom cap, filling it generously.

9. Bake in the preheated oven for 20-25 minutes until the mushrooms are tender, and the filling is slightly browned.

10. Remove from the oven and garnish with fresh parsley.

11. Serve the quinoa stuffed mushrooms as a delicious and nutritious appetizer or side dish.

Nutritional value (1 serving):

Calories: 150 Protein: 6g Fat: 6g Salt: 200mg

Greek Roasted Potatoes

Total servings: 1 serving
Preparation time: 10 minutes
Time to cook: 40 minutes

Ingredients:

- 1 medium-sized potato cut into wedges
- 1 tablespoon olive oil
- 1/2 teaspoon dried oregano
- 1/2 teaspoon dried thyme
- 1/4 teaspoon garlic powder
- Juice of 1/2 lemon
- Salt and pepper to taste
- Fresh parsley, chopped (for garnish)

Instructions:

1. Preheat the oven to 425°F (220°C).

2. Combine the potato wedges, olive oil, dried oregano, dried thyme, garlic powder, lemon juice, salt, and pepper in a bowl. Toss well to coat the potatoes evenly.

3. Place the seasoned potato wedges on a baking sheet in a single layer.

4. Roast in the oven for 35-40 minutes or until the potatoes are golden brown and crispy outside.

5. Remove the roasted potatoes from the oven and let them cool for a few minutes.

6. Garnish with fresh parsley.

7. Serve the Greek roasted potatoes as a flavorful and wholesome side dish.

Nutritional value (1 serving):

Calories: 180 Protein: 3g Fat: 6g Salt: 150mg

Charred Corn and Black Bean Salad

Total servings: 1 serving
Preparation time: 10 minutes
Time to cook: 15 minutes

Ingredients:

- 1 ear of corn, husked
- 1/2 cup black beans, rinsed and drained
- 1/4 cup diced red bell pepper
- 1/4 cup diced red onion
- 1/4 cup cherry tomatoes, halved
- 2 tablespoons chopped fresh cilantro
- 1 tablespoon lime juice
- 1 tablespoon olive oil
- 1/2 teaspoon ground cumin
- Salt and pepper to taste

Instructions:

1. Preheat the grill or stovetop grill pan over medium-high heat.

2. Place the corn on the grill and cook for about 10-12 minutes, rotating occasionally, until charred and tender. Remove from the grill and let it cool slightly.

3. Cut the kernels off the cob using a sharp knife and transfer them to a bowl.

4. Add the black beans, diced red bell pepper, red onion, cherry tomatoes, and chopped cilantro to the bowl with the corn.

5. Whisk together lime juice, olive oil, ground cumin, salt, and pepper in a small separate bowl.

6. Pour the dressing over the salad ingredients and toss well to combine.

7. Adjust the seasoning if needed.

8. Let the salad sit for a few minutes to allow the flavors to meld together.

9. Serve the charred corn and black bean salad as a refreshing and nutritious side dish.

Nutritional value (1 serving):

Calories: 230 Protein: 9g Fat: 7g Salt: 250mg

Grilled Balsamic Eggplant

Total servings: 1 serving
Preparation time: 10 minutes
Time to cook: 10 minutes

Ingredients:

- 1 small eggplant, sliced into 1/2-inch rounds
- 1 tablespoon balsamic vinegar
- 1 tablespoon olive oil
- 1 garlic clove, minced

- 1/4 teaspoon dried oregano
- Salt and pepper to taste
- Fresh basil leaves, chopped (for garnish)

Instructions:

1. Preheat the grill or stovetop grill pan over medium heat.

2. Whisk together balsamic vinegar, olive oil, minced garlic, dried oregano, salt, and pepper in a small bowl.

3. Brush both sides of the eggplant slices with the balsamic mixture.

4. Place the eggplant slices on the grill and cook for about 4-5 minutes per side or until tender and grill marks appear.

5. Remove from the grill and transfer the grilled eggplant to a serving plate.

6. Garnish with freshly chopped basil leaves.

7. Serve the grilled balsamic eggplant as a flavorful and healthy vegetable dish.

Nutritional value (1 serving):

Calories: 120 Protein: 2g Fat: 8g Salt: 150mg

Herb Roasted Tomato Slices

Total servings: 1 serving
Preparation time: 5 minutes
Time to cook: 20 minutes

Ingredients:

- 2 medium-sized tomatoes, sliced into rounds
- 1 tablespoon olive oil
- 1 teaspoon dried mixed herbs (such as thyme, oregano, and basil)
- Salt and pepper to taste

Instructions:

1. Preheat the oven to 400°F (200°C).

2. Place the tomato slices on a baking sheet lined with parchment paper.

3. Drizzle olive oil over the tomato slices.

4. Sprinkle the dried mixed herbs, salt, and pepper evenly over the tomatoes.

5. Gently toss the tomato slices to coat them with the oil and herbs.

6. Arrange the tomato slices in a single layer on the baking sheet.

7. Roast in the oven for 15-20 minutes or until the tomatoes are slightly shriveled and tender.

8. Remove from the oven and let them cool slightly.

9. Serve the herb-roasted tomato slices as a tasty and

healthy side dish, or use them as a topping for salads or sandwiches.

Nutritional value (1 serving):

Calories: 80 Protein: 1g Fat: 6g Salt: 100mg

Cilantro Lime Quinoa

Total servings: 1 serving
Preparation time: 5 minutes
Time to cook: 15 minutes

Ingredients:

- 1/2 cup quinoa, rinsed
- 1 cup water or low-sodium vegetable broth
- 1 tablespoon freshly squeezed lime juice
- 1 tablespoon chopped fresh cilantro
- Salt to taste

Instructions:

1. In a small saucepan, combine quinoa and water or vegetable broth.

2. Bring to a boil over medium heat.

3. Reduce the heat to low, cover the saucepan, and simmer for about 12-15 minutes or until the quinoa is tender and the liquid is absorbed.

4. Remove from heat and let it sit covered for 5 minutes.

5. Fluff the quinoa with a fork.

6. Add freshly squeezed lime juice and chopped cilantro to the cooked quinoa.

7. Season with salt to taste and toss well to combine.

8. Allow the flavors to meld together for a few minutes before serving.

9. Serve the cilantro lime quinoa as a nutritious and flavorful grain side dish.

Nutritional value (1 serving):

Calories: 180 Protein: 6g Fat: 3g Salt: 100mg

Roasted Brussels Sprout Slaw

Total servings: 1 serving
Preparation time: 10 minutes
Time to cook: 20 minutes

Ingredients:

- 1 cup Brussels sprouts, trimmed and thinly sliced
- 1 tablespoon olive oil
- 1 teaspoon of balsamic vinegar

- 1/4 teaspoon garlic powder
- Salt and pepper to taste
- 1 tablespoon chopped walnuts (optional, for garnish)

Instructions:

1. Preheat the oven to 400°F (200°C).

2. Combine the sliced Brussels sprouts, olive oil, balsamic vinegar, garlic powder, salt, and pepper in a mixing bowl. Toss well to coat the Brussels sprouts evenly.

3. Spread the coated Brussels sprouts in a single layer on a baking sheet lined with parchment paper.

4. Roast in the oven for about 20 minutes or until the Brussels sprouts are tender and lightly browned, stirring once halfway through.

5. Remove from the oven and let them cool slightly.

6. Transfer the roasted Brussels sprouts to a serving plate and garnish with chopped walnuts if desired.

7. Serve the roasted Brussels sprout slaw as a delicious and nutritious side dish.

Nutritional value (1 serving):

Calories: 120 Protein: 4g Fat: 7g Salt: 100mg

Lemon Dill Cucumber Ribbons

Total servings: 1 serving
Preparation time: 10 minutes
Time to cook: No cooking required

Ingredients:

- 1 medium cucumber, peeled
- 1 tablespoon freshly squeezed lemon juice
- 1 tablespoon chopped fresh dill
- Salt and pepper to taste

Instructions:

1. Using a vegetable peeler, slice the cucumber lengthwise into thin ribbons.

2. Add the freshly squeezed lemon juice, chopped dill, salt, and pepper to the bowl.

3. Serve the lemon dill cucumber ribbons as a refreshing, light salad or side dish.

Nutritional value (1 serving):

Calories: 25 Protein: 1g Fat: 0g Salt: 100mg

Chapter 7: Vegetables

Roasted Turmeric Cauliflower

Total Servings: 1
Preparation Time: 10 minutes
Cooking Time: 25 minutes

Ingredients:

- 1 cup cauliflower florets
- 1 tablespoon olive oil
- 1 teaspoon turmeric powder
- 1/2 teaspoon cumin powder
- 1/2 teaspoon paprika
- Salt, to taste
- Freshly ground black pepper, to taste

Instructions:

1. Preheat the oven to 400°F (200°C).

2. Combine the olive oil, turmeric powder, cumin powder, paprika, salt, and black pepper in a mixing bowl. Mix well to create a marinade.

3. Add the cauliflower florets to the bowl and toss them in the marinade until evenly coated.

4. Place the cauliflower florets on a baking sheet lined with parchment paper, spreading them out in a single layer.

5. Roast the cauliflower in the oven for 20-25 minutes or until tender and lightly golden brown.

6. Remove the roasted turmeric cauliflower from the oven and let it cool for a few minutes.

7. Transfer the cauliflower to a serving plate and garnish with fresh herbs if desired.

Nutritional Value (1 serving):

Calories: 120 Protein: 3g Fat: 7g Salt: 0.5g

Garlic Lemon Green Beans

Total Servings: 1
Preparation Time: 5 minutes
Cooking Time: 10 minutes

Ingredients:

- 1 cup green beans, trimmed
- 1 tablespoon olive oil
- 2 cloves garlic, minced
- 1 teaspoon lemon zest
- 1 tablespoon lemon juice
- Salt, to taste
- Freshly ground black pepper, to taste

Instructions:

1. Heat olive oil in a skillet over medium heat.

2. Add the minced garlic to the skillet and sauté for about 1 minute, until fragrant.

3. Add the green beans to the skillet and stir-fry for 3-4 minutes until tender-crisp.

4. Add lemon zest, lemon juice, salt, and black pepper to the skillet. Toss the green beans to coat them evenly with the seasoning.

5. Continue cooking for another 2-3 minutes, stirring occasionally, until the green beans are cooked through but retain their vibrant green color.

6. Remove the skillet from the heat and transfer the garlic, lemon green beans to a serving plate.

Nutritional Value (1 serving):

Calories: 70 Protein: 2g Fat: 4g Salt: 0.2g

Spiced Sweet Potato Wedges

Total Servings: 1
Preparation Time: 10 minutes
Cooking Time: 25 minutes

Ingredients:

- 1 small sweet potato
- 1 tablespoon olive oil
- 1/2 teaspoon paprika
- 1/2 teaspoon garlic powder
- 1/4 teaspoon cayenne pepper (optional, for spice)
- Salt, to taste
- Freshly ground black pepper, to taste

Instructions:

1. Preheat the oven to 425°F (220°C).

2. Wash and scrub the sweet potato thoroughly to remove any dirt. Cut it into wedges, about 1/2 inch thick.

3. In a large mixing bowl, combine olive oil, paprika, garlic powder, cayenne pepper (if using), salt, and black pepper. Mix well to create a seasoning blend.

4. Add the sweet potato wedges to the bowl and toss them in the seasoning blend until they are evenly coated.

5. Place the seasoned sweet potato wedges on a baking sheet lined with parchment paper, spreading them out in a single layer.

6. Roast the sweet potato wedges in the preheated oven for 20-25 minutes, flipping them halfway through, until they are golden brown and crispy, and tender on the inside.

7. Remove the roasted sweet potato wedges from the oven and let them cool for a few minutes before serving.

Nutritional Value(1 serving):

Calories: 180 Protein: 2g Fat: 6g Salt: 0.3g

Lemon Herb Quinoa Salad

Total Servings: 1
Preparation Time: 10 minutes
Cooking Time: 15 minutes

Ingredients:

- 1/2 cup cooked quinoa
- 1/4 cup cucumber, diced
- 1/4 cup cherry tomatoes, halved
- 2 tablespoons red onion, finely chopped
- 1 tablespoon fresh parsley, chopped
- 1 tablespoon fresh mint, chopped
- 1 tablespoon lemon juice
- 1 tablespoon extra-virgin olive oil
- Salt, to taste
- Freshly ground black pepper, to taste

Instructions:

1. Combine the cooked quinoa, cucumber, cherry tomatoes, red onion, parsley, and mint in a mixing bowl.

2. Whisk together lemon juice, olive oil, salt, and black pepper in a separate small bowl to create the dressing.

3. Pour the dressing over the quinoa mixture and toss gently to coat all ingredients evenly.

4. Let the lemon herb quinoa salad sit for a few minutes to allow the flavors to meld together.

5. Taste and adjust the seasoning if needed, adding more salt, black pepper, or lemon juice according to your preference.

6. Transfer the salad to a serving bowl or plate and garnish

with additional herbs if desired.

Nutritional Value (1 serving):

Calories: 200 Protein: 5g Fat: 8g Salt: 0.4g

Roasted Brussels Sprouts Medley

Total Servings: 1
Preparation Time: 10 minutes
Cooking Time: 20 minutes

Ingredients:

- 1 cup Brussels sprouts, halved
- 1/2 cup bell peppers, sliced
- 1/2 cup red onion, sliced
- 1 tablespoon olive oil
- 1/2 teaspoon dried thyme
- 1/2 teaspoon garlic powder
- Salt, to taste
- Freshly ground black pepper, to taste

Instructions:

1. Preheat the oven to 425°F (220°C).

2. Combine Brussels sprouts, bell peppers, and red onion in a mixing bowl.

3. Drizzle olive oil over the vegetables and toss them until they are evenly coated.

4. Sprinkle dried thyme, garlic powder, salt, and black pepper over the vegetables. Mix well to distribute the seasonings.

5. Place the seasoned Brussels sprouts medley on a baking sheet lined with parchment paper, spreading them out in a single layer.

6. Roast the vegetables in the oven for 20 minutes or until the Brussels sprouts are tender and lightly caramelized.

7. Remove the roasted Brussels sprouts medley from the oven and let them cool for a few minutes before serving.

Nutritional Value (1 serving):

Calories: 120 Protein: 5g Fat: 5g Salt: 0.4g

Grilled Zucchini Ribbons

Total Servings: 1
Preparation Time: 10 minutes
Cooking Time: 5 minutes

Ingredients:

- 1 medium zucchini
- 1 tablespoon olive oil
- 1/2 teaspoon lemon zest
- 1 tablespoon lemon juice
- 1/2 teaspoon dried oregano
- Salt, to taste
- Freshly ground black pepper, to taste

Instructions:

1. Preheat a grill or grill pan over medium heat.

2. Using a vegetable peeler, slice the zucchini into thin ribbons lengthwise. You can discard the outermost slices if desired.

3. Whisk together the olive oil, lemon zest, lemon juice, dried oregano, salt, and black pepper in a small bowl to create a marinade.

4. Place the zucchini ribbons in a shallow dish and drizzle the marinade. Gently toss to coat the zucchini ribbons evenly.

5. Place the marinated zucchini ribbons on the preheated grill or grill pan. Cook for 2-3 minutes on each side until they are tender and have grill marks.

6. Remove the grilled zucchini ribbons from the grill and transfer them to a serving plate.

Nutritional Value(1 serving):

Calories: 80 Protein: 2g Fat: 7g Salt: 0.2g

Stuffed Bell Peppers with Quinoa

Total Servings: 1
Preparation Time: 15 minutes
Cooking Time: 40 minutes

Ingredients:

- 1 bell pepper (any color)
- 1/4 cup cooked quinoa
- 2 tablespoons diced tomatoes
- 2 tablespoons diced zucchini
- 2 tablespoons diced onion
- 1 tablespoon chopped fresh parsley
- 1/2 teaspoon dried oregano
- Salt, to taste
- Freshly ground black pepper, to taste

Instructions:

1. Preheat the oven to 375°F (190°C).

2. Cut the bell pepper in half lengthwise and remove the seeds and membrane, creating two pepper halves that can be stuffed.

3. In a mixing bowl, combine the cooked quinoa, tomatoes, zucchini, diced onion, chopped fresh parsley, dried oregano, salt, and black pepper. Mix well to incorporate all the ingredients.

4. Spoon the quinoa mixture into the bell pepper halves, dividing it evenly between them.

5. Place the stuffed bell pepper halves in a baking dish and cover the dish with aluminum foil.

6. Bake the stuffed bell peppers in the oven for 30-35 minutes or until the peppers are tender and the filling is heated through.

7. Remove the dish from the oven and let the stuffed bell peppers cool for a few minutes before serving.

Nutritional Value (1 serving):

Calories: 180 Protein: 6g Fat: 2g Salt: 0.4g

Tomato Basil Caprese Skewers

Total Servings: 1
Preparation Time: 10 minutes
Cooking Time: No cooking required

Ingredients:

- 1 small tomato
- 2 small fresh mozzarella balls
- 4 fresh basil leaves
- 1 teaspoon balsamic glaze (optional)
- Salt, to taste
- Freshly ground black pepper, to taste

Instructions:

1. Wash the tomato and cut it into bite-sized pieces.

2. Drain the fresh mozzarella balls and cut them into bite-sized pieces as well.

3. Take a skewer and thread on one tomato piece, followed by one piece of mozzarella and then a basil leaf. Repeat this pattern until all the ingredients are used.

4. Arrange the tomato basil caprese skewers on a serving plate.

5. Drizzle balsamic glaze (if using) over the skewers for added flavor.

6. Season with salt and black pepper to taste.

7. Serve the tomato basil caprese skewers immediately.

Nutritional Value

(1 serving): Calories: 140 Protein: 9g Fat: 10g Salt: 0.2g

Greek Cucumber Quinoa Salad

Total Servings: 1
Preparation Time: 15 minutes
Cooking Time: 15 minutes

Ingredients:

- 1/2 cup cooked quinoa
- 1/2 cucumber, diced
- 1/4 cup cherry tomatoes, halved
- 2 tablespoons red onion, finely chopped
- 2 tablespoons Kalamata olives, pitted and sliced
- 2 tablespoons crumbled feta cheese
- 1 tablespoon fresh lemon juice
- 1 tablespoon extra-virgin olive oil
- 1/2 teaspoon dried oregano
- Salt, to taste
- Freshly ground black pepper, to taste

Instructions:

1. Combine the cooked quinoa, diced cucumber, cherry tomatoes, red onion, Kalamata olives, and crumbled feta cheese in a mixing bowl.

2. Whisk together the lemon juice, olive oil, dried oregano, salt, and black pepper in a separate small bowl to create the dressing.

3. Pour the dressing over the quinoa mixture and toss gently to coat all ingredients evenly.

4. Let the Greek cucumber quinoa salad sit for a few minutes to allow the flavors to meld together.

5. Taste and adjust the seasoning if needed, adding more salt, black pepper, or lemon juice according to your preference.

6. Transfer the salad to a serving bowl or plate.

Nutritional Value (1 serving):

Calories: 280 Protein: 9g Fat: 15g Salt: 0.8g

Citrus Kale Salad with Walnuts

Total Servings: 1
Preparation Time: 10 minutes
Cooking Time: No cooking required

Ingredients:

- 2 cups kale leaves torn into bite-sized pieces
- 1/2 orange, segmented
- 1/4 grapefruit, segmente
- 2 tablespoons chopped walnuts
- 1 tablespoon extra-virgin olive oil
- 1 tablespoon fresh lemon juice
- 1/2 teaspoon honey (optional)
- Salt, to taste
- Freshly ground black pepper, to taste

Instructions:

1. In a large mixing bowl, add the torn kale leaves.

2. Add the orange, grapefruit, and chopped walnuts to the bowl.

3. Whisk together the olive oil, lemon juice, honey (if using), salt, and black pepper to create the dressing in a separate small bowl.

4. Pour the dressing over the kale salad and toss well to coat the leaves and combine all the ingredients.

5. Massage the kale leaves gently with your hands for a few minutes to soften them.

6. Let the citrus kale salad sit for a few minutes to allow the flavors to meld together.

7. Taste and adjust the seasoning if needed, adding more salt, black pepper, or lemon juice according to your preference.

8. Transfer the salad to a serving bowl or plate.

Nutritional Value(1 serving):

Calories: 210 Protein: 7g Fat: 15g Salt: 0.4g

Ratatouille Stuffed Eggplant

Total Servings: 1
Preparation Time: 20 minutes
Cooking Time: 40 minutes

Ingredients:

- 1 small eggplant
- 1/4 cup diced zucchini
- 1/4 cup diced bell peppers
- 1/4 cup diced tomatoes
- 2 tablespoons diced red onion
- 1 garlic clove, minced
- 1 tablespoon fresh basil, chopped
- 1 tablespoon fresh parsley, chopped

- 1 tablespoon olive oil
- Salt, to taste
- Freshly ground black pepper, to taste

Instructions:

1. Preheat the oven to 375°F (190°C).

2. Slice the eggplant in half lengthwise and scoop out the flesh, leaving about a 1/4-inch border to create a hollow shell. Reserve the scooped-out meat.

3. In a skillet, heat olive oil over medium heat. Add the diced zucchini, bell peppers, tomatoes, red onion, minced garlic, and the reserved eggplant flesh. Sauté for about 5 minutes until the vegetables are softened.

4. Remove the skillet from the heat and stir in the fresh basil, parsley, salt, and black pepper. Mix well to combine all the flavors.

5. Spoon the vegetable mixture into the hollowed-out eggplant halves, dividing it evenly between them.

6. Place the stuffed eggplant halves on a baking sheet lined with parchment paper.

7. Bake in the oven for 30-35 minutes or until the eggplant is tender and the filling is heated.

8. Remove the stuffed eggplant from the oven and let it cool for a few minutes before serving.

Nutritional Value(1 serving):

Calories: 160 Protein: 4g Fat: 8g Salt: 0.3g

Balsamic Roasted Beetroot

Total Servings: 1
Preparation Time: 10 minutes
Cooking Time: 45 minutes

Ingredients:

- 1 medium beetroot
- 1 tablespoon balsamic vinegar
- 1 tablespoon olive oil
- 1/2 teaspoon dried thyme
- Salt, to taste
- Freshly ground black pepper, to taste

Instructions:

1. Preheat the oven to 400°F (200°C).

2. Peel the beetroot and cut it into bite-sized cubes or wedges.

3. Combine the balsamic vinegar, olive oil, dried thyme, salt, and black pepper in a mixing bowl. Mix well to create a marinade.

4. Add the beetroot cubes/wedges to the bowl and toss them in the marinade until evenly coated.

5. Place the marinated beetroot on a baking sheet lined with parchment paper, spreading them out in a single layer.

6. Roast the beetroot in the oven for 40-45 minutes or until tender and caramelized, stirring once or twice during cooking.

7. Remove the balsamic roasted beetroot from the oven and let it cool for a few minutes before serving.

Nutritional Value (1 serving):

Calories: 90 Protein: 2g Fat: 6g Salt: 0.4g

Mediterranean Lentil Soup

Total Servings: 1
Preparation Time: 10 minutes
Cooking Time: 30 minutes

Ingredients:

- 1/4 cup dried lentils
- 1 cup vegetable broth
- 1/4 cup diced onion
- 1/4 cup diced carrots
- 1/4 cup diced celery
- 1 garlic clove, minced
- 1/2 teaspoon dried oregano
- 1/2 teaspoon dried thyme
- 1/2 teaspoon paprika
- 1 tablespoon tomato paste
- 1 tablespoon olive oil
- Salt, to taste
- Freshly ground black pepper, to taste

Instructions:

1. Rinse the dried lentils under cold water and drain them.

2. In a medium-sized pot, heat olive oil over medium heat. Add the diced onion, carrots, celery, and minced garlic. Sauté for about 5 minutes until the vegetables are softened.

3. Add the pot's dried lentils, vegetable broth, oregano, dried thyme, paprika, tomato paste, salt, and black pepper. Stir well to combine all the ingredients.

4. Bring the soup to a boil, then reduce the heat to low. Cover the pot and let the soup simmer for 25-30 minutes or until the lentils are tender.

5. Remove the pot from the heat and let the soup cool for a few minutes before serving.

Nutritional Value(1 serving):

Calories: 220 Protein: 13g Fat: 5g Salt: 0.8g

Roasted Red Pepper Hummus

Total Servings: 1
Preparation Time: 10 minutes Cooking Time: 20 minutes

Ingredients:

- 1/2 cup canned chickpeas, rinsed and drained
- 1/4 cup roasted red peppers, drained and patted dry
- 1 tablespoon tahini
- 1 tablespoon lemon juice
- 1 garlic clove, minced
- 1/2 teaspoon ground cumi
- 1 tablespoon extra-virgin olive oil
- Salt, to taste
- Freshly ground black pepper, to taste

Instructions:

1. Combine chickpeas, roasted red peppers, tahini, lemon juice, minced garlic, ground cumin, salt, and black pepper in a food processor or blender.

2. Process the ingredients until smooth and well blended.

3. While the food processor is running, slowly drizzle in the extra-virgin olive oil until the hummus reaches a creamy consistency.

4. Taste and adjust the seasoning if needed, adding more salt, black pepper, or lemon juice according to your preference.

5. Transfer the roasted red pepper hummus to a serving bowl.

6. Serve the hummus with fresh vegetables, whole grain crackers, or pita bread.

Nutritional Value(1 serving):

Calories: 180 Protein: 6g Fat: 10g Salt: 0.6g

Herb-Roasted Carrot Fries

Total Servings: 1
Preparation Time: 10 minutes
Cooking Time: 20 minutes

Ingredients:

- 2 medium carrots
- 1 tablespoon olive oil
- 1/2 teaspoon dried rosemary
- 1/2 teaspoon dried thyme
- 1/4 teaspoon garlic powder
- Salt, to taste
- Freshly ground black pepper, to taste

Instructions:

1. Preheat the oven to 425°F (220°C).

2. Peel the carrots and cut them into thin strips resembling French fries.

3. Combine the carrot strips, olive oil, rosemary, dried thyme, garlic powder, salt, and black pepper in a mixing bowl. Toss well to coat the carrot strips evenly with the seasonings.

4. Place the seasoned carrot strips on a baking sheet lined with parchment paper, spreading them out in a single layer.

5. Roast the carrot fries in the oven for 15-20 minutes or until they are tender and lightly golden brown, flipping them once halfway through.

6. Remove the roasted carrot fries from the oven and let them cool for a few minutes before serving.

Nutritional Value (1 serving):

Calories: 120 Protein: 1g Fat: 7g Salt: 0.2g

Spinach Mushroom Quiche

Total Servings: 1
Preparation Time: 15 minutes
Cooking Time: 30 minutes

Ingredients:

- 1/2 cup fresh spinach leaves
- 1/4 cup sliced mushrooms
- 2 tablespoons diced onion
- 1 garlic clove, minced
- 2 large eggs
- 1/4 cup milk (low-fat or plant-based)
- 1/4 cup shredded low-fat cheese (such as mozzarella or Swiss)
- Salt, to taste
- Freshly ground black pepper, to taste

Instructions:

1. Preheat the oven to 375°F (190°C).

2. In a skillet, sauté the spinach, mushrooms, diced onion, and minced garlic over medium heat until the vegetables are tender and any excess moisture has evaporated.

3. Whisk together the eggs, milk, salt, and black pepper in a mixing bowl until well combined.

4. Stir in the sautéed vegetables and shredded cheese into the egg mixture.

5. Pour the mixture into a greased ramekin or small oven-safe dish

6. Place the quiche in the oven and bake for 25-30 minutes until the eggs are set and the top is lightly browned.

7. Remove the spinach mushroom quiche from the oven and let it cool for a few minutes before serving.

Nutritional Value (1 serving):

Calories: 220 Protein: 17g Fat: 10g Salt: 0.7g

Cilantro Lime Quinoa Salad

Total Servings: 1
Preparation Time: 15 minutes
Cooking Time: 15 minutes

Ingredients:

- 1/2 cup cooked quinoa
- 1/4 cup diced cucumber
- 1/4 cup diced bell peppers
- 2 tablespoons diced red onion
- 1 tablespoon chopped fresh cilantro
- 1 tablespoon fresh lime juice
- 1 tablespoon extra-virgin olive oil
- Salt, to taste
- Freshly ground black pepper, to taste

Instructions:

1. Combine the cooked quinoa, diced cucumber, bell peppers, red onion, and chopped fresh cilantro in a mixing bowl.

2. Whisk together the lime juice, olive oil, salt, and black pepper in a separate small bowl to create the dressing.

3. Pour the dressing over the quinoa mixture and toss gently to coat all ingredients evenly.

4. Let the cilantro lime quinoa salad sit for a few minutes to allow the flavors to meld together.

5. Taste and adjust the seasoning if needed, adding more salt, black pepper, or lime juice according to your preference.

6. Transfer the salad to a serving bowl or plate.

Nutritional Value (1 serving):

Calories: 210 Protein: 6g Fat: 9g Salt: 0.3g

Stuffed Portobello Mushrooms

Total Servings: 1
Preparation Time: 15 minutes
Cooking Time: 25 minutes

Ingredients:

- 2 large portobello mushrooms
- 1/4 cup diced bell peppers
- 1/4 cup diced zucchini
- 2 tablespoons diced red onion
- 1 garlic clove, minced
- 1 tablespoon chopped fresh basil
- 1 tablespoon chopped fresh parsley
- 1 tablespoon olive oil
- Salt, to taste
- Freshly ground black pepper, to taste

Instructions:

1. Preheat the oven to 375°F (190°C).

2. Remove the stems from the portobello mushrooms and gently scrape out the gills using a spoon.

3. In a skillet, heat olive oil over medium heat. Add the diced bell peppers, zucchini, red onion, and minced garlic. Sauté for about 5 minutes until the vegetables are softened.

4. Remove the skillet from the heat and stir in the fresh basil, parsley, salt, and black pepper. Mix well to combine all the flavors.

5. Spoon the vegetable mixture into the cavity of each portobello mushroom, dividing it evenly between them.

6. Place the stuffed portobello mushrooms on a baking sheet lined with parchment paper.

7. Bake in the oven for 20-25 minutes or until the mushrooms are tender and the filling is heated.

8. Remove the stuffed portobello mushrooms from the oven and let them cool for a few minutes before serving.

Nutritional Value (1 serving):

Calories: 160 Protein: 5g Fat: 8g Salt: 0.5g

Lemon Garlic Roasted Asparagus

Total Servings: 1
Preparation Time: 10 minutes
Cooking Time: 15 minutes

Ingredients:

- 6-8 asparagus spears
- 1 tablespoon olive oil
- 1 garlic clove, minced
- 1/2 teaspoon lemon zest
- 1 tablespoon fresh lemon juice
- Salt, to taste
- Freshly ground black pepper, to taste

Instructions:

1. Preheat the oven to 425°F (220°C).

2. Trim the woody ends of the asparagus spears by snapping off the tough bottoms.

3. Place the asparagus spears on a baking sheet lined with parchment paper.

4. In a small bowl, combine olive oil, minced garlic, lemon zest, lemon juice, salt, and black pepper. Mix well to create a marinade.

5. Drizzle the marinade over the asparagus spears, tossing them gently to coat them evenly.

6. Arrange the asparagus spears in a single layer on the baking sheet.

7. Roast in the oven for 12-15 minutes or until the asparagus is tender and slightly caramelized.

8. Remove the roasted asparagus from the oven and let it cool for a few minutes before serving.

Nutritional Value (1 serving):

Calories: 60 Protein: 3g Fat: 4g Salt: 0.2g

Grilled Eggplant and Tomato Stack

Total Servings: 1
Preparation Time: 10 minutes
Cooking Time: 10 minutes

Ingredients:

- 2 slices of eggplant (about 1/2 inch thick)
- 2 slices of tomato (about 1/2 inch thick)
- 1 tablespoon balsamic vinegar
- 1 tablespoon olive oil
- 1/2 teaspoon dried oregano
- Salt, to taste
- Freshly ground black pepper, to taste

Instructions:

1. Preheat a grill or grill pan over medium heat.

2. Brush both sides of the eggplant slices and tomato slices with olive oil.

3. Whisk together the balsamic vinegar, olive oil, dried oregano, salt, and black pepper in a small bowl to create a marinade.

4. Place the eggplant slices and tomato slices on the grill or grill pan. Cook for 4-5 minutes on each side until they are tender and grill marks appear.

5. Remove the eggplant and tomato slices from the grill and place them on a plate.

6. Drizzle the balsamic marinade over the grilled eggplant and tomato slices, allowing it to soak in.

7. Season with additional salt and black pepper to taste, if desired.

8. Stack the eggplant and tomato slices on each other to create a tower-like presentation.

Nutritional Value (1 serving):

Calories: 90 Protein: 2g Fat: 7g Salt: 0.3g

Spicy Roasted Chickpea Salad

Total Servings: 1
Preparation Time: 10 minutes
Cooking Time: 30 minutes

Ingredients:

- 1/2 cup canned chickpeas, rinsed and drained
- 1/2 teaspoon olive oil
- 1/4 teaspoon paprika
- 1/4 teaspoon cumin
- 1/8 teaspoon cayenne pepper (adjust to taste)
- Salt, to taste
- Freshly ground black pepper, to taste
- 2 cups mixed salad greens
- 1/4 cup cherry tomatoes, halved
- 1/4 cup diced cucumber
- 2 tablespoons diced red onion
- 1 tablespoon chopped fresh cilantro

- 1 tablespoon fresh lemon juice
- 1 tablespoon extra-virgin olive oil

Instructions:

1. Preheat the oven to 400°F (200°C).

2. Toss the rinsed and drained chickpeas in a bowl with olive oil, paprika, cumin, cayenne pepper, salt, and black pepper until well coated.

3. Spread the seasoned chickpeas in a single layer on a baking sheet lined with parchment paper.

4. Roast the chickpeas in the oven for 25-30 minutes or until they are crispy and golden brown.

5. Combine the mixed salad greens, cherry tomatoes, diced cucumber, red onion, and chopped fresh cilantro in a large bowl.

6. Whisk together the lemon juice and extra-virgin olive oil in a small bowl to create the dressing.

7. Add the roasted chickpeas to the salad bowl and drizzle the dressing over the salad. Toss gently to combine all the ingredients.

8. Taste and adjust the seasoning if needed, adding more salt, black pepper, or lemon juice according to your preference.

9. Transfer the spicy roasted chickpea salad to a serving plate or bowl.

Nutritional Value (1 serving):

Calories: 320 Protein: 12g Fat: 12g Salt: 0.8g

Zucchini Noodles with Pesto

Total Servings: 1
Preparation Time: 15 minutes
Cooking Time: No cooking required

Ingredients:

- 1 medium zucchini
- 2 tablespoons pesto sauce
- 1 tablespoon pine nuts (optional)
- Salt, to taste
- Freshly ground black pepper, to taste

Instructions:

1. Create zucchini noodles from medium zucchini using a spiralizer or julienne peeler.

2. Place the zucchini noodles in a large bowl.

3. Add the pesto sauce to the bowl and toss the zucchini noodles until they are well coated with the sauce.

4. If desired, toast the pine nuts in a dry skillet over medium heat until lightly browned.

5. Sprinkle the toasted pine nuts over the zucchini noodles.

6. Season with salt and black pepper to taste.

7. Serve the zucchini noodles with pesto immediately.

Nutritional Value (1 serving):

Calories: 200 Protein: 7g Fat: 18g Salt: 0.6g

Mediterranean Quinoa Stuffed Peppers

Total Servings: 1
Preparation Time: 15 minutes
Cooking Time: 30 minutes

Ingredients:

- 1 large bell pepper (any color)
- 1/4 cup cooked quinoa
- 2 tablespoons diced tomatoes
- 2 tablespoons diced cucumber
- 2 tablespoons diced Kalamata olives
- 1 tablespoon chopped fresh parsley
- 1 tablespoon crumbled feta cheese
- 1 tablespoon extra-virgin olive oil
- 1 tablespoon lemon juice
- 1/2 teaspoon dried oregano
- Salt, to taste
- Freshly ground black pepper, to taste

Instructions:

1. Preheat the oven to 375°F (190°C).

2. Cut the top off the bell pepper and remove the seeds and white pith from the inside.

3. In a mixing bowl, combine the cooked quinoa, diced tomatoes, diced cucumber, diced Kalamata olives, chopped fresh parsley, crumbled feta cheese, extra-virgin olive oil, lemon juice, dried oregano, salt, and black pepper. Mix well to combine all the ingredients.

4. Spoon the quinoa mixture into the hollowed-out bell pepper, pressing it down gently.

5. Cover the stuffed bell pepper in a baking dish with foil.

6. Bake in the preheated oven for 20 minutes.

7. Remove the foil and bake for 10 minutes until the bell pepper is tender and the filling is heated through.

8. Remove the stuffed bell pepper from the oven and let it cool for a few minutes before serving.

Nutritional Value (1 serving):

Herb-Roasted Tomato Slices

Total Servings: 1
Preparation Time: 5 minutes
Cooking Time: 15 minutes

Ingredients:

- 2 medium tomatoes, sliced into 1/2-inch thick rounds 1 tablespoon extra-virgin olive oil
- 1 teaspoon dried basil
- 1 teaspoon dried thyme
- 1/2 teaspoon garlic powder
- Salt, to taste
- Freshly ground black pepper, to taste

Instructions:

1. Preheat the oven to 400°F (200°C).

2. Place the tomato slices in a single layer on a baking sheet lined with parchment paper.

3. Drizzle the tomato slices with olive oil, ensuring they are well coated on both sides.

4. Combine the dried basil, dried thyme, garlic powder, salt, and black pepper in a small bowl. Mix well to create a herb seasoning blend.

5. Sprinkle the herb seasoning blend over the tomato slices, ensuring they are evenly coated.

6. Roast the tomato slices in the oven for 12-15 minutes or until they are slightly faded and the edges are lightly caramelized.

7. Remove the herb-roasted tomato slices from the oven and let them cool for a few minutes before serving.

Nutritional Value (1 serving):

Calories: 90 Protein: 2g Fat: 7g Salt: 0.3g

Greek Lemon Potatoes

Total Servings: 1
Preparation Time: 15 minutes
Cooking Time: 45 minutes

Ingredients:

- 2 small potatoes, cut into wedges
- 1 tablespoon extra-virgin olive oil
- 1 tablespoon fresh lemon juice

- 1 teaspoon dried oregano
- 1/2 teaspoon garlic powder
- Salt, to taste
- Freshly ground black pepper, to taste

Instructions:

1. Preheat the oven to 425°F (220°C).

2. Combine the potato wedges, olive oil, lemon juice, dried oregano, garlic powder, salt, and black pepper in a bowl. Toss well to coat the potatoes evenly with the seasonings.

3. Spread the seasoned potato wedges in a single layer on a baking sheet lined with parchment paper.

4. Roast the potatoes in the oven for 40-45 minutes, or until they are crispy and tender, flipping them once halfway through.

5. Remove the roasted lemon potatoes from the oven and let them cool for a few minutes before serving.

Nutritional Value(1 serving):

Calories: 200 Protein: 4g Fat: 8g Salt: 0.4g

Steamed Artichokes with Lemon Aioli

Total Servings: 1
Preparation Time: 10 minutes
Cooking Time: 20 minutes

Ingredients:

- 1 medium artichoke
- 1/4 cup water
- 1/2 lemon, sliced
- 1/4 cup low-fat mayonnaise
- 1 tablespoon fresh lemon juice
- 1 garlic clove, minced
- Salt, to taste
- Freshly ground black pepper, to taste

Instructions:

1. Fill a pot with a steamer basket and water, ensuring the water level is below the steamer basket. Bring the water to a boil.

2. Trim the stem of the artichoke and remove any tough outer leaves.

3. Place the artichoke in the steamer basket, stem-side down. Arrange the lemon slices on top of the artichoke.

4. Cover the pot and steam the artichoke over medium heat for about 20 minutes or until the leaves can be easily pulled off.

5. While the artichoke is steaming, prepare the lemon aioli by combining the low-fat mayonnaise, fresh lemon juice, minced garlic, salt, and black pepper in a small bowl. Mix well until smooth and creamy.

6. Once the artichoke is steamed, please remove it from the pot and let it cool slightly.

7. Serve the steamed artichoke with the lemon aioli for dipping.

Nutritional Value1 serving):

Calories: 120 Protein: 3g Fat: 6g Salt: 0.6g

Quinoa Stuffed Mushrooms

Total Servings: 1
Preparation Time: 15 minutes
Cooking Time: 25 minutes

Ingredients:

- 4 large mushrooms
- 1/4 cup cooked quinoa
- 2 tablespoons diced red bell pepper
- 2 tablespoons diced zucchini
- 2 tablespoons diced red onion
- 1 garlic clove, minced
- 1 tablespoon chopped fresh parsley
- 1 tablespoon grated Parmesan cheese
- 1 tablespoon extra-virgin olive oil
- Salt, to taste
- Freshly ground black pepper, to taste

Instructions:

1. Preheat the oven to 375°F (190°C).

2. Remove the stems from the mushrooms and set them aside. Place the mushroom caps on a baking sheet lined with parchment paper.

3. In a bowl, combine the cooked quinoa, diced red bell pepper, diced zucchini, diced red onion, minced garlic, chopped fresh parsley, grated Parmesan cheese, extra-virgin olive oil, salt, and black pepper. Mix well to combine all the ingredients.

4. Finely chop the mushroom stems and add them to the quinoa mixture. Mix well.

5. Spoon the quinoa mixture into the mushroom caps, filling them generously.

6. Bake in the oven for 20-25 minutes or until the mushrooms are tender and the filling is heated.

7. Remove the quinoa-stuffed mushrooms from the oven

and let them cool for a few minutes before serving.

Nutritional Value(1 serving):

Calories: 150 Protein: 7g Fat: 7g Salt: 0.5g

Roasted Parmesan Broccoli Florets

Total Servings: 1
Preparation Time: 10 minutes
Cooking Time: 15 minutes

Ingredients:

- 1 cup broccoli florets
- 1 tablespoon grated Parmesan cheese
- 1 tablespoon extra-virgin olive oil
- 1/2 teaspoon garlic powder
- Salt, to taste
- Freshly ground black pepper, to taste

Instructions:

1. Preheat the oven to 425°F (220°C).

2. Place the broccoli florets in a mixing bowl.

3. Combine the grated Parmesan cheese, extra-virgin olive oil, garlic powder, salt, and black pepper in a small bowl. Mix well to create a seasoned oil.

4. Drizzle the seasoned oil over the broccoli florets, tossing them gently to coat them evenly.

5. Spread the broccoli florets in a single layer on a baking sheet lined with parchment paper.

6. Roast in the oven for 12-15 minutes or until the broccoli is tender and lightly browned, stirring once halfway through.

7. Remove the roasted Parmesan broccoli florets from the oven and let them cool for a few minutes before serving.

Nutritional Value (1 serving):

Calories: 120 Protein: 6g Fat: 8g Salt: 0.4g

Lemon Dill Cucumber Ribbons

Total Servings: 1
Preparation Time: 10 minutes
Cooking Time: No cooking required

Ingredients:

- 1 large cucumber
- 1 tablespoon fresh lemon juice
- 1 tablespoon extra-virgin olive oil

- 1 tablespoon chopped fresh dill
- Salt, to taste
- Freshly ground black pepper, to taste

Instructions:

1. Using a vegetable peeler, create long cucumber ribbons by peeling them lengthwise.

2. Combine the cucumber ribbons, fresh lemon juice, extra-virgin olive oil, chopped fresh dill, salt, and black pepper in a bowl. Toss gently to coat the cucumber ribbons with the dressing.

3. Let the cucumber ribbons marinate in the dressing for a few minutes to allow the flavors to meld together.

4. Taste and adjust the seasoning if needed, adding more salt, black pepper, or lemon juice according to your preference.

5. Serve the lemon dill cucumber ribbons chilled as a refreshing side dish or salad.

Nutritional Value 1 serving):

Calories: 60 Protein: 1g Fat: 5g Salt: 0.2g

Charred Corn and Black Bean Salad

Total Servings: 1
Preparation Time: 15 minutes
Cooking Time: 10 minutes

Ingredients:

- 1/2 cup corn kernels (fresh or frozen)
- 1/4 cup black beans, rinsed and drained
- 2 tablespoons diced red bell pepper
- 2 tablespoons diced red onion
- 1 tablespoon chopped fresh cilantro
- 1 tablespoon fresh lime juice
- 1 tablespoon extra-virgin olive oil
- 1/2 teaspoon chili powder
- Salt, to taste
- Freshly ground black pepper, to taste

Instructions:

1. If using fresh corn, grill or boil it until it is cooked. If using frozen corn, thaw it according to package instructions.

2. Add the corn kernels in a skillet over medium heat and cook for 5-7 minutes, or until they are slightly charred, stirring occasionally.

3. In a mixing bowl, combine the charred corn kernels, black beans, diced red bell pepper, diced red onion, chopped

fresh cilantro, fresh lime juice, extra-virgin olive oil, chili powder, salt, and black pepper. Mix well to combine all the ingredients.

4. Let the charred corn and black bean salad sit for a few minutes to allow the flavors to meld together.

5. Taste and adjust the seasoning if needed, adding more salt, black pepper, or lime juice according to your preference.

6. Serve the salad at room temperature or chilled as a side dish or light meal.

Nutritional Value 1 serving):

Calories: 180 Protein: 6g Fat: 8g Salt: 0.4g

Grilled Balsamic Eggplant Slices

Total Servings: 1
Preparation Time: 10 minutes
Cooking Time: 10 minutes

Ingredients:

- 1 small eggplant, sliced into 1/2-inch thick rounds
- 2 tablespoons balsamic vinegar
- 1 tablespoon extra-virgin olive oil
- 1 garlic clove, minced
- 1/2 teaspoon dried oregano
- Salt, to taste
- Freshly ground black pepper, to taste

Instructions:

1. Preheat the grill or grill pan over medium heat.

2. Whisk together the balsamic vinegar, extra-virgin olive oil, minced garlic, dried oregano, salt, and black pepper in a small bowl to create a marinade.

3. Place the eggplant slices in a shallow dish and pour the marinade over them. Make sure both sides of the pieces are well coated.

4. Let the eggplant slices marinate for about 5 minutes to absorb the flavors.

5. Grill the eggplant slices for about 5 minutes on each side or until they are tender and grill marks appear.

6. Remove the grilled balsamic eggplant slices from the grill and let them cool for a few minutes before serving.

Nutritional Value (1 serving):

Calories: 120 Protein: 2g Fat: 7g   Salt: 0.4g

Marinated Grilled Portobello Caps

Total Servings: 1
Preparation Time: 15 minutes
Cooking Time: 10 minutes

Ingredients:

- 2 large Portobello mushroom caps
- 2 tablespoons balsamic vinegar
- 1 tablespoon low-sodium soy sauce
- 1 tablespoon extra-virgin olive oil
- 1 garlic clove, minced
- 1/2 teaspoon dried thyme
- Salt, to taste
- Freshly ground black pepper, to taste

Instructions:

1. Preheat the grill or grill pan over medium heat.

2. In a shallow dish, combine the balsamic vinegar, low-sodium soy sauce, extra-virgin olive oil, minced garlic, dried thyme, salt, and black pepper to create a marinade.

3. Remove the stems from the Portobello mushroom caps and gently scrape out the gills using a spoon.

4. Place the Portobello mushroom caps in the marinade, ensuring both sides are well coated. Let them marinate for about 10 minutes to absorb the flavors.

5. Grill the Portobello mushroom caps for about 5 minutes on each side or until they are tender and juicy.

6. Remove the grilled Portobello caps from the grill and let them cool for a few minutes before serving.

Nutritional Value (1 serving):

Calories: 90 Protein: 5g Fat: 5g Salt: 0.5g

Quinoa Cucumber Salad

Total Servings: 1
Preparation Time: 15 minutes
Cooking Time: 15 minutes

Ingredients:

- 1/2 cup cooked quinoa
- 1/2 cucumber, diced
- 1/4 cup cherry tomatoes, halved
- 2 tablespoons diced red onion
- 2 tablespoons chopped fresh parsley
- 1 tablespoon fresh lemon juice
- 1 tablespoon extra-virgin olive oil
- Salt, to taste
- Freshly ground black pepper, to taste

Instructions:

1. Combine the cooked quinoa, diced cucumber, halved cherry tomatoes, red onion, chopped fresh parsley, lemon juice, extra-virgin olive oil, salt, and black pepper in a bowl. Mix well to combine all the ingredients.

2. Taste and adjust the seasoning if needed, adding more salt, black pepper, or lemon juice according to your preference.

3. Let the quinoa cucumber salad sit for a few minutes to allow the flavors to meld together.

4. Serve the salad chilled as a refreshing side dish or light meal.

Nutritional Value (1 serving):

Calories: 200 Protein: 6g Fat: 8g Salt: 0.4g

Roasted Bell Pepper Quinoa

Total Servings: 1
Preparation Time: 15 minutes
Cooking Time: 25 minutes

Ingredients:

- 1/2 cup cooked quinoa
- 1 red bell pepper
- 1 tablespoon extra-virgin olive oil
- 1 tablespoon balsamic vinegar
- 1 garlic clove, minced
- 1/2 teaspoon dried basil
- Salt, to taste
- Freshly ground black pepper, to taste

Instructions:

1. Preheat the oven to 400°F (200°C).

2. Cut the red bell pepper in half and remove the seeds and white pith.

3. Place the red bell pepper halves on a baking sheet, cut side down.

4. Roast the red bell pepper in the oven for 20-25 minutes or until the skin is charred and blistered.

5. Remove the roasted red bell pepper from the oven and let it cool for a few minutes. Once cool enough to handle,

peel off the skin and dice the roasted pepper.

6. Combine the cooked quinoa, diced roasted bell pepper, extra-virgin olive oil, balsamic vinegar, minced garlic, dried basil, salt, and black pepper in a bowl. Mix well to combine all the ingredients.

7. Taste and adjust the seasoning if needed, adding more salt, black pepper, or balsamic vinegar according to your preference.

8. Let the roasted bell pepper quinoa sit for a few minutes to allow the flavors to meld together.

9. Serve the dish warm or at room temperature as a nutritious and satisfying meal.

Nutritional Valu (1 serving):

Calories: 250 Protein: 7g Fat: 10g Salt: 0.5g

Kale and White Bean Soup

Total Servings: 1
Preparation Time: 10 minutes
Cooking Time: 25 minutes

Ingredients:

- 1 cup kale, chopped
- 1/2 cup cooked white beans
- 1/4 cup diced carrots
- 1/4 cup diced celery
- 2 tablespoons diced onion
- 1 garlic clove, minced
- 2 cups vegetable broth
- 1 teaspoon dried thyme
- Salt, to taste
- Freshly ground black pepper, to taste

Instructions:

1. Heat a little vegetable broth or olive oil over medium heat in a pot.

2. Add the diced onion and minced garlic to the bank and sauté until the onion becomes translucent.

3. Add the diced carrots and celery to the pool and continue to sauté for another 3–4 minutes until they soften.

4. Pour in the vegetable broth and bring the soup to a boil. Reduce the heat to low.

5. Add the chopped kale, cooked white beans, and dried thyme to the pot. Stir well.

6. Simmer the soup for 15–20 minutes or until the vegetables are tender and the flavors have melded together.

7. Season the soup with salt and black pepper to taste.

8. Serve the hot kale and white bean soup as a comforting and nutritious meal.

Nutritional Value (1 serving):

Calories: 200 Protein: 10g Fat: 2g Salt: 0.6g

Grilled Zucchini Boats

Total Servings: 1
Preparation Time: 10 minutes
Cooking Time: 15 minutes

Ingredients:

- 1 medium zucchini
- 1/4 cup diced bell peppers (any color)
- 2 tablespoons diced red onion
- 2 tablespoons diced tomatoes
- 1 tablespoon chopped fresh basil
- 1 tablespoon grated Parmesan cheese
- 1 teaspoon extra-virgin olive oil
- Salt, to taste
- Freshly ground black pepper, to taste

Instructions:

1. Preheat the grill or grill pan over medium heat.

2. Cut the zucchini in half lengthwise and scoop out the seeds to create a hollow space in each half.

3. In a bowl, combine the diced bell peppers, red onion, tomatoes, chopped fresh basil, grated Parmesan cheese, extra-virgin olive oil, salt, and black pepper. Mix well.

4. Spoon the vegetable mixture evenly into the hollowed-out zucchini halves.

5. Grill the zucchini boats for about 7–8 minutes on each side or until the zucchini is tender and lightly charred.

6. Remove the grilled zucchini boats from the grill and let them cool for a few minutes before serving.

Nutritional Value (1 serving):

Calories: 120 Protein: 6g Fat: 5g Salt: 0.4g

Roasted Brussel Sprout Slaw

Total Servings: 1
Preparation Time: 10 minutes
Cooking Time: 15 minutes

Ingredients:

- 1 cup Brussels sprouts, thinly sliced
- 1/4 cup shredded carrots
- 2 tablespoons sliced almonds
- 2 tablespoons dried cranberries
- 1 tablespoon lemon juice
- 1 tablespoon extra-virgin olive oil
- 1/2 teaspoon Dijon mustard
- Salt, to taste
- Freshly ground black pepper, to taste

Instructions:

1. Preheat the oven to 400°F (200°C).

2. Place the thinly sliced Brussels sprouts on a baking sheet lined with parchment paper.

3. Roast the Brussels sprouts in the oven for 12-15 minutes or until lightly browned and crispy.

4. Combine the roasted Brussels sprouts, shredded carrots, sliced almonds, and dried cranberries in a bowl. Toss gently to mix the ingredients.

5. Whisk together the lemon juice, extra-virgin olive oil, Dijon mustard, salt, and black pepper in a small bowl to create a dressing.

6. Drizzle the dressing over the Brussels sprout slaw and toss to coat the ingredients evenly.

7. Taste and adjust the seasoning if needed, adding more salt, black pepper, or lemon juice according to your preference.

8. Serve the roasted Brussels sprout slaw as a crunchy and flavorful salad.

Nutritional Value (1 serving):

Calories: 160 Protein: 5g Fat: 9g Salt: 0.4g

Lemon Herb Green Peas

Total Servings: 1
Preparation Time: 5 minutes
Cooking Time: 10 minutes

Ingredients:

- 1 cup green peas (fresh or frozen)
- 1 tablespoon chopped fresh parsley
- 1 tablespoon chopped fresh mint
- 1 tablespoon lemon juice
- 1 tablespoon extra-virgin olive oil
- Salt, to taste

- Freshly ground black pepper, to taste

Instructions:

1. If using frozen green peas, cook them according to package instructions. If using fresh green peas, blanch them in boiling water for 2-3 minutes, then drain.

2. Combine the cooked green peas, chopped fresh parsley, chopped fresh mint, lemon juice, extra-virgin olive oil, salt, and black pepper in a bowl. Toss gently to mix the ingredients.

3. Taste and adjust the seasoning if needed, adding more salt, black pepper, or lemon juice according to your preference.

4. Serve the lemon herb green peas as a vibrant and nutritious side dish.

Nutritional Value (1 serving):

Calories: 90 Protein: 4g Fat: 5g Salt: 0.2g

Cauliflower Rice Stir-Fry

Total Servings: 1
Preparation Time: 10 minutes
Cooking Time: 10 minutes

Ingredients:

- 1 cup cauliflower florets
- 1/4 cup diced bell peppers (any color)
- 2 tablespoons diced carrots
- 2 tablespoons diced zucchini
- 2 tablespoons diced onion
- 1 garlic clove, minced
- 1 tablespoon low-sodium soy sauce
- 1 tablespoon sesame oil
- Salt, to taste
- Freshly ground black pepper, to taste

Instructions:

1. Place the cauliflower florets in a food processor and pulse until they resemble rice-like grains.

2. Heat the sesame oil over medium heat in a non-stick skillet or wok.

3. Add the minced garlic and diced onion to the skillet and sauté for 2-3 minutes, until the onion becomes translucent.

4. Add the diced bell peppers, carrots, and zucchini to the skillet. Sauté for another 2-3 minutes until the vegetables begin to soften.

5. Stir in the cauliflower rice and cook for 3-4 minutes or until the cauliflower is tender but still slightly crunchy.

6. Drizzle the low-sodium soy sauce over the cauliflower rice stir-fry. Season with salt and black pepper to taste. Stir well to combine all the ingredients.

7. Cook for 1-2 minutes, allowing the flavors to meld together.

8. Serve the cauliflower rice stir-fry hot as a delicious and satisfying meal.

Nutritional Value

(1 serving): Calories: 120 Protein: 4g Fat: 8g Salt: 0.6g

Cilantro Lime Grilled Corn

Total Servings: 1
Preparation Time: 5 minutes
Cooking Time: 10 minutes

Ingredients:

- 1 ear of corn
- 1 tablespoon chopped fresh cilantro
- 1 tablespoon fresh lime juice
- 1 teaspoon extra-virgin olive oil
- 1/4 teaspoon chili powder
- Salt, to taste
- Freshly ground black pepper, to taste

Instructions:

1. Preheat the grill to medium-high heat.

2. Remove the husk and silk from the ear of the corn.

3. In a small bowl, combine the chopped fresh cilantro, lime juice, extra-virgin olive oil, chili powder, salt, and black pepper to create a marinade.

4. Brush the marinade over the ear of corn, ensuring it is evenly coated.

5. Place the corn on the preheated grill and cook for about 8-10 minutes, turning occasionally, until the corn is lightly charred and tender.

6. Remove the grilled corn from the heat and let it cool for a few minutes.

7. Cut the grilled corn into smaller pieces, if desired, and drizzle any remaining marinade over the corn.

8. Serve the cilantro lime-grilled corn as a flavorful and nutritious side dish.

Nutritional Value 1 serving):

Calories: 100 Protein: 3g Fat: 3g Salt: 0.2g

Chapter 8: Meat

Grilled Chicken Breast

Total servings: 1 serving
Preparation time: 10 minutes
Time to cook: 15 minutes

Ingredients:

- 1 chicken breast (skinless, boneless)
- 1 tablespoon olive oil
- 1 teaspoon dried herbs (such as thyme, rosemary, or oregano)
- 1/2 teaspoon garlic powder
- Salt and pepper to taste

Instructions:

1. Preheat the grill to medium-high heat.

2. In a small bowl, mix together the olive oil, dried herbs, garlic powder, salt, and pepper to make a marinade.

3. Place the chicken breast in a shallow dish and pour the marinade over it. Ensure the chicken breast is coated evenly.

4. Let the chicken breast marinate for at least 15 minutes to allow the flavors to infuse.

5. Once the grill is preheated, place the chicken breast on the grill grates.

6. Grill the chicken for approximately 6-8 minutes per side or until the internal temperature reaches 165°F (74°C).

7. Remove the chicken breast from the grill and let it rest for a few minutes before slicing or serving.

8. Serve the grilled chicken breast with a side of your choice, such as steamed vegetables or a salad.

Nutritional value (1 serving):

Calories: 200 Protein: 30g Fat: 8g Salt: 300mg

Baked Salmon Fillet

Total servings: 1 serving
Preparation time: 10 minutes
Time to cook: 15 minutes

Ingredients:

- 1 salmon fillet (4-6 ounces)
- 1 tablespoon lemon juice
- 1 tablespoon olive oil
- 1/2 teaspoon dried dill
- 1/4 teaspoon garlic powder
- Salt and pepper to taste

Instructions:

1. Preheat the oven to 400°F (200°C).

2. Place the salmon fillet on a baking sheet lined with parchment paper or aluminum foil.

3. Drizzle the salmon fillet with lemon juice and olive oil, ensuring it is evenly coated.

4. Sprinkle the dried dill, garlic powder, salt, and pepper over the salmon fillet.

5. Gently rub the seasoning into the fish to enhance the flavors.

6. Bake the salmon in the preheated oven for 12-15 minutes or until the fish flakes easily with a fork.

7. Remove the salmon fillet from the oven and let it rest for a couple of minutes.

8. Serve the baked salmon fillet with a side of your choice, such as steamed vegetables or quinoa.

Nutritional value (1 serving):

Calories: 300 Protein: 30g Fat: 18g Salt: 400mg

Turkey Meatballs

Total servings: 1 serving
Preparation time: 15 minutes
Time to cook: 20 minutes

Ingredients:

- 4 ounces ground turkey
- 1/4 cup whole wheat bread crumbs
- 1/4 cup grated Parmesan cheese
- 1/4 cup finely chopped onion
- 1 garlic clove, minced
- 1 tablespoon chopped fresh parsley
- 1/2 teaspoon dried oregano
- 1/4 teaspoon salt
- 1/4 teaspoon black pepper
- 1 tablespoon olive oil
- 1/2 cup marinara sauce

Instructions:

1. In a mixing bowl, combine the ground turkey, bread crumbs, Parmesan cheese, onion, garlic, parsley, oregano, salt, and pepper. Mix well to incorporate all the ingredients.

2. Shape the mixture into small meatballs, about 1 inch in diameter.

3. Heat the olive oil in a non-stick skillet over medium heat.

4. Add the meatballs to the skillet and cook for about 10-12 minutes, turning occasionally, until browned on all sides and cooked through.

5. Pour the marinara sauce into the skillet with the meatballs. Reduce the heat to low and simmer for an additional 5 minutes, allowing the flavors to meld together.

6. Serve the turkey meatballs with a side of your choice, such as whole wheat pasta or steamed vegetables.

Nutritional value (1 serving):

Calories: 300 Protein: 24g Fat: 15g Salt: 600mg

Beef Stir Fry

Total servings: 1 serving
Preparation time: 15 minutes
Time to cook: 10 minutes

Ingredients:

- 4 ounces lean beef, thinly sliced
- 1 tablespoon low-sodium soy sauce
- 1 tablespoon hoisin sauce
- 1 tablespoon rice vinegar
- 1 garlic clove, minced
- 1/2 teaspoon grated fresh ginger
- 1/2 cup sliced bell peppers
- 1/2 cup broccoli florets
- 1/2 cup sliced carrots
- 1/4 cup sliced onions
- 1 tablespoon olive oil
- Sesame seeds for garnish (optional)

Instructions:

1. In a small bowl, whisk together the soy sauce, hoisin sauce, rice vinegar, garlic, and ginger to make the stir-fry sauce. Set aside.

2. Heat the olive oil in a wok or large skillet over medium-high heat.

3. Add the beef slices and stir-fry for 2-3 minutes until browned. Remove the beef from the pan and set aside.

4. In the same pan, add the bell peppers, broccoli, carrots, and onions. Stir-fry for 4-5 minutes until the vegetables are

crisp-tender.

5. Return the beef to the pan and pour the stir-fry sauce over the beef and vegetables. Stir-fry for an additional 1-2 minutes until everything is well-coated and heated through.

6. Remove from heat and garnish with sesame seeds, if desired.

7. Serve the beef stir-fry with a side of your choice, such as brown rice or quinoa.

Nutritional value (1 serving):

Calories: 350 Protein: 25g Fat: 12g Salt: 800mg

Lemon Garlic Shrimp

Total servings: 1 serving
Preparation time: 10 minutes
Time to cook: 5 minutes

Ingredients:

- 6 ounces shrimp, peeled and deveined
- 1 tablespoon olive oil
- 1 garlic clove, minced
- 1 tablespoon freshly squeezed lemon juice
- 1 teaspoon grated lemon zest
- 1 tablespoon chopped fresh parsley
- Salt and pepper to taste

Instructions:

1. In a bowl, combine the shrimp, olive oil, minced garlic, lemon juice, lemon zest, and parsley. Season with salt and pepper. Toss to coat the shrimp evenly.

2. Heat a non-stick skillet over medium-high heat.

3. Add the shrimp to the skillet and cook for about 2-3 minutes per side until they turn pink and opaque.

4. Remove the shrimp from the heat and serve immediately.

5. You can serve the lemon garlic shrimp over a bed of brown rice or with a side of steamed vegetables.

Nutritional value (1 serving):

Calories: 180 Protein: 22g Fat: 8g Salt: 400mg

Herb-Roasted Pork Tenderloin

Total servings: 1 serving
Preparation time: 10 minutes
Time to cook: 25-30 minutes

Ingredients:

- 4 ounces pork tenderloin

- 1 teaspoon olive oil
- 1 teaspoon dried thyme
- 1 teaspoon dried rosemary
- 1/2 teaspoon dried sage
- 1/2 teaspoon garlic powder
- Salt and pepper to taste

Instructions:

1. Preheat the oven to 400°F (200°C).

2. Rub the pork tenderloin with olive oil, ensuring it's evenly coated.

3. In a small bowl, combine the dried thyme, dried rosemary, dried sage, garlic powder, salt, and pepper.

4. Sprinkle the herb mixture over the pork tenderloin, pressing it into the meat to adhere.

5. Place the seasoned pork tenderloin on a baking sheet or in a roasting pan.

6. Roast in the preheated oven for 25-30 minutes or until the internal temperature reaches 145°F (63°C).

7. Remove the pork from the oven and let it rest for a few minutes before slicing.

8. Serve the herb-roasted pork tenderloin with a side of roasted vegetables or a fresh salad.

Nutritional value (1 serving):

Calories: 200 Protein: 30g   Fat: 7g Salt: 300mg

BBQ Chicken Skewers

Total servings: 1 serving
Preparation time: 15 minutes
Time to cook: 15-20 minutes

Ingredients:

- 4 ounces chicken breast, cut into cubes
- 1 tablespoon BBQ sauce (choose a low-sodium option)
- 1/2 tablespoon olive oil
- 1/2 teaspoon smoked paprika
- 1/4 teaspoon garlic powder
- Salt and pepper to taste
- Skewers (if using wooden skewers, soak them in water for 15 minutes to prevent burning)

Instructions:

1. Preheat the grill or grill pan to medium-high heat.

2. In a bowl, combine the BBQ sauce, olive oil, smoked paprika, garlic powder, salt, and pepper. Mix well.

3. Add the chicken cubes to the bowl and toss to coat them evenly with the BBQ sauce mixture. Let it marinate for about 10 minutes.

4. Thread the marinated chicken cubes onto the skewers.

5. Place the skewers on the preheated grill or grill pan and cook for about 6-8 minutes per side until the chicken is cooked through and slightly charred.

6. Remove the BBQ chicken skewers from the heat and let them rest for a few minutes before serving.

Nutritional value (1 serving):

Calories: 220 Protein: 28g Fat: 6g Salt: 350mg

Teriyaki Salmon

Total servings: 1 serving
Preparation time: 10 minutes
Time to cook: 12-15 minutes

Ingredients:

- 4 ounces salmon fillet
- 1 tablespoon low-sodium teriyaki sauce
- 1 teaspoon honey
- 1 teaspoon grated ginger
- 1 garlic clove, minced
- 1/2 tablespoon low-sodium soy sauce
- 1/2 tablespoon sesame oil
- Sesame seeds for garnish (optional)
- Green onions, chopped, for garnish (optional)

Instructions:

1. Preheat the oven to 400°F (200°C).

2. In a small bowl, whisk together the teriyaki sauce, honey, grated ginger, minced garlic, soy sauce, and sesame oil.

3. Place the salmon fillet in a baking dish and pour the teriyaki sauce mixture over it, making sure to coat it evenly.

4. Let the salmon marinate for about 10 minutes.

5. Bake the salmon in the preheated oven for 12-15 minutes or until it flakes easily with a fork.

6. Remove the salmon from the oven and sprinkle with sesame seeds and chopped green onions, if desired, for garnish.

Nutritional value (1 serving):

Calories: 280 Protein: 26g Fat: 16g Salt: 500mg

Baked Turkey Cutlets

Total servings: 1 serving
Preparation time: 10 minutes

Time to cook: 20 minutes

Ingredients:

- 4 ounces turkey cutlets
- 1 tablespoon olive oil
- 1/2 teaspoon dried thyme
- 1/2 teaspoon dried rosemary
- 1/2 teaspoon garlic powder
- Salt and pepper to taste

Instructions:

1. Preheat the oven to 375°F (190°C).

2. Place the turkey cutlets on a baking sheet lined with parchment paper.

3. Drizzle the olive oil over the turkey cutlets and season them with dried thyme, dried rosemary, garlic powder, salt, and pepper.

4. Gently rub the seasonings into the turkey cutlets, ensuring they are evenly coated.

5. Bake the turkey cutlets in the preheated oven for about 15-20 minutes or until they reach an internal temperature of 165°F (74°C).

6. Remove the turkey cutlets from the oven and let them rest for a few minutes before serving.

Nutritional value (1 serving):

Calories: 180 Protein: 32g Fat: 4g Salt: 300mg

Garlic Herb Roasted Chicken

Total servings: 1 serving
Preparation time: 10 minutes
Time to cook: 25-30 minutes

Ingredients:

- 4 ounces boneless, skinless chicken breast
- 1 tablespoon olive oil
- 1 garlic clove, minced
- 1/2 teaspoon dried thyme
- 1/2 teaspoon dried rosemary
- 1/2 teaspoon dried parsley
- Salt and pepper to taste

Instructions:

1. Preheat the oven to 400°F (200°C).

2. Place the chicken breast on a baking sheet lined with parchment paper.

3. In a small bowl, mix together the olive oil, minced garlic, dried thyme, dried rosemary, dried parsley, salt, and pepper.

4. Drizzle the garlic herb mixture over the chicken breast, making sure to coat it evenly.

5. Rub the mixture into the chicken breast, ensuring it is well coated.

6. Bake the chicken breast in the preheated oven for 25-30 minutes or until it reaches an internal temperature of 165°F (74°C).

7. Remove the chicken breast from the oven and let it rest for a few minutes before serving.

Nutritional value (1 serving):

Calories: 200 Protein: 32g Fat: 7g Salt: 350mg

Spicy Grilled Shrimp

Total servings: 1 serving
Preparation time: 10 minutes
Time to cook: 6-8 minutes

Ingredients:

- 6 ounces shrimp, peeled and deveined
- 1 tablespoon olive oil
- 1 teaspoon paprika
- 1/2 teaspoon cayenne pepper (adjust to desired spice level)
- 1/2 teaspoon garlic powder
- Salt and pepper to taste
- Lemon wedges, for serving

Instructions:

1. Preheat the grill to medium-high heat.

2. In a bowl, combine the shrimp, olive oil, paprika, cayenne pepper, garlic powder, salt, and pepper. Toss until the shrimp are evenly coated.

3. Thread the seasoned shrimp onto skewers.

4. Place the shrimp skewers on the preheated grill and cook for 2-4 minutes per side, or until the shrimp are opaque and cooked through.

5. Remove the shrimp skewers from the grill and serve immediately with lemon wedges.

Nutritional value (1 serving):

Calories: 160 Protein: 23g Fat: 7g Salt: 350mg

Lemon Pepper Chicken

Total servings: 1 serving
Preparation time: 10 minutes
Time to cook: 15-20 minutes

Ingredients:

- 4 ounces boneless, skinless chicken breast
- 1 tablespoon olive oil
- 1 teaspoon lemon zest
- 1/2 teaspoon black pepper
- 1/4 teaspoon garlic powder
- Salt to taste
- Lemon wedges, for serving

Instructions:

1. Preheat the oven to 400°F (200°C).

2. Place the chicken breast on a baking sheet lined with parchment paper.

3. In a small bowl, mix together the olive oil, lemon zest, black pepper, garlic powder, and salt.

4. Drizzle the lemon pepper mixture over the chicken breast, making sure to coat it evenly.

5. Rub the mixture into the chicken breast, ensuring it is well coated.

6. Bake the chicken breast in the preheated oven for 15-20 minutes or until it reaches an internal temperature of 165°F (74°C).

7. Remove the chicken breast from the oven and let it rest for a few minutes before serving.

8. Serve the lemon pepper chicken with lemon wedges on the side.

Nutritional value (1 serving):

Calories: 180 Protein: 30g Fat: 5g Salt: 300mg

Ginger Soy Beef

Total servings: 1 serving
Preparation time: 10 minutes
Time to cook: 10 minutes

Ingredients:

- 4 ounces lean beef steak, thinly sliced
- 1 tablespoon low-sodium soy sauce
- 1 teaspoon grated fresh ginger

- 1 clove garlic, minced
- 1 teaspoon sesame oil
- 1/2 teaspoon honey or alternative sweetener
- 1/2 teaspoon cornstarch
- 1/2 teaspoon vegetable oil
- 1/4 cup sliced bell peppers (any color)
- 1/4 cup sliced onions
- Salt and pepper to taste
- Sesame seeds for garnish (optional)
- Chopped green onions for garnish (optional)

Instructions:

1. In a bowl, combine the soy sauce, grated ginger, minced garlic, sesame oil, honey, and cornstarch. Stir well to make a marinade.

2. Add the sliced beef to the marinade and toss until the beef is well coated. Allow it to marinate for at least 10 minutes.

3. Heat the vegetable oil in a skillet or wok over medium-high heat.

4. Add the marinated beef to the hot skillet and stir-fry for 2-3 minutes, or until the beef is cooked to your desired level of doneness. Remove the beef from the skillet and set aside.

5. In the same skillet, add the sliced bell peppers and onions. Stir-fry for 2-3 minutes, or until the vegetables are crisp-tender.

6. Return the cooked beef to the skillet with the vegetables. Stir-fry for another minute to heat everything through.

7. Season with salt and pepper to taste. Garnish with sesame seeds and chopped green onions, if desired.

8. Serve the ginger soy beef over steamed brown rice or with a side of steamed vegetables.

Nutritional value (1 serving):

Calories: 280 Protein: 25g Fat: 14g Salt: 500mg

Orange Glazed Salmon

Total servings: 1 serving
Preparation time: 10 minutes
Time to cook: 15 minutes

Ingredients:

- 4 ounces salmon fillet
- 2 tablespoons freshly squeezed orange juice
- 1 tablespoon low-sodium soy sauce

- 1 teaspoon grated orange zest
- 1 teaspoon honey or alternative sweetener
- 1/2 teaspoon minced fresh ginger
- 1/2 teaspoon cornstarch
- Salt and pepper to taste
- Sliced green onions for garnish (optional)

Instructions:

1. Preheat the oven to 400°F (200°C).

2. In a small bowl, whisk together the orange juice, soy sauce, orange zest, honey, ginger, cornstarch, salt, and pepper to make the glaze.

3. Place the salmon fillet on a baking sheet lined with parchment paper.

4. Brush the glaze over the salmon, making sure it is evenly coated.

5. Bake the salmon in the preheated oven for 12-15 minutes, or until it is cooked through and flakes easily with a fork.

6. Remove the salmon from the oven and let it rest for a minute before serving.

7. Garnish with sliced green onions, if desired.

8. Serve the orange glazed salmon with a side of steamed vegetables or a mixed green salad.

Nutritional value (1 serving):

Calories: 290 Protein: 28g Fat: 14g Salt: 500mg

Honey Mustard Turkey

Total servings: 1 serving
Preparation time: 5 minutes
Time to cook: 20 minutes

Ingredients:

- 4 ounces turkey breast, boneless and skinless
- 1 tablespoon Dijon mustard
- 1 tablespoon honey or alternative sweetener
- 1 teaspoon lemon juice
- 1/2 teaspoon dried thyme
- Salt and pepper to taste
- Cooking spray

Instructions:

1. Preheat the oven to 375°F (190°C).

2. In a small bowl, whisk together the Dijon mustard, honey, lemon juice, dried thyme, salt, and pepper to make the honey mustard sauce.

3. Place the turkey breast on a baking sheet lined with foil and lightly coated with cooking spray.

4. Brush the honey mustard sauce over the turkey, making sure it is evenly coated.

5. Bake the turkey in the preheated oven for 18-20 minutes, or until it reaches an internal temperature of 165°F (74°C) and is cooked through.

6. Remove the turkey from the oven and let it rest for a few minutes before slicing.

7. Serve the honey mustard turkey with a side of steamed vegetables or a fresh salad.

Nutritional value (1 serving):

Calories: 180 Protein: 26g Fat: 3g Salt: 400mg

Rosemary Roasted Pork

Total servings: 1 serving
Preparation time: 5 minutes
Time to cook: 25 minutes

Ingredients:

- 4 ounces pork tenderloin
- 1 teaspoon olive oil
- 1 teaspoon dried rosemary
- 1/2 teaspoon minced garlic
- Salt and pepper to taste
- Cooking spray

Instructions:

1. Preheat the oven to 400°F (200°C).

2. Rub the pork tenderloin with olive oil, dried rosemary, minced garlic, salt, and pepper.

3. Place the seasoned pork tenderloin on a baking sheet lined with foil and lightly coated with cooking spray.

4. Roast the pork in the preheated oven for 20-25 minutes, or until it reaches an internal temperature of 145°F (63°C) and is cooked through.

5. Remove the pork from the oven and let it rest for a few minutes before slicing.

6. Serve the rosemary roasted pork with a side of roasted vegetables or a quinoa salad.

Nutritional value (1 serving):

Calories: 240 Protein: 26g Fat: 11g Salt: 300mg

Chipotle Chicken Skewers

Total servings: 1 serving
Preparation time: 10 minutes
Time to cook: 15 minutes

Ingredients:

- 4 ounces boneless, skinless chicken breast, cut into cubes
- 1 tablespoon chipotle seasoning (low-sodium)
- 1 tablespoon olive oil
- 1/2 lime, juiced
- Salt and pepper to taste
- Wooden skewers, soaked in water for 30 minutes

Instructions:

1. Preheat the grill or grill pan to medium-high heat.

2. In a bowl, combine the chicken cubes, chipotle seasoning, olive oil, lime juice, salt, and pepper. Toss well to coat the chicken evenly.

3. Thread the marinated chicken onto the soaked wooden skewers, leaving a little space between each piece.

4. Place the chicken skewers on the preheated grill or grill pan. Cook for about 6-8 minutes, turning occasionally, until the chicken is cooked through and nicely charred on the outside.

5. Remove the chicken skewers from the grill and let them rest for a few minutes before serving.

6. Serve the chipotle chicken skewers with a side of grilled vegetables or a fresh salad.

Nutritional value (1 serving):

Calories: 180 Protein: 24g Fat: 8g Salt: 300mg

Citrus Herb Baked Fish

Total servings: 1 serving
Preparation time: 10 minutes
Time to cook: 15 minutes

Ingredients:

- 4 ounces white fish fillet (such as tilapia or cod)
- 1 tablespoon olive oil
- 1 tablespoon lemon juice
- 1 teaspoon fresh herbs (such as thyme, rosemary, or dill), chopped
- 1/2 teaspoon minced garlic
- Salt and pepper to taste
- Lemon slices for garnish

Instructions:

1. Preheat the oven to 375°F (190°C).

2. Place the fish fillet on a baking sheet lined with foil and lightly coated with cooking spray or olive oil.

3. In a small bowl, mix together the olive oil, lemon juice, fresh herbs, minced garlic, salt, and pepper to make a marinade.

4. Drizzle the marinade over the fish fillet, making sure it is evenly coated.

5. Place a few lemon slices on top of the fish for added flavor.

6. Bake the fish in the preheated oven for about 12-15 minutes, or until it is cooked through and flakes easily with a fork.

7. Remove the fish from the oven and let it rest for a few minutes before serving.

8. Serve the citrus herb baked fish with a side of steamed vegetables or quinoa.

Nutritional value (1 serving):

Calories: 150 Protein: 24g Fat: 6g Salt: 300mg

Turkey and Spinach Patties

Total servings: 1 serving
Preparation time: 15 minutes
Time to cook: 15 minutes

Ingredients:

- 4 ounces ground turkey
- 1 cup fresh spinach, finely chopped
- 1/4 cup whole wheat breadcrumbs
- 1/4 cup onion, finely chopped
- 1 clove garlic, minced
- 1/2 teaspoon dried oregano
- 1/4 teaspoon ground cumin
- Salt and pepper to taste
- Cooking spray

Instructions:

1. In a mixing bowl, combine the ground turkey, chopped spinach, breadcrumbs, onion, garlic, dried oregano, ground cumin, salt, and pepper. Mix well until all the ingredients are evenly incorporated.

2. Divide the mixture into two portions and shape each portion into a patty.

3. Preheat a non-stick skillet or grill pan over medium heat. Lightly coat it with cooking spray.

4. Place the turkey patties on the preheated skillet and cook for about 6-8 minutes per side, or until they are cooked through and reach an internal temperature of 165°F (74°C).

5. Remove the patties from the skillet and let them rest for a few minutes before serving.

6. Serve the turkey and spinach patties with a side of steamed vegetables or a whole grain bun if desired.

Nutritional value (1 serving):

Calories: 180 Protein: 22g Fat: 7g Salt: 300mg

Mediterranean Grilled Lamb

Total servings: 1 serving
Preparation time: 10 minutes
Time to cook: 10 minutes

Ingredients:

- 4 ounces lamb loin or chop
- 1 tablespoon olive oil
- 1 tablespoon lemon juice
- 1 teaspoon dried oregano
- 1/2 teaspoon minced garlic
- Salt and pepper to taste

Instructions:

1. Preheat the grill or grill pan to medium-high heat.

2. In a small bowl, combine the olive oil, lemon juice, dried oregano, minced garlic, salt, and pepper to make a marinade.

3. Rub the marinade all over the lamb loin or chop, ensuring it is evenly coated.

4. Place the lamb on the preheated grill or grill pan. Cook for about 4-5 minutes per side, or until the lamb reaches your desired level of doneness.

5. Remove the lamb from the grill and let it rest for a few minutes before serving.

6. Slice the grilled lamb and serve it with a side of Greek salad or roasted vegetables.

Nutritional value (1 serving):

Calories: 220 Protein: 25g Fat: 13g Salt: 350mg

Cajun Shrimp Skewers

Total servings: 1 serving
Preparation time: 15 minutes

Time to cook: 8 minutes

Ingredients:

- 8 large shrimp, peeled and deveined
- 1 teaspoon Cajun seasoning
- 1/2 teaspoon paprika
- 1/4 teaspoon garlic powder
- 1/4 teaspoon onion powder
- 1/4 teaspoon dried thyme
- 1/4 teaspoon dried oregano
- Pinch of cayenne pepper (optional)
- 1 tablespoon olive oil
- 1/2 lemon, juiced
- Salt and pepper to taste
- Wooden skewers, soaked in water for 30 minutes

Instructions:

1. 1Preheat the grill or grill pan to medium-high heat.

2. In a bowl, combine the Cajun seasoning, paprika, garlic powder, onion powder, dried thyme, dried oregano, cayenne pepper (if using), salt, and pepper.

3. Thread the shrimp onto the soaked wooden skewers, ensuring they are secure.

4. Drizzle the shrimp skewers with olive oil and sprinkle the spice mixture evenly over the shrimp, pressing gently to adhere.

5. Grill the shrimp skewers for about 2-4 minutes per side, or until the shrimp are opaque and cooked through.

6. Remove the shrimp skewers from the grill and squeeze the lemon juice over them.

7. Serve the Cajun shrimp skewers with a side of steamed vegetables or a fresh salad.

Nutritional value (1 serving):

Calories: 150 Protein: 20g Fat: 6g Salt: 400mg

Garlic Herb Roasted Beef

Total servings: 1 serving
Preparation time: 10 minutes
Time to cook: 20 minutes

Ingredients:

- 4 ounces beef tenderloin or sirloin steak
- 1 tablespoon olive oil
- 2 cloves garlic, minced

- 1/2 teaspoon dried rosemary
- 1/2 teaspoon dried thyme
- Salt and pepper to taste

Instructions:

1. Preheat the oven to 425°F (220°C).

2. Rub the beef tenderloin or sirloin steak with olive oil, minced garlic, dried rosemary, dried thyme, salt, and pepper. Ensure the steak is evenly coated with the seasonings.

3. Place the seasoned beef on a baking sheet or in an oven-safe skillet.

4. Roast the beef in the preheated oven for about 15-20 minutes, or until it reaches your desired level of doneness. The cooking time may vary depending on the thickness of the steak.

5. Remove the beef from the oven and let it rest for a few minutes before slicing.

6. Slice the roasted beef and serve it with a side of roasted vegetables or a mixed green salad.

Nutritional value (1 serving):

Calories: 240 Protein: 30g Fat: 12g Salt: 400mg

Sweet and Spicy Chicken

Total servings: 1 serving
Preparation time: 10 minutes
Time to cook: 20 minutes

Ingredients:

- 4 ounces boneless, skinless chicken breast
- 1 tablespoon honey
- 1 tablespoon low-sodium soy sauce
- 1 teaspoon Sriracha sauce (adjust to taste)
- 1/2 teaspoon garlic powder
- 1/2 teaspoon ground ginger
- 1/4 teaspoon red pepper flakes (optional)
- Salt and pepper to taste
- 1 teaspoon olive oil

Instructions:

1. Preheat the oven to 400°F (200°C).

2. In a small bowl, mix together the honey, low-sodium soy sauce, Sriracha sauce, garlic powder, ground ginger, red pepper flakes (if using), salt, and pepper.

3. Place the chicken breast in a baking dish and pour the sauce mixture over it, ensuring it is evenly coated.

4. Heat the olive oil in a skillet over medium heat. Once hot, add the chicken breast and sear for 2-3 minutes on each side until lightly browned.

5. Transfer the skillet with the chicken to the preheated oven and bake for approximately 12-15 minutes, or until the chicken is cooked through and reaches an internal temperature of 165°F (74°C).

6. Remove the chicken from the oven and let it rest for a few minutes before serving.

7. Slice the sweet and spicy chicken and serve it with a side of steamed vegetables or a whole grain of your choice.

Nutritional value (1 serving):

Calories: 200 Protein: 25g Fat: 4g Salt: 500mg

Teriyaki Glazed Salmon

Total servings: 1 serving
Preparation time: 10 minutes
Time to cook: 15 minutes

Ingredients:

- 4 ounces salmon fillet
- 1 tablespoon low-sodium soy sauce
- 1 tablespoon honey or maple syrup
- 1 tablespoon rice vinegar
- 1 teaspoon grated ginger
- 1 clove garlic, minced
- 1/2 teaspoon cornstarch (optional, for thickening)
- Sesame seeds and chopped green onions for garnish (optional)

Instructions:

1. Preheat the oven to 400°F (200°C).

2. In a small bowl, whisk together the low-sodium soy sauce, honey or maple syrup, rice vinegar, grated ginger, minced garlic, and cornstarch (if desired) until well combined.

3. Place the salmon fillet in a baking dish and pour the teriyaki sauce mixture over it, ensuring it is evenly coated.

4. Bake the salmon in the preheated oven for approximately 12-15 minutes, or until it is cooked through and flakes easily with a fork.

5. Remove the salmon from the oven and let it rest for a few minutes.

6. Garnish with sesame seeds and chopped green onions, if desired, and serve with a side of steamed vegetables or brown rice.

Nutritional value (1 serving):

Calories: 250 Protein: 25g Fat: 12g Salt: 500mg

Turkey Sausage Patties

Total servings: 1 serving
Preparation time: 10 minutes
Time to cook: 12 minutes

Ingredients:

- 4 ounces ground turkey
- 1/2 teaspoon dried sage
- 1/2 teaspoon dried thyme
- 1/4 teaspoon garlic powder
- 1/4 teaspoon onion powder
- 1/4 teaspoon paprika
- Salt and pepper to taste
- 1 teaspoon olive oil

Instructions:

1. In a mixing bowl, combine the ground turkey, dried sage, dried thyme, garlic powder, onion powder, paprika, salt, and pepper. Mix well until all the ingredients are evenly incorporated.

2. Divide the turkey mixture into two equal portions and shape each portion into a patty.

3. Heat the olive oil in a non-stick skillet over medium heat.

4. Once the skillet is hot, place the turkey patties in the skillet and cook for approximately 5-6 minutes per side, or until the patties are cooked through and reach an internal temperature of 165°F (74°C).

5. Remove the turkey sausage patties from the skillet and let them rest for a few minutes before serving.

6. Serve the turkey sausage patties with a side of sautéed vegetables or whole grain toast.

Nutritional value (1 serving):

Calories: 150 Protein: 20g Fat: 7g Salt: 400mg

Herb-Marinated Grilled Chicken

Total servings: 1 serving
Preparation time: 10 minutes
Time to cook: 15 minutes

Ingredients:

- 4 ounces boneless, skinless chicken breast
- 1 tablespoon lemon juice
- 1 tablespoon olive oil
- 1 clove garlic, minced
- 1/2 teaspoon dried rosemary
- 1/2 teaspoon dried thyme
- Salt and pepper to taste

Instructions:

1. In a small bowl, whisk together the lemon juice, olive oil, minced garlic, dried rosemary, dried thyme, salt, and pepper to create the marinade.

2. Place the chicken breast in a shallow dish and pour the marinade over it, ensuring it is evenly coated. Let it marinate for at least 30 minutes, or up to 4 hours in the refrigerator.

3. Preheat the grill to medium-high heat.

4. Remove the chicken breast from the marinade and discard the excess marinade.

5. Grill the chicken breast for approximately 6-8 minutes per side, or until it is cooked through and reaches an internal temperature of 165°F (74°C).

6. Remove the grilled chicken from the heat and let it rest for a few minutes before serving.

7. Slice the herb-marinated grilled chicken and serve it with a side of steamed vegetables or a fresh salad.

Nutritional value (1 serving):

Calories: 180 Protein: 25g Fat: 8g Salt: 300mg

Lemon Garlic Shrimp Scampi

Total servings: 1 serving
Preparation time: 10 minutes
Time to cook: 10 minutes

Ingredients:

- 4 ounces shrimp, peeled and deveined
- 2 cloves garlic, minced
- 1 tablespoon olive oil
- 1 tablespoon lemon juice
- 1/4 teaspoon red pepper flakes (optional)
- Salt and pepper to taste
- 1 tablespoon chopped fresh parsley

Instructions:

1. In a bowl, combine the minced garlic, olive oil, lemon juice, red pepper flakes (if using), salt, and pepper. Mix well to make the marinade.

2. Add the shrimp to the marinade and toss until they are well-coated. Let the shrimp marinate for about 10 minutes.

3. Heat a non-stick skillet over medium heat.

4. Add the marinated shrimp to the skillet and cook for about 2-3 minutes per side, or until they are pink and opaque.

5. Remove the shrimp from the skillet and transfer them to a plate.

6. Garnish the shrimp with chopped fresh parsley.

7. Serve the lemon garlic shrimp scampi with a side of whole grain pasta or steamed vegetables.

Nutritional value (1 serving):

Calories: 180 Protein: 20g Fat: 7g Salt: 300mg

Balsamic Glazed Pork Chops

Total servings: 1 serving
Preparation time: 5 minutes
Time to cook: 15 minutes

Ingredients:

- 4 ounces boneless pork chop
- 1 tablespoon balsamic vinegar
- 1 teaspoon Dijon mustard
- 1 teaspoon honey
- 1/2 teaspoon dried thyme
- Salt and pepper to taste
- 1 teaspoon olive oil

Instructions:

1. In a small bowl, whisk together the balsamic vinegar, Dijon mustard, honey, dried thyme, salt, and pepper to create the glaze.

2. Season the pork chop with salt and pepper on both sides.

3. Heat the olive oil in a non-stick skillet over medium-high heat.

4. Add the pork chop to the skillet and cook for about 5-6 minutes per side, or until it reaches an internal temperature of 145°F (63°C).

5. Reduce the heat to low and pour the balsamic glaze over the pork chop.

6. Cook for an additional 1-2 minutes, flipping the pork chop once to ensure it is evenly coated with the glaze.

7. Remove the pork chop from the skillet and let it rest for a few minutes before serving.

8. Serve the balsamic glazed pork chop with a side of roasted vegetables or a fresh salad.

Nutritional value (1 serving):

Calories: 250 Protein: 25g Fat: 10g Salt: 400mg

Honey Sriracha Chicken

Total servings: 1 serving
Preparation time: 10 minutes
Time to cook: 20 minutes

Ingredients:

- 4 ounces boneless, skinless chicken breast
- 1 tablespoon honey
- 1 tablespoon Sriracha sauce
- 1 tablespoon low-sodium soy sauce
- 1 teaspoon minced garlic
- 1 teaspoon grated ginger
- 1 teaspoon olive oil
- Salt and pepper to taste
- Chopped green onions for garnish

Instructions:

1. Preheat the oven to 400°F (200°C).

2. In a small bowl, whisk together the honey, Sriracha sauce, soy sauce, minced garlic, grated ginger, olive oil, salt, and pepper to make the marinade.

3. Place the chicken breast in a shallow dish and pour the marinade over it. Make sure the chicken is well-coated. Let it marinate for about 10 minutes.

4. Heat an oven-safe skillet over medium-high heat.

5. Add the chicken breast to the skillet and cook for about 2-3 minutes on each side, or until it gets a golden brown sear.

6. Transfer the skillet to the preheated oven and bake for 12-15 minutes, or until the chicken is cooked through and reaches an internal temperature of 165°F (74°C).

7. Remove the skillet from the oven and let the chicken rest for a few minutes.

8. Garnish the chicken with chopped green onions before serving.

Nutritional value (1 serving):

Calories: 250 Protein: 25g Fat: 5g Salt: 600mg

Blackened Salmon

Total servings: 1 serving
Preparation time: 5 minutes
Time to cook: 10 minutes

Ingredients:

- 4 ounces salmon fillet
- 1 teaspoon paprika
- 1/2 teaspoon dried thyme
- 1/2 teaspoon garlic powder
- 1/2 teaspoon onion powder
- 1/4 teaspoon cayenne pepper
- 1/4 teaspoon salt
- 1/4 teaspoon black pepper
- 1 teaspoon olive oil
- Lemon wedges for serving

Instructions:

1. In a small bowl, mix together the paprika, dried thyme, garlic powder, onion powder, cayenne pepper, salt, and black pepper to create the blackened seasoning.

2. Rub the salmon fillet with the blackened seasoning, making sure it is evenly coated on both sides.

3. Heat the olive oil in a non-stick skillet over medium-high heat.

4. Add the seasoned salmon fillet to the skillet, skin-side down.

5. Cook the salmon for about 4-5 minutes on each side, or until it is cooked to your desired level of doneness.

6. Remove the salmon from the skillet and let it rest for a few minutes before serving.

7. Serve the blackened salmon with lemon wedges on the side.

Nutritional value (1 serving):

Calories: 300 Protein: 25g Fat: 20g Salt: 400mg

Italian Turkey Meatloaf

Total servings: 4 servings
Preparation time: 15 minutes
Time to cook: 45 minutes

Ingredients:

- 1 pound ground turkey
- 1/2 cup whole wheat breadcrumbs
- 1/4 cup grated Parmesan cheese
- 1/4 cup finely chopped onion
- 1/4 cup finely chopped bell pepper
- 1/4 cup finely chopped carrot
- 1/4 cup chopped fresh parsley
- 1 egg

- 2 cloves garlic, minced
- 1 teaspoon dried oregano
- 1/2 teaspoon dried basil
- 1/2 teaspoon salt
- 1/4 teaspoon black pepper
- 1/4 cup low-sodium marinara sauce

Instructions:

1. Preheat the oven to 375°F (190°C).

2. In a large bowl, combine ground turkey, breadcrumbs, Parmesan cheese, onion, bell pepper, carrot, parsley, egg, garlic, oregano, basil, salt, and black pepper. Mix well until all ingredients are evenly incorporated.

3. Transfer the mixture to a loaf pan and shape it into a loaf.

4. Spread the marinara sauce evenly over the top of the meatloaf.

5. Bake in the preheated oven for 40-45 minutes, or until the internal temperature reaches 165°F (74°C).

6. Remove the meatloaf from the oven and let it rest for a few minutes before slicing.

7. Serve the Italian turkey meatloaf slices with your choice of side dishes.

Nutritional value (1 serving):

Calories: 250 Protein: 25g Fat: 10g Salt: 600mg

Asian Beef Stir-Fry

Total servings: 1 serving
Preparation time: 10 minutes
Time to cook: 15 minutes

Ingredients:

- 4 ounces beef sirloin, thinly sliced
- 1 cup mixed vegetables (broccoli florets, bell peppers, snap peas, carrots)
- 1 tablespoon low-sodium soy sauce
- 1 tablespoon hoisin sauce
- 1 teaspoon cornstarch
- 1 teaspoon sesame oil
- 1 teaspoon minced garlic
- 1/2 teaspoon grated ginger
- 1/2 teaspoon honey
- 1/4 teaspoon red pepper flakes (optional)
- 1 teaspoon vegetable oil for cooking

Instructions:

1. In a small bowl, whisk together soy sauce, hoisin sauce, cornstarch, sesame oil, minced garlic, grated ginger, honey, and red pepper flakes (if using) to make the sauce.

2. Heat vegetable oil in a large skillet or wok over medium-high heat.

3. Add the beef slices to the hot skillet and cook for 2-3 minutes until browned. Remove the beef from the skillet and set it aside.

4. In the same skillet, add the mixed vegetables and stir-fry for 3-4 minutes until they are crisp-tender.

5. Return the beef to the skillet and pour the sauce over the beef and vegetables.

6. Stir-fry for an additional 2-3 minutes until the sauce thickens and coats the beef and vegetables.

7. Remove from heat and serve the Asian beef stir-fry immediately with steamed rice or your choice of grains.

Nutritional value (1 serving):

Calories: 300 Protein: 25g Fat: 10g Salt: 800mg

Dijon Herb Baked Chicken

Total servings: 1 serving
Preparation time: 10 minutes
Time to cook: 25 minutes

Ingredients:

- 1 chicken breast (about 4 ounces)
- 1 tablespoon Dijon mustard
- 1 teaspoon dried Italian herbs
- 1 teaspoon olive oil
- 1 clove garlic, minced
- Salt and black pepper to taste

Instructions:

1. Preheat the oven to 400°F (200°C).

2. Season the chicken breast with salt and black pepper.

3. In a small bowl, mix together the Dijon mustard, dried Italian herbs, olive oil, and minced garlic.

4. Place the chicken breast on a baking sheet lined with parchment paper.

5. Brush the Dijon herb mixture evenly over the chicken breast.

6. Bake in the preheated oven for 20-25 minutes, or until the chicken is cooked through and reaches an internal temperature of 165°F (74°C).

7. Remove the chicken from the oven and let it rest for a few minutes before serving.

Nutritional value (1 serving):

Calories: 200 Protein: 28g Fat: 8g Salt: 500mg

Garlic Butter Shrimp

Total servings: 1 serving
Preparation time: 10 minutes
Time to cook: 5 minutes

Ingredients:

- 6-8 large shrimp, peeled and deveined
- 1 tablespoon unsalted butter
- 2 cloves garlic, minced
- 1 tablespoon chopped fresh parsley
- Juice of half a lemon
- Salt and black pepper to taste

Instructions:

1. In a skillet, melt the butter over medium heat.

2. Add the minced garlic to the skillet and sauté for 1 minute until fragrant.

3. Add the shrimp to the skillet and cook for 2-3 minutes, flipping once, until they turn pink and opaque.

4. Add the chopped parsley, lemon juice, salt, and black pepper to the skillet. Stir to coat the shrimp evenly.

5. Remove from heat and transfer the garlic butter shrimp to a serving plate.

6. Serve immediately with a side of steamed vegetables or your choice of grains.

Nutritional value (1 serving):

Calories: 150 Protein: 20g Fat: 7g Salt: 300mg

Rosemary Lemon Pork Chops

Total servings: 1 serving
Preparation time: 10 minutes
Time to cook: 15 minutes

Ingredients:

- 1 pork chop (about 4 ounces)
- 1 tablespoon fresh rosemary, chopped
- Juice of half a lemon
- 1 teaspoon olive oil
- 1 clove garlic, minced
- Salt and black pepper to taste

Instructions:

1. Preheat the grill or a skillet over medium-high heat.

2. Season the pork chop with salt, black pepper, and chopped rosemary.

3. In a small bowl, combine the lemon juice, olive oil, and minced garlic.

4. Brush the lemon juice mixture onto both sides of the pork chop.

5. Place the pork chop on the grill or skillet and cook for about 6-8 minutes per side, or until the internal temperature reaches 145°F (63°C).

6. Remove the pork chop from the heat and let it rest for a few minutes before serving.

Nutritional value (1 serving):

Calories: 220 Protein: 26g Fat: 10g Salt: 400mg

BBQ Turkey Burgers

Total servings: 1 serving
Preparation time: 10 minutes
Time to cook: 15 minutes

Ingredients:

- 4 ounces ground turkey
- 1 tablespoon BBQ sauce
- 1 green onion, finely chopped
- 1/4 teaspoon garlic powder
- Salt and black pepper to taste
- Whole wheat burger bun
- Lettuce, tomato, and other desired toppings for serving

Instructions:

1. In a bowl, combine the ground turkey, BBQ sauce, chopped green onion, garlic powder, salt, and black pepper. Mix well until all ingredients are evenly incorporated.

2. Form the turkey mixture into a patty shape, making sure it is slightly larger than the size of the burger bun.

3. Preheat the grill or a skillet over medium heat.

4. Cook the turkey burger patty for about 6-8 minutes per side, or until it reaches an internal temperature of 165°F (74°C).

5. Assemble the turkey burger by placing the cooked patty on a whole wheat bun. Add lettuce, tomato, and any other desired toppings.

6. Serve immediately.

Nutritional value (1 serving):

Calories: 280 Protein: 25g Fat: 10g Salt: 450mg

Herb-Encrusted Baked Fish

Total servings: 1 serving
Preparation time: 10 minutes
Time to cook: 15-20 minutes

Ingredients:

- 1 fish fillet (such as salmon, trout, or tilapia)
- 1 tablespoon fresh herbs (such as parsley, thyme, or dill), chopped
- 1 teaspoon olive oil
- 1/2 teaspoon lemon zest
- Salt and black pepper to taste

Instructions:

1. Preheat the oven to 400°F (200°C).

2. Place the fish fillet on a baking sheet lined with parchment paper.

3. In a small bowl, combine the chopped herbs, olive oil, lemon zest, salt, and black pepper.

4. Spread the herb mixture evenly over the fish fillet, pressing it gently to adhere.

5. Bake the fish in the preheated oven for 15-20 minutes or until it flakes easily with a fork and reaches an internal temperature of 145°F (63°C).

6. Remove the baked fish from the oven and let it rest for a few minutes before serving.

Nutritional value (1 serving):

Calories: 200 Protein: 25g Fat: 8g Salt: 300mg

Lemon Herb Grilled Chicken

Total servings: 1 serving
Preparation time: 10 minutes
Time to cook: 10-12 minutes

Ingredients:

- 1 chicken breast (about 4 ounces)
- Juice of half a lemon
- 1 tablespoon fresh herbs (such as rosemary, thyme, or basil), chopped
- 1 teaspoon olive oil
- 1 clove garlic, minced
- Salt and black pepper to taste

Instructions:

1. Preheat the grill or a skillet over medium-high heat.

2. Season the chicken breast with salt, black pepper, and chopped herbs.

3. In a small bowl, combine the lemon juice, olive oil, and minced garlic.

4. Brush the lemon juice mixture onto both sides of the chicken breast.

5. Place the chicken breast on the grill or skillet and cook for about 5-6 minutes per side or until the internal temperature reaches 165°F (74°C).

6. Remove the chicken breast from the heat and let it rest for a few minutes before serving.

Nutritional value (1 serving):

Calories: 220 Protein: 30g Fat: 8g Salt: 350mg

Spicy Lime Shrimp

Total servings: 1 serving
Preparation time: 10 minutes
Time to cook: 5-6 minutes

Ingredients:

- 8-10 large shrimp, peeled and deveined
- Juice of 1 lime
- 1 teaspoon olive oil
- 1 clove garlic, minced
- 1/2 teaspoon chili powder
- 1/4 teaspoon cayenne pepper (adjust according to spice preference)
- Salt and black pepper to taste
- Fresh cilantro for garnish (optional)

Instructions:

1. In a bowl, combine the lime juice, olive oil, minced garlic, chili powder, cayenne pepper, salt, and black pepper.

2. Add the shrimp to the bowl and toss to coat them evenly with the marinade. Let them marinate for about 10 minutes.

3. Preheat a skillet over medium-high heat.

4. Add the marinated shrimp to the skillet and cook for about 2-3 minutes on each side or until they turn pink and opaque.

5. Remove the cooked shrimp from the skillet and transfer them to a serving plate.

6. Garnish with fresh cilantro, if desired, and serve immediately.

Nutritional value (1 serving):

Calories: 120 Protein: 20g Fat: 3g Salt: 300mg

Greek Turkey Meatballs

Total servings: 1 serving
Preparation time: 10 minutes
Time to cook: 15-20 minutes

Ingredients:

- 4 ounces ground turkey
- 1/4 cup whole wheat breadcrumbs
- 1/4 cup finely chopped onion
- 1 clove garlic, minced
- 1 tablespoon chopped fresh parsley
- 1/2 teaspoon dried oregano
- 1/4 teaspoon dried basil
- Salt and black pepper to taste
- Cooking spray

Instructions:

1. Preheat the oven to 400°F (200°C).

2. In a mixing bowl, combine the ground turkey, breadcrumbs, chopped onion, minced garlic, chopped parsley, dried oregano, dried basil, salt, and black pepper. Mix well until all the ingredients are evenly incorporated.

3. Shape the mixture into small meatballs, about 1 inch in diameter.

4. Place the meatballs on a baking sheet lined with parchment paper. Make sure to space them out so they don't touch each other.

5. Lightly spray the meatballs with cooking spray to promote browning.

6. Bake the meatballs in the preheated oven for 15-20 minutes or until they are cooked through and browned on the outside.

7. Remove the cooked meatballs from the oven and let them cool for a few minutes before serving.

Nutritional value (1 serving):

Calories: 180 Protein: 20g Fat: 8g Salt: 350mg

Chapter 9: Seafood

Grilled Salmon Fillet

Total servings: 1 serving
Preparation time: 5 minutes
Time to cook: 10-12 minutes

Ingredients:

- 1 salmon fillet (4-6 ounces)
- 1 teaspoon olive oil
- 1 teaspoon lemon juice
- 1/2 teaspoon minced garlic
- Salt and black pepper to taste
- Fresh dill or parsley for garnish (optional)

Instructions:

1. Preheat the grill to medium heat.

2. In a small bowl, mix together the olive oil, lemon juice, minced garlic, salt, and black pepper.

3. Brush the mixture evenly over the salmon fillet, ensuring it's coated on all sides.

4. Place the salmon fillet on the preheated grill, skin-side down if it has skin. Close the grill and cook for 5-6 minutes.

5. Carefully flip the salmon fillet using a spatula and continue grilling for another 5-6 minutes or until the fish flakes easily with a fork.

6. Remove the grilled salmon from the heat and transfer it to a serving plate.

7. Garnish with fresh dill or parsley, if desired, and serve immediately.

Nutritional value (1 serving):

Calories: 280 Protein: 25g Fat: 18g Salt: 350mg

Lemon Garlic Shrimp

Total servings: 1 serving
Preparation time: 10 minutes
Time to cook: 5-6 minutes

Ingredients:

- 8-10 large shrimp, peeled and deveined
- 1 teaspoon olive oil
- 1 clove garlic, minced
- Juice of 1/2 lemon
- 1/2 teaspoon lemon zest
- Salt and black pepper to taste
- Fresh parsley for garnish (optional)

Instructions:

1. In a bowl, combine the olive oil, minced garlic, lemon juice, lemon zest, salt, and black pepper.

2. Add the shrimp to the bowl and toss to coat them evenly with the mixture. Let them marinate for about 5 minutes.

3. Preheat a skillet over medium-high heat.

4. Add the marinated shrimp to the skillet and cook for 2-3 minutes on each side or until they turn pink and opaque.

5. Remove the cooked shrimp from the skillet and transfer them to a serving plate.

6. Garnish with fresh parsley, if desired, and serve immediately.

Nutritional value (1 serving):

Calories: 120 Protein: 20g Fat: 4g Salt: 300mg

Baked Cod Fish

Total servings: 1 serving
Preparation time: 10 minutes
Time to cook: 15-18 minutes

Ingredients:

- 1 cod fillet (4-6 ounces)
- 1 teaspoon olive oil
- 1/2 teaspoon lemon juice
- 1/2 teaspoon dried thyme
- 1/2 teaspoon dried oregano
- 1/4 teaspoon garlic powder
- Salt and black pepper to taste
- Lemon wedges for serving (optional)

Instructions:

1. Preheat the oven to 400°F (200°C).

2. Pat dry the cod fillet using a paper towel to remove excess moisture.

3. Place the cod fillet on a baking sheet lined with parchment paper.

4. Drizzle the olive oil and lemon juice over the cod fillet, ensuring it's evenly coated.

5. In a small bowl, mix together the dried thyme, dried oregano, garlic powder, salt, and black pepper. Sprinkle the herb mixture over the cod fillet, pressing it gently to adhere.

6. Bake the cod in the preheated oven for 15-18 minutes or until it flakes easily with a fork and is opaque throughout.

7. Remove the baked cod from the oven and let it rest for a few minutes before serving.

8. Serve with lemon wedges on the side, if desired.

Nutritional value (1 serving):

Calories: 180 Protein: 30g Fat: 5g Salt: 400mg

Garlic Herb Tilapia

Total servings: 1 serving
Preparation time: 10 minutes
Time to cook: 10-12 minutes

Ingredients:

- 1 tilapia fillet (4-6 ounces)
- 1 teaspoon olive oil
- 1 clove garlic, minced
- 1/2 teaspoon dried parsley
- 1/4 teaspoon dried dill
- 1/4 teaspoon paprika
- Salt and black pepper to taste
- Lemon wedges for serving (optional)

Instructions:

1. Preheat a skillet over medium heat.

2. Pat dry the tilapia fillet using a paper towel.

3. In a small bowl, combine the olive oil, minced garlic, dried parsley, dried dill, paprika, salt, and black pepper.

4. Brush both sides of the tilapia fillet with the herb mixture, ensuring it's evenly coated.

5. Place the coated tilapia fillet in the preheated skillet and cook for 4-6 minutes on each side or until it flakes easily with a fork and is opaque throughout.

6. Remove the cooked tilapia from the skillet and transfer it to a serving plate.

7. Squeeze fresh lemon juice over the tilapia or serve it with lemon wedges on the side, if desired.

Nutritional value (1 serving):

Calories: 150 Protein: 28g Fat: 3g Salt: 300mg

Spicy Cajun Prawns

Total servings: 1 serving
Preparation time: 10 minutes
Time to cook: 6-8 minutes

Ingredients:

- 6-8 large prawns or shrimp, peeled and deveined
- 1 tablespoon olive oil
- 1 teaspoon Cajun seasoning
- 1/2 teaspoon paprika
- 1/4 teaspoon cayenne pepper (adjust according to spice preference)
- Salt to taste
- Fresh lemon wedges for serving (optional)
- Chopped fresh parsley for garnish (optional)

Instructions:

1. In a bowl, combine the Cajun seasoning, paprika, cayenne pepper, and a pinch of salt.

2. Add the prawns to the bowl and toss them gently until they are evenly coated with the spice mixture.

3. Heat olive oil in a skillet over medium-high heat.

4. Add the seasoned prawns to the skillet and cook for 2-3 minutes on each side or until they turn pink and are cooked through.

5. Remove the cooked prawns from the skillet and transfer them to a serving plate.

6. Squeeze fresh lemon juice over the prawns and garnish with chopped fresh parsley, if desired.

7. Serve hot with lemon wedges on the side, if desired.

Nutritional value (1 serving):

Calories: 150 Protein: 20g Fat: 6g Salt: 400mg

Teriyaki Glazed Salmon

Total servings: 1 serving
Preparation time: 10 minutes
Time to cook: 12-15 minutes

Ingredients:

- 1 salmon fillet (4-6 ounces)
- 2 tablespoons low-sodium soy sauce
- 1 tablespoon honey or maple syrup
- 1 tablespoon rice vinegar
- 1/2 teaspoon minced garlic
- 1/2 teaspoon grated ginger
- 1/4 teaspoon sesame oil
- Sesame seeds for garnish (optional)

Instructions:

1. Preheat the oven to 400°F (200°C).

2. In a small bowl, whisk together the soy sauce, honey or maple syrup, rice vinegar, minced garlic, grated ginger, and sesame oil.

3. Place the salmon fillet in a baking dish or on a baking sheet lined with parchment paper.

4. Pour the teriyaki sauce over the salmon, ensuring it's evenly coated.

5. Bake the salmon in the preheated oven for 12-15 minutes or until it flakes easily with a fork and is cooked to your desired doneness.

6. Remove the cooked salmon from the oven and let it rest for a few minutes.

7. Sprinkle sesame seeds and sliced green onions over the salmon for garnish, if desired.

8. Serve hot.

Nutritional value (1 serving):

Calories: 300 Protein: 25g Fat: 15g Salt: 700mg

Lemon Dill Trout

Total servings: 1 serving
Preparation time: 5 minutes
Time to cook: 10-12 minutes

Ingredients:

• 1 trout fillet (4-6 ounces)

• 1 tablespoon lemon juice

• 1 teaspoon olive oil

• 1/2 teaspoon dried dill (or 1 teaspoon fresh dill)

• Salt and pepper to taste

• Lemon slices for garnish (optional)

• Fresh dill sprigs for garnish (optional)

Instructions:

1. Preheat the oven to 400°F (200°C).

2. Place the trout fillet on a baking sheet lined with parchment paper.

3. Drizzle the lemon juice and olive oil over the trout.

4. Sprinkle the dried dill (or fresh dill) evenly over the fillet.

5. Season with salt and pepper to taste.

6. Bake the trout in the preheated oven for 10-12 minutes or until it flakes easily with a fork and is cooked through.

7. Remove the cooked trout from the oven and let it rest for a few minutes.

8. Garnish with lemon slices and fresh dill sprigs, if desired.

9. Serve hot.

Nutritional value (1 serving):

Calories: 200 Protein: 25g Fat: 9g Salt: 300mg

Shrimp Stir-Fry

Total servings: 1 serving
Preparation time: 10 minutes
Time to cook: 10 minutes

Ingredients:

• 8-10 large shrimp, peeled and deveined

• 1 tablespoon olive oil

• 1/2 cup sliced bell peppers (any color)

• 1/2 cup sliced zucchini

• 1/2 cup sliced mushrooms

• 1/4 cup sliced onions

• 1 garlic clove, minced

• 1/2 teaspoon grated ginger

• 1 tablespoon low-sodium soy sauce

• 1 tablespoon lemon juice

• Salt and pepper to taste

• Chopped fresh cilantro for garnish (optional)

Instructions:

1. Heat olive oil in a skillet or wok over medium-high heat.

2. Add the garlic and ginger to the skillet and cook for 1 minute until fragrant.

3. Add the shrimp to the skillet and cook for 2-3 minutes until they turn pink and are cooked through. Remove the shrimp from the skillet and set aside.

4. In the same skillet, add the sliced bell peppers, zucchini, mushrooms, and onions. Stir-fry for 3-4 minutes until the vegetables are tender-crisp.

5. Return the cooked shrimp to the skillet and stir in the soy sauce and lemon juice. Cook for an additional 1-2 minutes to heat through and allow the flavors to blend.

6. Season with salt and pepper to taste.

7. Garnish with chopped fresh cilantro, if desired.

8. Serve hot.

Nutritional value (1 serving):

Calories: 180 Protein: 20g Fat: 7g Salt: 400mg

Grilled Tuna Steak

Total servings: 1 serving
Preparation time: 10 minutes

Ingredients:

- 1 tuna steak (6-8 ounces)
- 1 tablespoon olive oil
- 1 tablespoon lemon juice
- 1 teaspoon soy sauce (low-sodium)
- 1/2 teaspoon dried herbs (such as thyme, oregano, or rosemary)
- Salt and pepper to taste
- Lemon wedges for serving
- Fresh herbs for garnish (optional)

Instructions:

1. Preheat the grill to medium-high heat.

2. Pat dry the tuna steak with a paper towel to remove any excess moisture.

3. In a small bowl, whisk together the olive oil, lemon juice, soy sauce, dried herbs, salt, and pepper.

4. Brush both sides of the tuna steak with the marinade.

5. Place the tuna steak on the grill and cook for 3-4 minutes per side for medium-rare or adjust the cooking time according to your preference.

6. Remove the tuna steak from the grill and let it rest for a few minutes.

7. Slice the grilled tuna steak and serve with lemon wedges.

8. Garnish with fresh herbs, if desired.

9. Serve hot.

Nutritional value (1 serving):

Calories: 250 Protein: 40g Fat: 8g Salt: 400mg

Citrus Herb Baked Fish

Total servings: 1 serving
Preparation time: 10 minutes
Time to cook: 15-20 minutes

Ingredients:

- 1 white fish fillet (such as cod, halibut, or tilapia) (6-8 ounces)
- 1 tablespoon olive oil
- 1 tablespoon lemon juice
- 1 teaspoon orange juice
- 1/2 teaspoon dried herbs (such as dill, basil, or parsley)
- 1/2 teaspoon lemon zest
- Salt and pepper to taste
- Lemon slices for garnish (optional)
- Fresh herbs for garnish (optional)

Instructions:

1. Preheat the oven to 400°F (200°C).

2. Place the fish fillet on a baking sheet lined with parchment paper.

3. In a small bowl, whisk together the olive oil, lemon juice, orange juice, dried herbs, lemon zest, salt, and pepper.

4. Brush the marinade evenly over the fish fillet.

5. Bake the fish in the preheated oven for 15-20 minutes or until it flakes easily with a fork and is cooked through.

6. Remove the baked fish from the oven and let it rest for a few minutes.

7. Garnish with lemon slices and fresh herbs, if desired.

8. Serve hot.

Nutritional value (1 serving):

Calories: 180 Protein: 30g Fat: 6g Salt: 300mg

Pan-Seared Scallops

Total servings: 1 serving
Preparation time: 5 minutes
Time to cook: 5 minutes

Ingredients:

- 4-6 large sea scallops
- 1 tablespoon olive oil
- Salt and pepper to taste
- Lemon wedges for serving
- Fresh herbs for garnish (optional)

Instructions:

1. Pat dry the scallops with a paper towel to remove any excess moisture.

2. Season both sides of the scallops with salt and pepper.

3. Heat the olive oil in a skillet over medium-high heat.

4. Once the oil is hot, add the scallops to the skillet, making sure they are not crowded.

5. Sear the scallops for 2-3 minutes on each side, or until they are golden brown and opaque in the center.

6. Remove the scallops from the skillet and let them rest for a minute.

7. Serve the pan-seared scallops with lemon wedges.

8. Garnish with fresh herbs, if desired.

9. Serve hot.

Nutritional value (1 serving):

Garlic Butter Shrimp

Total servings: 1 serving
Preparation time: 5 minutes
Time to cook: 5 minutes

Ingredients:

- **6-8 large shrimp, peeled and deveined**
- **1 tablespoon butter**
- **1 clove garlic, minced**
- **1 tablespoon lemon juice**
- **Salt and pepper to taste**
- **Lemon wedges for serving**
- **Fresh parsley for garnish (optional)**

Instructions:

1. Season the shrimp with salt and pepper.

2. In a skillet, melt the butter over medium heat.

3. Add the minced garlic to the skillet and sauté for about 1 minute until fragrant.

4. Add the shrimp to the skillet and cook for 2-3 minutes, turning once, until they are pink and opaque.

5. Drizzle the shrimp with lemon juice and toss to coat.

6. Remove the skillet from heat and let the shrimp rest for a minute.

7. Serve the garlic butter shrimp with lemon wedges.

8. Garnish with fresh parsley, if desired.

9. Serve hot.

Nutritional value (1 serving):

Calories: 150 Protein: 20g Fat: 7g Salt: 300mg

Sesame Ginger Salmon

Total servings: 1 serving.
Preparation time: 10 minutes.
Time to cook: 15 minutes.

Ingredients:

- 1 salmon fillet (4-6 ounces)
- 1 tablespoon low-sodium soy sauce
- 1 tablespoon fresh ginger, grated
- 1 tablespoon sesame oil
- 1 teaspoon honey
- 1 teaspoon toasted sesame seeds
- 1 green onion, thinly sliced

Instructions:

1. Preheat the oven to 400°F (200°C).

2. Place the salmon fillet on a baking sheet lined with parchment paper.

3. In a small bowl, whisk together the soy sauce, grated ginger, sesame oil, and honey.

4. Pour the sauce over the salmon fillet, ensuring it is evenly coated.

5. Sprinkle the toasted sesame seeds over the salmon.

6. Bake the salmon in the preheated oven for 12-15 minutes or until it flakes easily with a fork.

7. Remove the salmon from the oven and garnish with sliced green onions.

8. Serve the sesame ginger salmon with a side of steamed vegetables or brown rice.

Nutritional value (1 serving):

Calories: 300 Protein: 25g Fat: 18g Salt: 500mg

Spicy Sriracha Shrimp

Total servings: 1 serving.
Preparation time: 10 minutes.
Time to cook: 10 minutes.

Ingredients:

- 8-10 large shrimp, peeled and deveined
- 1 tablespoon olive oil
- 1 tablespoon low-sodium soy sauce
- 1 tablespoon sriracha sauce
- 1 garlic clove, minced
- 1 teaspoon honey
- 1 teaspoon lime juice
- Fresh cilantro, for garnish

Instructions:

1. In a bowl, combine the olive oil, soy sauce, sriracha sauce, minced garlic, honey, and lime juice.

2. Add the shrimp to the bowl and toss until they are evenly coated with the marinade. Let it marinate for 5 minutes.

3. Heat a skillet over medium-high heat and add the marinated shrimp, reserving the marinade.

4. Cook the shrimp for 2-3 minutes on each side until they turn pink and opaque.

5. Pour the reserved marinade into the skillet and cook for

an additional minute, allowing it to thicken slightly.

6. Remove the skillet from heat and transfer the spicy sriracha shrimp to a serving plate.

7. Garnish with fresh cilantro.

Nutritional value (1 serving):

Calories: 150 Protein: 18g Fat: 6g Salt: 600mg

Grilled Halibut Fillet

Total servings: 1 serving.
Preparation time: 10 minutes.
Time to cook: 12-15 minutes.

Ingredients:

- 1 halibut fillet (4-6 ounces)
- 1 tablespoon lemon juice
- 1 tablespoon olive oil
- 1 teaspoon dried dill
- 1/2 teaspoon garlic powder
- Salt and pepper to taste
- Fresh lemon wedges, for serving

Instructions:

1. Preheat the grill to medium heat.

2. In a small bowl, whisk together the lemon juice, olive oil, dried dill, garlic powder, salt, and pepper.

3. Brush the halibut fillet with the marinade, ensuring it is evenly coated.

4. Place the halibut fillet on the grill and cook for 6-8 minutes per side, or until it is opaque and flakes easily with a fork.

5. Remove the grilled halibut from the heat and let it rest for a few minutes.

6. Serve the halibut fillet with fresh lemon wedges for an extra burst of flavor.

Nutritional value (1 serving):

Calories: 200 Protein: 30g Fat: 8g Salt: 300mg

Herb-Roasted Sea Bass

Total servings: 1 serving.
Preparation time: 10 minutes.
Time to cook: 15-18 minutes.

Ingredients:

- 1 sea bass fillet (4-6 ounces)
- 1 tablespoon olive oil
- 1 tablespoon fresh lemon juice
- 1 garlic clove, minced
- 1 teaspoon dried thyme
- 1/2 teaspoon dried rosemary
- Salt and pepper to taste
- Fresh parsley, for garnish

Instructions:

1. Preheat the oven to 400°F (200°C).

2. In a small bowl, combine the olive oil, lemon juice, minced garlic, dried thyme, dried rosemary, salt, and pepper.

3. Place the sea bass fillet in a baking dish lined with parchment paper.

4. Brush the herb mixture over the sea bass, making sure it is evenly coated.

5. Roast the sea bass in the preheated oven for 15-18 minutes, or until it is cooked through and flakes easily with a fork.

6. Remove the herb-roasted sea bass from the oven and let it rest for a few minutes.

7. Garnish with fresh parsley before serving.

Nutritional value (1 serving):

Calories: 180 Protein: 25g Fat: 7g Salt: 400mg

Lemon Pepper Cod

Total servings: 1 serving.
Preparation time: 10 minutes.
Time to cook: 12-15 minutes.

Ingredients:

- 1 cod fillet (4-6 ounces)
- 1 tablespoon lemon juice
- 1 tablespoon olive oil
- 1 teaspoon lemon zest
- 1/2 teaspoon ground black pepper
- Salt to taste
- Fresh parsley, for garnish

Instructions:

1. Preheat the oven to 400°F (200°C).

2. Place the cod fillet on a baking sheet lined with parchment paper.

3. In a small bowl, whisk together the lemon juice, olive oil, lemon zest, ground black pepper, and salt.

4. Brush the lemon pepper mixture over the cod fillet, ensuring it is evenly coated.

5. Bake the cod in the preheated oven for 12-15 minutes, or until it is opaque and flakes easily with a fork.

6. Remove the lemon pepper cod from the oven and let it rest for a few minutes.

7. Garnish with fresh parsley before serving.

Nutritional value (1 serving):

Calories: 180 Protein: 25g Fat: 8g Salt: 400mg

Teriyaki Shrimp Skewers

Total servings: 1 serving.
Preparation time: 10 minutes.
Time to cook: 6-8 minutes.

Ingredients:

- 8-10 large shrimp, peeled and deveined
- 2 tablespoons low-sodium soy sauce
- 1 tablespoon honey
- 1 tablespoon rice vinegar
- 1 teaspoon minced garlic
- 1/2 teaspoon grated ginger
- 1/2 teaspoon sesame oil
- Bamboo skewers, soaked in water
- Sesame seeds and sliced green onions for garnish

Instructions:

1. In a bowl, whisk together the soy sauce, honey, rice vinegar, minced garlic, grated ginger, and sesame oil to make the teriyaki marinade.

2. Add the shrimp to the bowl and let them marinate for 5 minutes.

3. Preheat a grill or grill pan over medium heat.

4. Thread the marinated shrimp onto the soaked bamboo skewers.

5. Grill the shrimp skewers for 2-3 minutes per side until they turn pink and opaque.

6. Brush the shrimp with any remaining teriyaki marinade while grilling.

7. Remove the teriyaki shrimp skewers from the grill and let them rest for a minute.

8. Sprinkle sesame seeds and sliced green onions over the skewers before serving.

Nutritional value (1 serving):

Calories: 160 Protein: 20g Fat: 4g Salt: 500mg

Cajun Blackened Catfish

Total servings: 1 serving.
Preparation time: 10 minutes.
Time to cook: 8-10 minutes.

Ingredients:

- 1 catfish fillet (4-6 ounces)
- 1 teaspoon paprika
- 1/2 teaspoon dried thyme
- 1/2 teaspoon dried oregano
- 1/2 teaspoon garlic powder
- 1/4 teaspoon cayenne pepper
- 1/4 teaspoon salt
- 1 tablespoon olive oil
- Fresh lemon wedges, for serving

Instructions:

1. In a small bowl, mix together the paprika, dried thyme, dried oregano, garlic powder, cayenne pepper, and salt to create the Cajun spice blend.

2. Pat the catfish fillet dry with a paper towel and sprinkle both sides with the Cajun spice blend, pressing it gently into the fish.

3. Heat the olive oil in a skillet over medium-high heat.

4. Place the seasoned catfish fillet in the hot skillet and cook for 4-5 minutes per side until it is blackened and flakes easily with a fork.

5. Remove the Cajun blackened catfish from the skillet and let it rest for a minute.

6. Serve with fresh lemon wedges for a tangy kick.

Nutritional value (1 serving):

Calories: 180 Protein: 25g Fat: 7g

Baked Lemon Herb Tilapia

Total servings: 1 serving.
Preparation time: 10 minutes.
Time to cook: 12-15 minutes.

Ingredients:

- 1 tilapia fillet (4-6 ounces)
- 1 tablespoon lemon juice
- 1 tablespoon olive oil

- 1/2 teaspoon dried basil
- 1/2 teaspoon dried thyme
- 1/4 teaspoon garlic powder
- Salt and pepper to taste
- Fresh parsley, for garnish

Instructions:

1. Preheat the oven to 400°F (200°C).

2. Place the tilapia fillet on a baking sheet lined with parchment paper.

3. In a small bowl, whisk together the lemon juice, olive oil, dried basil, dried thyme, garlic powder, salt, and pepper.

4. Brush the lemon herb mixture over the tilapia fillet, ensuring it is evenly coated.

5. Bake the tilapia in the preheated oven for 12-15 minutes, or until it is cooked through and flakes easily with a fork.

6. Remove the baked lemon herb tilapia from the oven and let it rest for a few minutes.

7. Garnish with fresh parsley before serving.

Nutritional value (1 serving):

Calories: 150 Protein: 25g Fat: 5g Salt: 300mg

Honey Glazed Salmon

Total servings: 1 serving.
Preparation time: 10 minutes.
Time to cook: 12-15 minutes.

Ingredients:

- 1 salmon fillet (4-6 ounces)
- 1 tablespoon honey
- 1 tablespoon low-sodium soy sauce
- 1 teaspoon Dijon mustard
- 1/2 teaspoon minced garlic
- Salt and pepper to taste
- Fresh dill or parsley, for garnish

Instructions:

1. Preheat the oven to 400°F (200°C).

2. Place the salmon fillet on a baking sheet lined with parchment paper.

3. In a small bowl, whisk together the honey, soy sauce, Dijon mustard, minced garlic, salt, and pepper to create the honey glaze.

4. Brush the honey glaze over the salmon fillet, ensuring it is evenly coated.

5. Bake the salmon in the preheated oven for 12-15 minutes, or until it is cooked through and flakes easily with a fork.

6. Remove the honey glazed salmon from the oven and let it rest for a minute.

7. g. Garnish with fresh dill or parsley **before serving.**

Nutritional value (1 serving):

Calories: 250 Protein: 25g Fat: 10g

Garlic Parmesan Shrimp

Total servings: 1 serving.
Preparation time: 10 minutes.
Time to cook: 6-8 minutes.

Ingredients:

- 8-10 large shrimp, peeled and deveined
- 1 tablespoon olive oil
- 1 teaspoon minced garlic
- 1 tablespoon grated Parmesan cheese
- 1 tablespoon chopped fresh parsley
- Salt and pepper to taste
- Lemon wedges, for serving

Instructions:

1. In a bowl, toss the shrimp with olive oil, minced garlic, Parmesan cheese, chopped fresh parsley, salt, and pepper.

2. Heat a skillet over medium-high heat.

3. Add the seasoned shrimp to the hot skillet and cook for 2-3 minutes per side until they turn pink and opaque.

4. Remove the garlic Parmesan shrimp from the skillet and let them rest for a minute.

5. Serve with lemon wedges for a bright, citrusy flavor.

Nutritional value (1 serving):

Calories: 180 Protein: 20g Fat: 8g Salt: 400mg

Grilled Swordfish Steak

Total servings: 1 serving.
Preparation time: 10 minutes.
Time to cook: 8-10 minutes.

Ingredients:

- 1 swordfish steak (4-6 ounces)
- 1 tablespoon olive oil
- 1 teaspoon lemon juice

- 1/2 teaspoon dried oregano
- 1/4 teaspoon garlic powder
- Salt and pepper to taste
- Fresh lemon wedges, for serving

Instructions:

1. Preheat the grill to medium-high heat.

2. Brush both sides of the swordfish steak with olive oil and lemon juice.

3. In a small bowl, mix together the dried oregano, garlic powder, salt, and pepper.

4. Sprinkle the oregano mixture over the swordfish steak, pressing it gently into the fish.

5. Place the seasoned swordfish steak on the preheated grill and cook for 4-5 minutes per side until it is cooked through and easily flakes with a fork.

6. Remove the grilled swordfish steak from the grill and let it rest for a minute.

7. Serve with fresh lemon wedges for added zest.

Nutritional value (1 serving):

Calories: 240 Protein: 30g Fat: 10g

Orange Glazed Mahi Mahi

Total servings: 1 serving.
Preparation time: 10 minutes.
Time to cook: 12-15 minutes.

Ingredients:

- 1 mahi mahi fillet (4-6 ounces)
- 2 tablespoons orange juice
- 1 tablespoon low-sodium soy sauce
- 1 tablespoon honey
- 1 teaspoon grated ginger
- 1/2 teaspoon minced garlic
- Salt and pepper to taste
- Sesame seeds and sliced green onions, for garnish

Instructions:

1. Preheat the oven to 400°F (200°C).

2. Place the mahi mahi fillet on a baking sheet lined with parchment paper.

3. In a small bowl, whisk together the orange juice, soy sauce, honey, grated ginger, minced garlic, salt, and pepper to create the orange glaze.

4. Brush the orange glaze over the mahi mahi fillet, ensuring it is evenly coated.

5. Bake the mahi mahi in the preheated oven for 12-15 minutes, or until it is cooked through and flakes easily with a fork.

6. Remove the orange glazed mahi mahi from the oven and let it rest for a minute.

7. Garnish with sesame seeds and sliced green onions before serving.

Nutritional value (1 serving):

Calories: 220 Protein: 25g Fat: 7g Salt: 400mg

Spicy Thai Coconut Shrimp

Total servings: 1 serving.
Preparation time: 10 minutes.
Time to cook: 10 minutes.

Ingredients:

- 8-10 large shrimp, peeled and deveined
- 1 tablespoon red curry paste
- 1/2 cup light coconut milk
- 1 tablespoon low-sodium soy sauce
- 1 tablespoon lime juice
- 1/2 teaspoon grated ginger
- 1/2 teaspoon minced garlic
- 1/2 teaspoon honey
- Fresh cilantro, for garnish
- Lime wedges, for serving

Instructions:

1. In a bowl, whisk together the red curry paste, coconut milk, soy sauce, lime juice, grated ginger, minced garlic, and honey to create the spicy Thai coconut sauce.

2. Heat a skillet over medium heat and add the spicy Thai coconut sauce.

3. Add the shrimp to the skillet and cook for 3-4 minutes, or until the shrimp turn pink and are cooked through.

4. Remove the skillet from heat and let the shrimp rest in the sauce for a minute.

5. Transfer the spicy Thai coconut shrimp to a serving plate, garnish with fresh cilantro, and serve with lime wedges for an extra burst of citrus flavor.

Nutritional value (1 serving):

Calories: 200 Protein: 20g Fat: 10g Salt: 600mg

Herb-Crusted Salmon

Total servings: 1 serving.
Preparation time: 10 minutes.
Time to cook: 12-15 minutes.

Ingredients:

- 1 salmon fillet (4-6 ounces)
- 1 tablespoon Dijon mustard
- 1 tablespoon chopped fresh herbs (such as parsley, dill, or basil)
- 1 tablespoon whole wheat breadcrumbs
- 1 teaspoon olive oil
- Salt and pepper to taste
- Lemon wedges, for serving

Instructions:

1. Preheat the oven to 400°F (200°C).

2. Place the salmon fillet on a baking sheet lined with parchment paper.

3. Spread a thin layer of Dijon mustard over the top of the salmon fillet.

4. In a small bowl, mix together the chopped fresh herbs, breadcrumbs, olive oil, salt, and pepper to create the herb crust mixture.

5. Press the herb crust mixture onto the mustard-coated side of the salmon fillet.

6. Bake the salmon in the preheated oven for 12-15 minutes, or until it is cooked through and flakes easily with a fork.

7. Remove the herb-crusted salmon from the oven and let it rest for a minute.

8. Serve with lemon wedges for a tangy touch.

Nutritional value (1 serving):

Calories: 280 Protein: 30g Fat: 15g Salt: 400mg

Lemon Butter Scallops

Total servings: 1 serving.
Preparation time: 10 minutes.
Time to cook: 5-7 minutes.

Ingredients:

- 6-8 large sea scallops
- 1 tablespoon butter
- 1 tablespoon fresh lemon juice

- 1 teaspoon minced garlic
- 1/2 teaspoon lemon zest
- Salt and pepper to taste
- Fresh parsley, for garnish

Instructions:

1. Pat dry the scallops with a paper towel to remove excess moisture.

2. In a skillet, melt the butter over medium heat.

3. Add the scallops to the skillet and cook for 2-3 minutes on each side, or until they are golden brown and cooked through.

4. Remove the cooked scallops from the skillet and set them aside on a plate.

5. In the same skillet, add the lemon juice, minced garlic, and lemon zest. Cook for 1-2 minutes to combine the flavors.

6. Pour the lemon butter sauce over the scallops.

7. Garnish with fresh parsley before serving.

Nutritional value (1 serving):

Calories: 200 Protein: 20g Fat: 8g Salt: 400mg

Teriyaki Glazed Tuna

Total servings: 1 serving.
Preparation time: 10 minutes.
Time to cook: 8-10 minutes.

Ingredients:

- 1 tuna steak (4-6 ounces)
- 1 tablespoon low-sodium soy sauce
- 1 tablespoon honey
- 1 tablespoon rice vinegar
- 1/2 teaspoon minced ginger
- 1/2 teaspoon minced garlic
- 1/4 teaspoon sesame oil
- Fresh green onions, for garnish
- Sesame seeds, for garnish

Instructions:

1. Preheat a grill or grill pan over medium-high heat.

2. In a bowl, whisk together the soy sauce, honey, rice vinegar, minced ginger, minced garlic, and sesame oil to create the teriyaki glaze.

3. Brush both sides of the tuna steak with the teriyaki glaze.

4. Place the tuna steak on the preheated grill and cook for 3-4 minutes per side, or until it reaches your desired level of doneness.

5. Remove the grilled tuna steak from the grill and let it rest for a minute.

6. Slice the tuna steak into thin strips.

7. Garnish with fresh green onions and sesame seeds before serving.

Nutritional value (1 serving):

Calories: 250 Protein: 30g Fat: 8g Salt: 600mg

Cajun Grilled Shrimp

Total servings: 1 serving.
Preparation time: 10 minutes.
Time to cook: 6-8 minutes.

Ingredients:

- 8-10 large shrimp, peeled and deveined
- 1 teaspoon Cajun seasoning
- 1 tablespoon olive oil
- 1 tablespoon lemon juice
- Salt and pepper to taste
- Fresh parsley, for garnish
- Lemon wedges, for serving

Instructions:

1. Preheat the grill to medium-high heat.

2. In a bowl, toss the shrimp with Cajun seasoning, olive oil, lemon juice, salt, and pepper until well coated.

3. Thread the seasoned shrimp onto skewers, if desired, for easier grilling.

4. Place the shrimp on the preheated grill and cook for 2-4 minutes per side, or until they are pink and opaque.

5. Remove the grilled shrimp from the grill and let them rest for a minute.

6. Garnish with fresh parsley and serve with lemon wedges for an added zing.

Nutritional value (1 serving):

Calories: 180 Protein: 20g Fat: 8g Salt: 500mg

Garlic Dijon Salmon

Total servings: 1 serving.
Preparation time: 10 minutes.
Time to cook: 12-15 minutes.

Ingredients:

- 1 salmon fillet (4-6 ounces)
- 1 tablespoon Dijon mustard
- 1 tablespoon minced garlic
- 1 tablespoon lemon juice
- 1/2 teaspoon dried dill
- Salt and pepper to taste
- Fresh dill, for garnish

Instructions:

1. Preheat the oven to 400°F (200°C).

2. Place the salmon fillet on a baking sheet lined with parchment paper.

3. In a small bowl, mix together the Dijon mustard, minced garlic, lemon juice, dried dill, salt, and pepper to create the garlic Dijon marinade.

4. Spread the garlic Dijon marinade evenly over the top of the salmon fillet.

5. Bake the salmon in the preheated oven for 12-15 minutes, or until it is cooked through and flakes easily with a fork.

6. Remove the garlic Dijon salmon from the oven and let it rest for a minute.

7. Garnish with fresh dill before serving.

Nutritional value (1 serving):

Calories: 280 Protein: 30g Fat: 15g Salt: 400mg

Sesame Crusted Ahi Tuna

Total servings: 1 serving.
Preparation time: 10 minutes.
Time to cook: 4-5 minutes.

Ingredients:

- 1 ahi tuna steak (4-6 ounces)
- 1 tablespoon sesame seeds
- 1/2 tablespoon low-sodium soy sauce
- 1/2 tablespoon sesame oil
- 1/2 teaspoon grated ginger
- 1/2 teaspoon minced garlic
- Salt and pepper to taste
- Fresh cilantro, for garnish
- Wasabi and soy sauce, for serving

Instructions:

1. Pat dry the ahi tuna steak with a paper towel to remove excess moisture.

2. In a shallow dish, spread the sesame seeds evenly.

3. In another shallow dish, mix together the soy sauce, sesame oil, grated ginger, minced garlic, salt, and pepper to create the marinade.

4. Dip the ahi tuna steak into the marinade, making sure to coat both sides.

5. Press the marinated tuna steak onto the sesame seeds, ensuring the seeds stick to both sides.

6. Heat a skillet or grill pan over high heat.

7. Place the sesame-crusted ahi tuna steak on the hot skillet and cook for 1-2 minutes on each side, or until it is seared on the outside and remains rare in the center.

8. Remove the cooked tuna steak from the skillet and let it rest for a minute.

9. Slice the sesame-crusted ahi tuna steak into thin strips.

10. Garnish with fresh cilantro and serve with wasabi and soy sauce for dipping.

Nutritional value (1 serving):

Calories: 200 Protein: 25g Fat: 8g Salt: 400mg

Baked Parmesan Crusted Cod

Total servings: 1 serving.
Preparation time: 10 minutes.
Time to cook: 12-15 minutes.

Ingredients:

- 1 cod fillet (4-6 ounces)
- 1 tablespoon grated Parmesan cheese
- 1 tablespoon whole wheat breadcrumbs
- 1/2 tablespoon olive oil
- 1/2 teaspoon dried Italian herbs (such as oregano, basil, or thyme)
- Salt and pepper to taste
- Lemon wedges, for serving

Instructions:

1. Preheat the oven to 400°F (200°C).

2. Place the cod fillet on a baking sheet lined with parchment paper.

3. In a small bowl, mix together the grated Parmesan cheese, breadcrumbs, olive oil, dried Italian herbs, salt, and pepper to create the Parmesan crust mixture.

4. Press the Parmesan crust mixture onto the top of the cod fillet, covering it evenly.

5. Bake the cod in the preheated oven for 12-15 minutes, or until it is cooked through and the crust is golden brown.

6. Remove the baked Parmesan crusted cod from the oven and let it rest for a minute.

7. Serve with lemon wedges for a tangy touch.

Nutritional value (1 serving):

Calories: 220 Protein: 30g Fat: 8g Salt: 500mg

Honey Lime Shrimp

Total servings: 1 serving.
Preparation time: 10 minutes
Cooking time: 10 minutes

Ingredients:

- 8 large shrimp, peeled and deveined
- 1 tablespoon honey
- 1 tablespoon lime juice
- 1 teaspoon low-sodium soy sauce
- 1 teaspoon minced garlic
- 1/2 teaspoon grated fresh ginger
- 1/4 teaspoon red pepper flakes (optional)
- 1 teaspoon olive oil
- Fresh cilantro, for garnish (optional)

Instructions:

1. In a small bowl, whisk together honey, lime juice, soy sauce, minced garlic, grated ginger, and red pepper flakes (if using).

2. Place the shrimp in a zip-top bag and pour half of the marinade over them. Seal the bag and gently massage to ensure all shrimp are coated. Let marinate in the refrigerator for at least 10 minutes, or up to 30 minutes for more flavor.

3. Preheat a grill or grill pan over medium-high heat. Lightly grease the grill grates with olive oil to prevent sticking.

4. Remove the shrimp from the marinade, discarding the used marinade. Thread the shrimp onto skewers, if desired.

5. Grill the shrimp for about 2-3 minutes per side, or until they turn pink and opaque. Baste with the remaining marinade while grilling.

6. Once cooked, remove the shrimp from the grill and let them rest for a minute.

7. Serve the honey lime shrimp hot, garnished with fresh cilantro (if desired).

Nutritional value (1 serving):

Calories: 180 Protein: 20g Fat: 3g Salt: 210mg

Grilled Snapper Fillet

Total servings: 1 serving.
Preparation time: 5 minutes
Cooking time: 10 minutes

Ingredients:

- 1 snapper fillet (approximately 4-6 ounces)

- 1 teaspoon olive oil
- 1/2 teaspoon lemon zest
- 1/2 teaspoon dried thyme
- 1/4 teaspoon garlic powder
- 1/4 teaspoon paprika
- Salt and pepper, to taste
- Lemon wedges, for serving

Instructions:

1. Preheat a grill or grill pan over medium-high heat. Lightly grease the grill grates with olive oil to prevent sticking.

2. In a small bowl, combine olive oil, lemon zest, dried thyme, garlic powder, paprika, salt, and pepper. Mix well to make a paste.

3. Pat the snapper fillet dry with a paper towel. Brush the paste evenly over both sides of the fillet.

4. Place the snapper fillet on the preheated grill and cook for about 4-5 minutes per side, or until the fish is opaque and flakes easily with a fork.

5. Once cooked, remove the snapper fillet from the grill and let it rest for a minute.

6. Serve the grilled snapper fillet hot, with lemon wedges on the side for squeezing over the fish.

Nutritional value (1 serving):

Calories: 220 Protein: 30g Fat: 8g Salt: 180mg

Lemon Herb Grilled Shrimp

Total servings: 1 serving.
Preparation time: 10 minutes
Cooking time: 5 minutes

Ingredients:

- 8 large shrimp, peeled and deveined
- 1 tablespoon lemon juice
- 1 tablespoon olive oil
- 1 garlic clove, minced
- 1/2 teaspoon dried thyme
- 1/2 teaspoon dried oregano
- Salt and pepper, to taste
- Lemon wedges, for serving
- Fresh parsley, for garnish (optional)

Instructions:

1. In a small bowl, whisk together lemon juice, olive oil, minced garlic, dried thyme, dried oregano, salt, and

pepper.

2. Place the shrimp in a zip-top bag and pour the marinade over them. Seal the bag and gently massage to ensure all shrimp are coated. Let marinate in the refrigerator for at least 10 minutes.

3. Preheat a grill or grill pan over medium-high heat. Lightly grease the grill grates with olive oil to prevent sticking.

4. Remove the shrimp from the marinade, discarding the used marinade. Thread the shrimp onto skewers, if desired.

5. Grill the shrimp for about 2-3 minutes per side, or until they turn pink and opaque.

6. Once cooked, remove the shrimp from the grill and let them rest for a minute.

7. Serve the lemon herb grilled shrimp hot, with lemon wedges on the side for squeezing over the shrimp. Garnish with fresh parsley, if desired.

Nutritional value (1 serving):

Calories: 160 Protein: 24g Fat: 7g Salt: 200mg

Spicy Chipotle Salmon

Total servings: 1 serving.
Preparation time: 10 minutes
Cooking time: 15 minutes

Ingredients:

- 1 salmon fillet (approximately 4-6 ounces)
- 1 tablespoon olive oil
- 1 teaspoon chipotle chili powder
- 1/2 teaspoon smoked paprika
- 1/2 teaspoon garlic powder
- 1/4 teaspoon cayenne pepper (adjust to desired spiciness)
- Salt and pepper, to taste
- Fresh cilantro, for garnish (optional)
- Lime wedges, for serving

Instructions:

1. Preheat a grill or grill pan over medium-high heat. Lightly grease the grill grates with olive oil to prevent sticking.

2. In a small bowl, combine olive oil, chipotle chili powder, smoked paprika, garlic powder, cayenne pepper, salt, and pepper. Mix well to make a paste.

3. Pat the salmon fillet dry with a paper towel. Brush the spice paste evenly over the flesh side of the fillet.

4. Place the salmon fillet on the preheated grill, skin-side down, and cook for about 6-8 minutes.

5. Carefully flip the salmon fillet using a spatula and cook for an additional 6-8 minutes, or until the fish is opaque and flakes easily with a fork.

6. Once cooked, remove the salmon fillet from the grill and let it rest for a minute.

7. Serve the spicy chipotle salmon hot, garnished with fresh cilantro (if desired) and lime wedges on the side for squeezing over the fish.

Nutritional value (1 serving):

Calories: 280 Protein: 28g Fat: 17g Salt: 220mg

Teriyaki Glazed Sea Bass

Total Servings: 1 serving.
Preparation Time: 10 minutes
Cooking Time: 15 minutes

Ingredients:

- 1 sea bass fillet (4-6 ounces)
- 2 tablespoons low-sodium soy sauce
- 1 tablespoon honey
- 1 tablespoon rice vinegar
- 1 garlic clove, minced
- 1 teaspoon grated fresh ginger
- 1 teaspoon cornstarch
- 1 teaspoon water
- 1/2 teaspoon sesame oil
- 1/2 teaspoon sesame seeds (optional)
- Fresh cilantro or green onions for garnish (optional)

Instructions:

1. Preheat the oven to 400°F (200°C).

2. In a small bowl, whisk together the soy sauce, honey, rice vinegar, minced garlic, and grated ginger to make the teriyaki glaze.

3. In a separate small bowl, mix the cornstarch and water to create a slurry.

4. Heat a non-stick skillet over medium heat and add the sesame oil.

5. Place the sea bass fillet in the skillet, skin side down, and cook for 2-3 minutes until the skin becomes crispy.

6. Flip the fillet and pour the teriyaki glaze over the fish.

7. Cook for an additional 2 minutes, then transfer the skillet to the preheated oven.

8. Bake for 10 minutes or until the fish flakes easily with a fork.

9. Remove the skillet from the oven and transfer the fish to a serving plate.

10. Meanwhile, heat the remaining teriyaki glaze over medium heat.

11. Add the cornstarch slurry to the glaze and cook for 1-2 minutes until the sauce thickens.

12. Drizzle the thickened glaze over the sea bass fillet.

13. Sprinkle sesame seeds, fresh cilantro, or green onions on top for added flavor and garnish (optional).

14. Serve the Teriyaki Glazed Sea Bass immediately.

Nutritional Value (1 serving):

Calories: 250 Protein: 30g Fat: 10g Salt: 600mg

Cajun Grilled Catfish

Total Servings: 1 serving.
Preparation Time: 10 minutes
Cooking Time: 10 minutes

Ingredients:

- 1 catfish fillet (4-6 ounces)
- 1 teaspoon paprika
- 1/2 teaspoon garlic powder
- 1/2 teaspoon onion powder
- 1/2 teaspoon dried thyme
- 1/2 teaspoon dried oregano
- 1/4 teaspoon cayenne pepper (adjust according to spice preference)
- 1/4 teaspoon salt
- 1/4 teaspoon black pepper
- 1 tablespoon olive oil
- Lemon wedges for serving (optional)
- Fresh parsley for garnish (optional)

Instructions:

1. Preheat the grill to medium-high heat.

2. In a small bowl, combine paprika, garlic powder, onion powder, dried thyme, dried oregano, cayenne pepper, salt, and black pepper to make the Cajun seasoning.

3. Rub both sides of the catfish fillet with olive oil.

4. Sprinkle the Cajun seasoning evenly over both sides of the catfish fillet, pressing gently to adhere.

5. Place the seasoned catfish fillet on the preheated grill.

6. Grill for approximately 4-5 minutes on each side or until the fish is cooked through and flakes easily with a fork.

7. Remove the catfish fillet from the grill and transfer it to a serving plate.

8. Squeeze fresh lemon juice over the grilled catfish if desired.

9. Garnish with fresh parsley for added flavor (optional).

10. Serve the Cajun Grilled Catfish immediately.

Nutritional Value (1 serving):

Calories: 220 Protein: 30g Fat: 9g Salt: 400mg

Garlic Lemon Scallops

Total Servings: 1 serving.
Preparation Time: 10 minutes
Cooking Time: 5 minutes

Ingredients:

- 4 large scallops
- 1 tablespoon olive oil
- 2 cloves garlic, minced
- 1 tablespoon fresh lemon juice
- 1/2 teaspoon lemon zest
- Salt and black pepper to taste
- Fresh parsley for garnish (optional)

Instructions:

1. Pat dry the scallops with a paper towel to remove any excess moisture.

2. Heat the olive oil in a skillet over medium-high heat.

3. Add the minced garlic to the skillet and sauté for about 1 minute until fragrant.

4. Season the scallops with salt and black pepper on both sides.

5. Carefully place the scallops in the skillet, making sure they are not touching each other.

6. Cook the scallops for 2-3 minutes on each side until they turn golden brown and opaque in the center.

7. Remove the scallops from the skillet and drizzle them with fresh lemon juice.

8. Sprinkle lemon zest over the scallops for an extra burst of flavor.

9. Garnish with fresh parsley if desired.

10. Serve the Garlic Lemon Scallops immediately.

Nutritional Value (1 serving):

Calories: 180 Protein: 20g Fat: 8g Salt: 300mg

Lemon Dill Grilled Trout

Total Servings: 1 serving.
Preparation Time: 10 minutes
Cooking Time: 10 minutes

Ingredients:

- 1 trout fillet (6-8 ounces)
- 1 tablespoon olive oil
- 1 tablespoon fresh lemon juice
- 1/2 teaspoon lemon zest
- 1 tablespoon fresh dill, chopped
- Salt and black pepper to taste
- Lemon slices for serving (optional)
- Fresh dill sprigs for garnish (optional)

Instructions:

1. Preheat the grill to medium-high heat.

2. Brush the trout fillet with olive oil on both sides to prevent sticking.

3. Drizzle fresh lemon juice over the trout fillet.

4. Sprinkle lemon zest, chopped fresh dill, salt, and black pepper evenly over the fillet.

5. Place the seasoned trout fillet on the grill, skin side down.

6. Grill for approximately 4-5 minutes on each side or until the fish is cooked through and flakes easily with a fork.

7. Transfer the grilled trout to a serving plate.

8. Squeeze fresh lemon juice over the trout if desired.

9. Garnish with lemon slices and fresh dill sprigs for an elegant presentation (optional).

10. Serve the Lemon Dill Grilled Trout immediately.

Nutritional Value (1 serving):

Calories: 250 Protein: 30g Fat: 12g Salt: 400mg

Chapter 10: Soups

Tomato Basil Soup

Total Servings: 1 serving.
Preparation Time: 10 minutes
Cooking Time: 25 minutes

Ingredients:

- 1 tablespoon olive oil
- 1 small onion, chopped
- 2 cloves garlic, minced
- 1 can (14 ounces) diced tomatoes
- 1 cup low-sodium vegetable broth
- 1/2 teaspoon dried basil
- 1/2 teaspoon dried oregano
- Salt and black pepper to taste
- 1 tablespoon fresh basil, chopped (for garnish)

Instructions:

1. Heat the olive oil in a saucepan over medium heat.

2. Add the chopped onion and minced garlic to the saucepan and sauté for about 5 minutes until they become soft and translucent.

3. Add the diced tomatoes (with their juices) to the saucepan and stir well.

4. Pour the vegetable broth and add the dried basil and oregano.

5. Season with salt and black pepper to taste.

6. Bring the mixture to a boil, then reduce the heat and let it simmer for 15 minutes, allowing the flavors to blend together.

7. Remove the saucepan from heat and use an immersion or countertop blender to puree the soup until smooth.

8. Return the soup to the saucepan and reheat gently if needed.

9. Ladle the tomato basil soup into a bowl and garnish with fresh chopped basil.

10. Serve the Tomato Basil Soup immediately.

Nutritional Value (1 serving):

Calories: 150 Protein: 4g Fat: 6g Salt: 400mg

Lentil Vegetable Soup

Total Servings: 1 serving
Preparation Time: 10 minutes
Cooking Time: 30 minutes

Ingredients:

- 1/4 cup dried green lentils
- 1 cup low-sodium vegetable broth
- 1/4 cup diced onion
- 1/4 cup diced carrot
- 1/4 cup diced celery
- 1 garlic clove, minced
- 1/2 teaspoon ground cumin
- 1/2 teaspoon dried thyme
- 1/4 teaspoon paprika
- 1 bay leaf
- 1 cup chopped fresh spinach
- Salt and pepper to taste

Instructions:

1. Rinse the dried green lentils under cold water and drain them.

2. Combine the lentils, vegetable broth, diced onion, carrot, celery, minced garlic, ground cumin, dried thyme, paprika, and bay leaf in a medium-sized pot.

3. Bring the mixture to a boil over medium-high heat. Once boiling, reduce the heat to low and cover the pot.

4. Simmer the soup for about 20-25 minutes or until the lentils and vegetables are tender.

5. Remove the bay leaf from the soup and discard it.

6. Stir in the chopped fresh spinach and cook for 2-3 minutes until the spinach wilts.

7. Season the soup with salt and pepper according to your taste preferences.

Nutritional Value (1 serving):

Calories: 180 Protein: 12g Fat: 1g Salt: 200mg

‖Chicken Noodle Soup

Total Servings: 1 serving
Preparation Time: 10 minutes
Cooking Time: 25 minutes

Ingredients:

- 1 boneless, skinless chicken breast, cooked and shredded
- 2 cups low-sodium chicken broth
- 1/2 cup sliced carrots
- 1/2 cup sliced celery
- 1/4 cup diced onion
- 1 garlic clove, minced
- 1/2 teaspoon dried thyme
- 1/2 teaspoon dried rosemary
- 1/2 cup cooked egg noodles
- Salt and pepper to taste
- Fresh parsley for garnish (optional)

Instructions:

1. Combine the chicken broth, sliced carrots, sliced celery, diced onion, minced garlic, dried thyme, and dried rosemary in a medium-sized pot.

2. Bring the mixture to a boil over medium-high heat. Once boiling, reduce the heat to low and let it simmer for 10 minutes until the vegetables are tender.

3. Add the shredded chicken to the pot and simmer for 5 minutes to heat through.

4. Stir in the cooked egg noodles and cook for another 2-3 minutes until the noodles are warmed.

5. Season the soup with salt and pepper according to your taste preferences.

6. Serve the chicken noodle soup hot, garnished with fresh parsley if desired.

Nutritional Value (1 serving):

Calories: 250 Protein: 25g Fat: 4g Salt: 400mg

Minestrone Soup

Total Servings: 1 serving
Preparation Time: 10 minutes
Cooking Time: 25 minutes

Ingredients:

- 1 tablespoon olive oil
- 1/4 cup diced onion
- 1 garlic clove, minced
- 1/4 cup diced carrot
- 1/4 cup diced celery
- 1/4 cup diced zucchini
- 1/4 cup canned kidney beans, rinsed and drained
- 1/4 cup canned diced tomatoes
- 2 cups low-sodium vegetable broth
- 1/2 teaspoon dried basil
- 1/2 teaspoon dried oregano
- 1/2 cup cooked whole wheat pasta
- Salt and pepper to taste
- Fresh basil leaves for garnish (optional)

Instructions:

1. In a medium-sized pot, heat the olive oil over medium heat.

2. Add the diced onion and minced garlic to the pot and sauté for 2-3 minutes until they become translucent.

3. Add the diced carrot, celery, zucchini, kidney beans, tomatoes, vegetable broth, dried basil, and dried oregano to the pot. Bring the mixture to a boil.

4. Reduce the heat to low and let the soup simmer for 15 minutes until the vegetables are tender.

5. Stir in the cooked whole wheat pasta and simmer for 2-3 minutes.

6. Season the soup with salt and pepper according to your taste preferences.

7. Serve the minestrone hot, garnished with fresh basil leaves if desired.

Nutritional Value (1 serving):

Calories: 220 Protein: 10g Fat: 5g Salt: 400mg

Butternut Squash Soup

Total Servings: 1 serving
Preparation Time: 10 minutes
Cooking Time: 30 minutes

Ingredients:

- 1 cup cubed butternut squash
- 1/4 cup diced onion
- 1 garlic clove, minced
- 1/2 cup low-sodium vegetable broth

- 1/4 teaspoon ground cinnamon
- 1/4 teaspoon ground nutmeg
- Salt and pepper to taste
- 1 tablespoon Greek yogurt (optional)
- Fresh parsley or chives for garnish (optional)

Instructions:

1. Combine the cubed butternut squash, diced onion, minced garlic, vegetable broth, ground cinnamon, and ground nutmeg in a medium-sized pot.

2. Bring the mixture to a boil over medium-high heat. Once boiling, reduce the heat to low and let it simmer for 20-25 minutes until the butternut squash is tender.

3. Use an immersion blender or transfer the mixture to a blender and blend until smooth.

4. Season the soup with salt and pepper according to your taste preferences.

5. If desired, swirl in a tablespoon of Greek yogurt for added creaminess.

6. Serve hot butternut squash soup, garnished with fresh parsley or chives if desired.

Nutritional Value (1 serving):

Calories: 120 Protein: 3g Fat: 1g Salt: 300mg

Black Bean Soup

Total Servings: 1 serving
Preparation Time: 10 minutes
Cooking Time: 30 minutes

Ingredients:

- 1/4 cup diced onion
- 1 garlic clove, minced
- 1/2 cup canned black beans, rinsed and drained
- 1/4 cup diced tomatoes
- 1/4 cup diced bell pepper
- 1/4 cup low-sodium vegetable broth
- 1/4 teaspoon ground cumin
- 1/4 teaspoon chili powder
- Juice of 1/2 lime
- Salt and pepper to taste
- Fresh cilantro for garnish (optional)

Instructions:

1. In a medium-sized pot, sauté the diced onion and minced garlic over medium heat until they become fragrant and slightly softened.

2. Add the black beans, diced tomatoes, diced bell pepper, vegetable broth, ground cumin, and chili powder to the pot. Stir to combine.

3. Bring the mixture to a boil over medium-high heat. Once boiling, reduce the heat to low and let it simmer for 20-25 minutes to allow the flavors to meld together.

4. Add the lime juice to the soup and stir to incorporate.

5. Season the soup with salt and pepper according to your taste preferences.

6. Serve the black bean soup hot, garnished with fresh cilantro if desired.

Nutritional Value (1 serving):

Calories: 150 Protein: 8g Fat: 1g Salt: 400mg

Broccoli Cheddar Soup

Total Servings: 1 serving
Preparation Time: 10 minutes
Cooking Time: 25 minutes

Ingredients:

- 1 cup broccoli florets
- 1/4 cup diced onion
- 1 garlic clove, minced
- 1 cup low-sodium vegetable broth
- 1/2 cup low-fat milk
- 1/2 cup shredded reduced-fat cheddar cheese
- Salt and pepper to taste
- Fresh chives or parsley for garnish (optional)

Instructions:

1. In a medium-sized pot, steam the broccoli florets until tender. Set aside.

2. In the same pot, sauté the diced onion and minced garlic over medium heat until they become fragrant and slightly softened.

3. Add the steamed broccoli, low-sodium vegetable broth, and low-fat milk to the pot. Bring the mixture to a boil.

4. Reduce the heat to low and let the soup simmer for 10 minutes.

5. Using an immersion blender or transferring the mixture to a blender, blend until smooth.

6. Stir in the shredded reduced-fat cheddar cheese until melted and well combined.

7. Season the soup with salt and pepper according to your taste preferences.

8. Serve the broccoli cheddar soup hot, garnished with fresh chives or parsley if desired.

Mushroom Soup

Total Servings: 1 serving
Preparation Time: 10 minutes
Cooking Time: 25 minutes

Ingredients:

- 1 cup sliced mushrooms (such as cremini or button mushrooms)
- 1/4 cup diced onion
- 1 garlic clove, minced
- 1 cup low-sodium vegetable broth
- 1/2 cup low-fat milk
- 1/4 teaspoon dried thyme
- 1/4 teaspoon dried rosemary
- Salt and pepper to taste
- Fresh parsley for garnish (optional)

Instructions:

1. In a medium-sized pot, sauté the sliced mushrooms, diced onion, and minced garlic over medium heat until they become tender and slightly browned.

2. Add the low-sodium vegetable broth, low-fat milk, dried thyme, and rosemary to the pot. Bring the mixture to a boil.

3. Reduce the heat to low and let the soup simmer for 15 minutes.

4. Blend half the soup using an immersion blender or transfer the mixture to a blender until smooth. This step adds creaminess while leaving some mushroom chunks for texture.

5. Return the blended mixture to the pot and stir to combine.

6. Season the soup with salt and pepper according to your taste preferences.

7. Serve the mushroom soup hot, garnished with fresh parsley if desired.

Nutritional Value (1 serving):

Calories: 120 Protein: 8g Fat: 3g Salt: 300mg

Spinach Tortellini Soup

Total Servings: 4 servings
Preparation Time: 10 minutes
Cooking Time: 25 minutes

Ingredients:

- 1 tablespoon olive oil
- 1 small onion, diced
- 2 cloves garlic, minced
- 4 cups low-sodium vegetable broth
- 1 can diced tomatoes, undrained
- 1 teaspoon dried basil
- 1 teaspoon dried oregano
- 1/2 teaspoon salt
- 1/4 teaspoon black pepper
- 1 package (9 ounces) refrigerated spinach tortellini
- 4 cups fresh spinach leaves
- 1/4 cup grated Parmesan cheese, for garnish (optional)

Instructions:

1. Heat the olive oil in a large pot over medium heat. Add the diced onion, minced garlic, and sauté until the onion becomes translucent and fragrant for about 3-4 minutes.

2. Pour in the vegetable broth and diced tomatoes with their juice. Stir in the dried basil, oregano, salt, and black pepper. Bring the mixture to a boil, then reduce the heat and let it simmer for 10 minutes to allow the flavors to meld.

3. Add the spinach tortellini to the pot and cook according to the package instructions, usually around 5-7 minutes or until the tortellini is tender.

4. Stir in the fresh spinach leaves and cook for 2 minutes until the spinach wilts.

5. Remove the pot from heat and ladle the soup into bowls. If desired, sprinkle grated Parmesan cheese on top for added flavor.

Nutritional Value (Per Serving):

Calories: 280 Protein: 12g Fat: 8g Salt: 800mg

Corn Chowder

Total Servings: 6 servings
Preparation Time: 15 minutes
Cooking Time: 25 minutes

Ingredients:

- 2 tablespoons olive oil
- 1 medium onion, diced
- 2 cloves garlic, minced
- 4 cups low-sodium vegetable broth
- 4 cups frozen corn kernels
- 2 medium potatoes, peeled and diced
- 1 cup unsweetened almond milk (or any plant-based

milk)

- 1 teaspoon dried thyme
- 1/2 teaspoon smoked paprika
- Salt and pepper to taste
- Fresh parsley, chopped, for garnish (optional)

Instructions:

1. In a large pot, heat the olive oil over medium heat. Add the diced onion, minced garlic, and sauté until the onion becomes translucent and fragrant for about 3-4 minutes.

2. Pour the vegetable broth and add the frozen corn kernels and diced potatoes. Bring the mixture to a boil, then reduce the heat and let it simmer for 15 minutes or until the potatoes are tender.

3. Using an immersion or regular blender, puree half of the soup until creamy while leaving some chunks for texture.

4. Stir in the almond milk, dried thyme, smoked paprika, salt, and pepper. Cook for 5 minutes, stirring occasionally, until the flavors combine.

5. Remove the pot from heat and spoon the corn chowder into bowls. Garnish with fresh parsley if desired.

Nutritional Value (Per Serving):

Calories: 220 Protein: 6g Fat: 7g Salt: 300mg

Potato Leek Soup

Total Servings: 4 servings
Preparation Time: 15 minutes
Cooking Time: 30 minutes

Ingredients:

- 2 tablespoons olive oil
- 2 leeks, white and light green parts only, thinly sliced
- 3 cloves garlic, minced
- 4 medium potatoes, peeled and diced
- 4 cups low-sodium vegetable broth
- 1 cup unsweetened almond milk (or any plant-based milk)
- 1 teaspoon dried thyme
- Salt and pepper to taste
- Fresh chives, chopped, for garnish (optional)

Instructions:

1. Heat the olive oil in a large pot over medium heat. Add the sliced leeks, minced garlic, and sauté until the leeks become tender and fragrant for about 5 minutes.

2. Add the diced potatoes to the pot and pour in the vegetable broth. Bring the mixture to a boil, then reduce the heat and let it simmer for 20-25 minutes or until the

potatoes are soft and cooked through.

3. Using an immersion or regular blender, puree the soup until smooth and creamy.

4. Stir in the almond milk and dried thyme—season with salt and pepper to taste. Cook for 5 minutes, stirring occasionally, to allow the flavors to blend.

5. Remove the pot from heat and ladle the potato leek soup into bowls. Garnish with fresh chives if desired.

Nutritional Value (Per Serving):

Calories: 220 Protein: 5g Fat: 8g Salt: 300mg

Gazpacho Soup

Total Servings: 4 servings
Preparation Time: 15 minutes
Time to Chill: 2 hours

Ingredients:

- 4 large ripe tomatoes, diced
- 1 cucumber, peeled and diced
- 1 red bell pepper, diced
- 1 small red onion, diced
- 2 cloves garlic, minced
- 2 tablespoons olive oil
- 2 tablespoons red wine vinegar
- 1 teaspoon dried basil
- 1 teaspoon dried oregano
- Salt and pepper to taste
- Fresh basil leaves, chopped, for garnish (optional)

Instructions:

1. Combine the diced tomatoes, cucumber, red bell pepper, red onion, minced garlic, olive oil, red wine vinegar, dried basil, and dried oregano in a blender or food processor. Blend until smooth and well combined.

2. Season the gazpacho soup with salt and pepper to taste. Adjust the seasoning as needed.

3. Transfer the soup to a large bowl and cover it. Refrigerate for at least 2 hours to allow the flavors to meld and the soup to chill.

4. Once chilled, give the gazpacho soup a good stir before serving. Ladle it into bowls and garnish with fresh basil leaves if desired.

Nutritional Value (Per Serving):

Calories: 120 Protein: 2g Fat: 7g Salt: 150mg

Cabbage Soup

Total Servings: 4 servings
Preparation Time: 15 minutes
Cooking Time: 30 minutes

Ingredients:

- 1 tablespoon olive oil
- 1 medium onion, diced
- 3 cloves garlic, minced
- 4 cups low-sodium vegetable broth
- 4 cups shredded cabbage
- 2 carrots, peeled and diced
- 2 celery stalks, diced
- 1 can diced tomatoes, undrained
- 1 teaspoon dried thyme
- 1/2 teaspoon smoked paprika
- Salt and pepper to taste
- Fresh parsley, chopped, for garnish (optional)

Instructions:

1. Heat the olive oil in a large pot over medium heat. Add the diced onion, minced garlic, and sauté until the onion becomes translucent and fragrant for about 3-4 minutes.

2. Pour in the vegetable broth and add the shredded cabbage, diced carrots, celery, tomatoes with their juice, dried thyme, and smoked paprika. Bring the mixture to a boil, then reduce the heat and let it simmer for 20-25 minutes or until the vegetables are tender.

3. Season the cabbage soup with salt and pepper to taste. Adjust the seasoning as needed.

4. Remove the pot from heat and ladle the soup into bowls. Garnish with fresh parsley if desired.

Nutritional Value (Per Serving):

Calories: 120 Protein: 3g Fat: 4g Salt: 400mg

Carrot Ginger Soup

Total Servings: 4 servings
Preparation Time: 10 minutes
Cooking Time: 25 minutes

Ingredients:

- 1 tablespoon olive oil
- 1 small onion, diced
- 3 cloves garlic, minced
- 4 cups low-sodium vegetable broth
- 4 large carrots, peeled and chopped
- 1 tablespoon freshly grated ginger
- 1/2 teaspoon ground turmeric
- 1/2 teaspoon ground cumin
- Salt and pepper to taste
- Fresh cilantro, chopped, for garnish (optional)

Instructions:

1. Heat the olive oil in a large pot over medium heat. Add the diced onion, minced garlic, and sauté until the onion becomes translucent and fragrant for about 3-4 minutes.

2. Pour the vegetable broth and add the chopped carrots, grated ginger, ground turmeric, and ground cumin. Bring the mixture to a boil, then reduce the heat and let it simmer for 20-25 minutes or until the carrots are soft and cooked through.

3. Using an immersion or regular blender, puree the soup until smooth and creamy.

4. Season the carrot ginger soup with salt and pepper to taste. Adjust the seasoning as needed.

5. Remove the pot from heat and ladle the soup into bowls. Garnish with fresh cilantro if desired.

Nutritional Value (Per Serving):

Calories: 100 Protein: 2g Fat: 4g Salt: 300mg

Chicken and Rice Soup

Total Servings: 4 servings
Preparation Time: 10 minutes
Cooking Time: 40 minutes

Ingredients:

- 1 tablespoon olive oil
- 1 small onion, diced
- 2 carrots, peeled and diced
- 2 celery stalks, diced
- 2 cloves garlic, minced
- 4 cups low-sodium chicken broth
- 2 cups cooked chicken breast, shredded
- 1/2 cup uncooked brown rice
- 1 teaspoon dried thyme
- Salt and pepper to taste
- Fresh parsley, chopped, for garnish (optional)

Instructions:

1. Heat the olive oil in a large pot over medium heat. Add the diced onion, carrots, celery, and minced garlic. Sauté until the vegetables become tender and fragrant, about 5 minutes.

2. Pour the chicken broth and add the shredded chicken breast, uncooked brown rice, dried thyme, salt, and pepper. Bring the mixture to a boil, then reduce the heat and let it simmer for 30-35 minutes or until the rice is cooked and tender.

3. Taste the soup and adjust the seasoning with salt and pepper if needed.

4. Remove the pot from heat and ladle the chicken and rice soup into bowls. Garnish with fresh parsley if desired.

Nutritional Value (Per Serving):

Calories: 250 Protein: 25g Fat: 6g Salt: 500mg

Split Pea Soup

Total Servings: 4 servings
Preparation Time: 15 minutes
Cooking Time: 1 hour 30 minutes

Ingredients:

- 1 tablespoon olive oil
- 1 small onion, diced
- 2 carrots, peeled and diced
- 2 celery stalks, diced
- 2 cloves garlic, minced
- 1 cup dried green split peas, rinsed and drained
- 4 cups low-sodium vegetable broth
- 1 bay leaf
- 1 teaspoon dried thyme
- Salt and pepper to taste
- Fresh parsley, chopped, for garnish (optional)

Instructions:

1. Heat the olive oil in a large pot over medium heat. Add the diced onion, carrots, celery, and minced garlic. Sauté until the vegetables become tender and fragrant, about 5 minutes.

2. Add the dried green split peas to the pot and pour in the vegetable broth. Stir in the bay leaf and dried thyme. Bring the mixture to a boil, then reduce the heat and let it simmer for 1 hour to 1 hour 30 minutes, or until the split peas are soft and fully cooked.

3. Stir the soup occasionally to prevent sticking, and add more water or broth if needed to reach your desired consistency.

4. Season the split pea soup with salt and pepper to taste. Remove the bay leaf before serving.

5. Ladle the soup into bowls and garnish with fresh parsley if desired.

Nutritional Value (Per Serving):

Calories: 220 Protein: 10g Fat: 4g Salt: 400mg

Thai Coconut Soup

Total Servings: 4 servings
Preparation Time: 10 minutes
Cooking Time: 25 minutes

Ingredients:

- 1 tablespoon olive oil
- 1 small onion, diced
- 2 cloves garlic, minced
- 2 teaspoons grated ginger
- 1 red bell pepper, thinly sliced
- 4 cups low-sodium vegetable broth
- 1 can (13.5 oz) coconut milk
- 2 tablespoons low-sodium soy sauce
- 2 tablespoons lime juice
- 1 tablespoon brown sugar
- 1 tablespoon Thai red curry paste
- 1 cup sliced mushrooms
- 1 cup thinly sliced bok choy
- 1/2 cup shredded carrots
- Fresh cilantro, chopped, for garnish (optional)
- Lime wedges for serving (optional)

Instructions:

1. Heat the olive oil in a large pot over medium heat. Add the diced onion, minced garlic, and grated ginger. Sauté until the onion becomes translucent and fragrant, about 3-4 minutes.

2. Add the sliced red bell pepper to the pot and cook for 2 minutes.

3. Pour the vegetable broth and add the coconut milk, low-sodium soy sauce, lime juice, brown sugar, and Thai red curry paste. Stir well to combine and bring the mixture to a simmer.

4. Add the sliced mushrooms, thinly sliced bok choy, and shredded carrots to the pot. Simmer for 10-15 minutes or until the vegetables are tender.

5. Taste the soup and adjust the seasoning with more soy sauce, lime juice, or curry paste if desired.

6. Remove the pot from heat and spoon the Thai coconut soup into bowls. Garnish with fresh cilantro and serve with

lime wedges, if desired.

Cauliflower Soup

Total Servings: 4 servings
Preparation Time: 10 minutes
Cooking Time: 25 minutes

Ingredients:

- 1 tablespoon olive oil
- 1 small onion, diced
- 2 cloves garlic, minced
- 1 head cauliflower, chopped into florets
- 4 cups low-sodium vegetable broth
- 1 cup unsweetened almond milk (or any plant-based milk)
- 1 teaspoon dried thyme
- Salt and pepper to taste
- Fresh chives, chopped, for garnish (optional)

Instructions:

1. Heat the olive oil in a large pot over medium heat. Add the diced onion, minced garlic, and sauté until the onion becomes translucent and fragrant for about 3-4 minutes.

2. Add the cauliflower florets to the pot and pour in the vegetable broth. Bring the mixture to a boil, then reduce the heat and let it simmer for 20-25 minutes or until the cauliflower is tender.

3. Using an immersion or regular blender, puree the soup until smooth and creamy.

4. Stir in the almond milk and dried thyme—season with salt and pepper to taste. Cook for 5 minutes, stirring occasionally, to allow the flavors to blend.

5. Remove the pot from heat and ladle the cauliflower soup into bowls. Garnish with fresh chives if desired.

Nutritional Value (Per Serving):

Calories: 100 Protein: 3g Fat: 5g Salt: 400mg

Italian Wedding Soup

Total Servings: 4 servings
Preparation Time: 20 minutes
Time to Cook: 30 minutes

Ingredients:

- 1 tablespoon olive oil

- 1 small onion, finely diced
- 2 cloves garlic, minced
- 2 carrots, peeled and diced
- 2 celery stalks, diced
- 4 cups low-sodium chicken broth
- 1 cup small pasta (such as orzo or acini di pepe)
- 1 cup cooked turkey or chicken meatballs, sliced
- 2 cups baby spinach, chopped
- 1 teaspoon dried basil
- Salt and pepper to taste
- Grated Parmesan cheese for serving (optional)

Instructions:

1. Heat the olive oil in a large pot over medium heat. Add the diced onion, minced garlic, carrots, and celery. Sauté until the vegetables are tender, about 5 minutes.

2. Pour in the chicken broth and bring it to a boil. Add the small pasta and cook according to package instructions until al dente.

3. Add the sliced turkey or chicken meatballs, chopped baby spinach, dried basil, salt, and pepper to the pot. Stir well, let it simmer for 5 minutes to heat through, and allow the flavors to meld together.

4. Taste the soup and adjust the seasoning with salt and pepper if needed.

5. Remove the pot from heat and spoon the Italian Wedding Soup into bowls. Serve with grated Parmesan cheese on top, if desired.

Nutritional Value (Per Serving):

Calories: 250 Protein: 15g Fat: 6g Salt: 600mg

Pumpkin Soup

Total Servings: 4 servings
Preparation Time: 10 minutes
Time to Cook: 30 minutes

Ingredients:

- 1 tablespoon olive oil
- 1 small onion, diced
- 2 cloves garlic, minced
- 2 cups pumpkin puree
- 4 cups low-sodium vegetable broth
- 1 teaspoon ground cumin
- 1/2 teaspoon ground cinnamon
- 1/4 teaspoon ground nutmeg

- Salt and pepper to taste
- Greek yogurt or sour cream for serving (optional)
- Fresh parsley or chives, chopped, for garnish (optional)

Instructions:

1. Heat the olive oil in a large pot over medium heat. Add the diced onion, minced garlic, and sauté until the onion becomes translucent and fragrant for about 3-4 minutes.

2. Add the pumpkin puree, vegetable broth, ground cumin, ground cinnamon, and ground nutmeg to the pot. Stir well to combine all the ingredients.

3. Bring the mixture to a boil, then reduce the heat and let it simmer for 20-25 minutes, allowing the flavors to meld together.

4. Season the pumpkin soup with salt and pepper to taste. Adjust the seasoning as needed.

5. Remove the pot from heat and use an immersion or regular blender to puree the soup until smooth and creamy.

6. Ladle the pumpkin soup into bowls and garnish with a dollop of Greek yogurt or sour cream, if desired. Sprinkle with fresh parsley or chives for added flavor and presentation.

Nutritional Value (Per Serving):

Calories: 150 Protein: 4g Fat: 6g Salt: 400mg

White Bean Soup

Total Servings: 4 servings
Preparation Time: 10 minutes
Time to Cook: 30 minutes

Ingredients:

- 1 tablespoon olive oil
- 1 small onion, diced
- 2 cloves garlic, minced
- 2 carrots, peeled and diced
- 2 celery stalks, diced
- 2 cans (15 oz each) of white beans, drained and rinsed
- 4 cups low-sodium vegetable broth
- 1 teaspoon dried rosemary
- Salt and pepper to taste
- Fresh parsley, chopped, for garnish (optional)

Instructions:

1. Heat the olive oil in a large pot over medium heat. Add the diced onion, minced garlic, carrots, and celery. Sauté until the vegetables are tender, about 5 minutes.

2. Add the white beans to the pot and pour in the vegetable broth. Stir in the dried rosemary and bring the mixture to a boil.

3. Reduce the heat and let the soup simmer for 20-25 minutes, allowing the flavors to blend.

4. Using an immersion or regular blender, puree a portion of the soup to create a creamy texture. Leave some beans and vegetables intact for added texture.

5. Season the white bean soup with salt and pepper to taste. Adjust the seasoning if needed.

6. Remove the pot from heat and ladle the soup into bowls. Garnish with fresh parsley, if desired.

Nutritional Value (Per Serving):

Calories: 200 Protein: 10g Fat: 4g Salt: 400mg

Creamy Asparagus Soup

Total Servings: 4 servings
Preparation Time: 10 minutes
Time to Cook: 25 minutes

Ingredients:

- 1 tablespoon olive oil
- 1 small onion, diced
- 2 cloves garlic, minced
- 1 lb asparagus, woody ends removed and chopped
- 4 cups low-sodium vegetable broth
- 1 cup low-fat milk
- Salt and pepper to taste
- Lemon zest, for garnish (optional)
- Toasted almond slices for garnish (optional)

Instructions:

1. Heat the olive oil in a large pot over medium heat. Add the diced onion, minced garlic, and sauté until the onion becomes translucent and fragrant for about 3-4 minutes.

2. Add the chopped asparagus to the pot and sauté for another 2 minutes.

3. Pour in the vegetable broth and bring it to a boil. Reduce the heat and let the soup simmer for 15-20 minutes or until the asparagus is tender.

4. Using an immersion or regular blender, puree the soup until smooth and creamy.

5. Return the soup to the pot and stir in the low-fat milk—season with salt and pepper to taste. Cook for an additional 5 minutes to heat through.

6. Remove the pot from heat and ladle the creamy asparagus soup into bowls. Garnish with lemon zest and toasted almond slices, if desired.

Nutritional Value (Per Serving):

Calories: 150 Protein: 6g Fat: 6g Salt: 400mg

Moroccan Lentil Soup

Total Servings: 4 servings
Preparation Time: 10 minutes
Time to Cook: 30 minutes

Ingredients:

- 1 tablespoon olive oil
- 1 small onion, diced
- 2 cloves garlic, minced
- 2 carrots, peeled and diced
- 2 celery stalks, diced
- 1 cup red lentils, rinsed
- 4 cups low-sodium vegetable broth
- 1 can (14 oz) diced tomatoes
- 1 teaspoon ground cumin
- 1 teaspoon ground coriander
- 1/2 teaspoon ground turmeric
- 1/2 teaspoon paprika
- Salt and pepper to taste
- Fresh cilantro, chopped, for garnish (optional)
- Lemon wedges for serving (optional)

Instructions:

1. Heat the olive oil in a large pot over medium heat. Add the diced onion, minced garlic, carrots, and celery. Sauté until the vegetables are tender, about 5 minutes.

2. Add the red lentils to the pot and pour in the vegetable broth. Stir in the diced tomatoes, ground cumin, coriander, turmeric, and paprika.

3. Bring the mixture to a boil, then reduce the heat and let it simmer for 20-25 minutes or until the lentils are cooked and tender.

4. Season the Moroccan lentil soup with salt and pepper to taste. Adjust the seasoning if needed.

5. Remove the pot from heat and ladle the soup into bowls. Garnish with fresh cilantro and serve with lemon wedges for a burst of freshness, if desired.

Nutritional Value (Per Serving):

Calories: 250 Protein: 15g Fat: 4g Salt: 400mg

Sweet Potato Soup

Total Servings: 4 servings
Preparation Time: 10 minutes
Time to Cook: 25 minutes

Ingredients:

- 1 tablespoon olive oil
- 1 small onion, diced
- 2 cloves garlic, minced
- 2 medium sweet potatoes, peeled and cubed
- 4 cups low-sodium vegetable broth
- 1 teaspoon ground cumin
- 1/2 teaspoon ground cinnamon
- 1/4 teaspoon ground nutmeg
- Salt and pepper to taste
- Greek yogurt or coconut cream for serving (optional)
- Toasted pumpkin seeds for garnish (optional)

Instructions:

1. Heat the olive oil in a large pot over medium heat. Add the diced onion, minced garlic, and sauté until the onion becomes translucent and fragrant for about 3-4 minutes.

2. Add the cubed sweet potatoes to the pot and pour in the vegetable broth. Stir in the ground cumin, ground cinnamon, and ground nutmeg.

3. Bring the mixture to a boil, then reduce the heat and let it simmer for 15-20 minutes or until the sweet potatoes are soft and cooked through.

4. Using an immersion or regular blender, puree the soup until smooth and creamy.

5. Return the soup to the pot and season with salt and pepper to taste. Cook for an additional 5 minutes to heat through.

6. Remove the pot from heat and spoon the sweet potato soup into bowls. Serve with a dollop of Greek yogurt or coconut cream on top, if desired. Garnish with toasted pumpkin seeds for added texture and flavor.

Nutritional Value (Per Serving):

Calories: 200 Protein: 4g Fat: 6g Salt: 400mg

Chicken Tortilla Soup

Total Servings: 4 servings
Preparation Time: 10 minutes
Time to Cook: 30 minutes

Ingredients:

- 1 tablespoon olive oil

- 1 small onion, diced
- 2 cloves garlic, minced
- 1 jalapeno pepper, seeds removed and finely chopped (optional)
- 2 boneless, skinless chicken breasts, cooked and shredded
- 4 cups low-sodium chicken broth
- 1 can (14 oz) diced tomatoes
- 1 can (14 oz) black beans, drained and rinsed
- 1 cup frozen corn kernels
- 1 teaspoon ground cumin
- 1 teaspoon chili powder
- Salt and pepper to taste
- Fresh cilantro, chopped, for garnish (optional)
- Baked tortilla chips, crushed, for topping (optional)
- Lime wedges for serving (optional)

Instructions:

1. Heat the olive oil in a large pot over medium heat. Add the diced onion, minced garlic, and jalapeno pepper. Sauté until the onion becomes translucent and fragrant, about 3-4 minutes.

2. Add the shredded chicken to the pot and stir to combine with the onions and garlic.

3. Pour the chicken broth and add the diced tomatoes, black beans, frozen corn kernels, ground cumin, and chili powder. Stir well to combine all the ingredients.

4. Bring the soup to a boil, then reduce the heat and let it simmer for 20-25 minutes to allow the flavors to meld together.

5. Season the chicken tortilla soup with salt and pepper to taste. Adjust the seasoning if needed.

6. Remove the pot from heat and ladle the soup into bowls. Garnish with fresh cilantro and crushed baked tortilla chips for added crunch, if desired. Serve with lime wedges on the side for a tangy twist.

Nutritional Value (Per Serving):

Calories: 300 Protein: 25g Fat: 8g Salt: 600mg

Vegetable Barley Soup

Total Servings: 4 servings
Preparation Time: 10 minutes
Time to Cook: 45 minutes

Ingredients:
- 1 tablespoon olive oil

- 1 small onion, diced
- 2 cloves garlic, minced
- 2 carrots, peeled and diced
- 2 celery stalks, diced
- 1 zucchini, diced
- 1 cup pearl barley, rinsed
- 4 cups low-sodium vegetable broth
- 1 can (14 oz) diced tomatoes
- 1 teaspoon dried thyme
- 1 teaspoon dried oregano
- Salt and pepper to taste
- Fresh parsley, chopped, for garnish (optional)

Instructions:

1. Heat the olive oil in a large pot over medium heat. Add the diced onion, minced garlic, carrots, celery, and zucchini. Sauté until the vegetables are tender, about 5 minutes.

2. Add the pearl barley to the pot and pour in the vegetable broth. Stir in the diced tomatoes, dried thyme, and dried oregano.

3. Bring the mixture to a boil, then reduce the heat and let it simmer for 40-45 minutes or until the barley is cooked and tender.

4. Season the vegetable barley soup with salt and pepper to taste. Adjust the seasoning if needed.

5. Remove the pot from heat and ladle the soup into bowls. Garnish with fresh parsley, if desired.

Nutritional Value (Per Serving):

Calories: 250 Protein: 6g Fat: 4g Salt: 400mg

Creamy Tomato Soup

Total Servings: 4 servings
Preparation Time: 10 minutes
Time to Cook: 30 minutes

Ingredients:
- 1 tablespoon olive oil
- 1 small onion, diced
- 2 cloves garlic, minced
- 2 cans (14 oz each) of diced tomatoes
- 2 cups low-sodium vegetable broth
- 1 teaspoon dried basil
- 1 teaspoon dried oregano
- 1/2 teaspoon dried thyme

- 1/2 cup low-fat milk or unsweetened almond milk

- Salt and pepper to taste

- Fresh basil leaves, chopped, for garnish (optional)

Instructions:

1. Heat the olive oil in a large pot over medium heat. Add the diced onion and minced garlic. Sauté until the onion becomes translucent and fragrant, about 3-4 minutes.

2. Add the diced tomatoes (with their juice) to the pot. Pour the vegetable broth and stir in the dried basil, oregano, and thyme.

3. Bring the mixture to a boil, then reduce the heat and let it simmer for 20 minutes to allow the flavors to meld together.

4. Using an immersion or regular blender, puree the soup until smooth and creamy.

5. Return the soup to the pot and stir in the low-fat milk or unsweetened almond milk—season with salt and pepper to taste. Heat the soup for an additional 5 minutes.

6. Remove the pot from heat and ladle the creamy tomato soup into bowls. Garnish with fresh basil leaves, if desired.

Nutritional Value (Per Serving):

Calories: 150 Protein: 5g Fat: 5g Salt: 500mg

Black Bean and Quinoa Soup

Total Servings: 4 servings
Preparation Time: 10 minutes
Time to Cook: 30 minutes

Ingredients:

- 1 tablespoon olive oil

- 1 small onion, diced

- 2 cloves garlic, minced

- 2 carrots, peeled and diced

- 2 celery stalks, diced

- 1 can (14 oz) black beans, drained and rinsed

- 1/2 cup uncooked quinoa, rinsed

- 4 cups low-sodium vegetable broth

- 1 teaspoon ground cumin

- 1/2 teaspoon chili powder

- Salt and pepper to taste

- Fresh cilantro, chopped, for garnish (optional)

- Lime wedges for serving (optional)

Instructions:

1. Heat the olive oil in a large pot over medium heat. Add the diced onion, minced garlic, carrots, and celery. Sauté until the vegetables are tender, about 5 minutes.

2. Add the black beans and quinoa to the pot. Pour the vegetable broth and stir in the ground cumin and chili powder.

3. Bring the mixture to a boil, then reduce the heat and let it simmer for 20-25 minutes or until the quinoa is cooked and tender.

4. Season the black bean and quinoa soup with salt and pepper to taste. Adjust the seasoning if needed.

5. Remove the pot from heat and ladle the soup into bowls. Garnish with fresh cilantro and serve with lime wedges on the side for a tangy twist, if desired.

Nutritional Value (Per Serving):

Calories: 250 Protein: 10g Fat: 5g Salt: 500mg

Beet Soup

Total Servings: 4 servings
Preparation Time: 15 minutes
Time to Cook: 45 minutes

Ingredients:

- 1 tablespoon olive oil

- 1 small onion, diced

- 2 cloves garlic, minced

- 4 medium beets, peeled and diced

- 2 carrots, peeled and diced

- 2 cups low-sodium vegetable broth

- 2 cups water

- 1 tablespoon lemon juice

- Salt and pepper to taste

- Greek yogurt or sour cream for garnish (optional)

- Fresh dill, chopped, for garnish (optional)

Instructions:

1. Heat the olive oil in a large pot over medium heat. Add the diced onion and minced garlic. Sauté until the onion becomes translucent and fragrant, about 3-4 minutes.

2. Add the diced beets and carrots to the pot. Stir well to coat the vegetables with the oil and cook for another 5 minutes.

3. Pour in the vegetable broth and water. Bring the mixture to a boil, then reduce the heat and let it simmer for 30-35 minutes or until the beets and carrots are tender.

4. Using an immersion or regular blender, puree the soup until smooth and creamy.

5. Stir in the lemon juice and season with salt and pepper to taste. Adjust the seasoning if needed.

6. Remove the pot from heat and ladle the beet soup into bowls. Garnish with a dollop of Greek yogurt or sour cream, and sprinkle fresh dill on top, if desired.

Nutritional Value (Per Serving):

Calories: 120 Protein: 3g Fat: 4g Salt: 400mg

Chicken and Vegetable Soup

Total Servings: 4 servings
Preparation Time: 10 minutes
Time to Cook: 30 minutes

Ingredients:

- 1 tablespoon olive oil
- 1 small onion, diced
- 2 cloves garlic, minced
- 2 carrots, peeled and diced
- 2 celery stalks, diced
- 2 cups cooked chicken breast, shredded
- 4 cups low-sodium chicken broth
- 1 cup frozen green peas
- 1 cup chopped green beans
- 1 teaspoon dried thyme
- Salt and pepper to taste
- Fresh parsley, chopped, for garnish (optional)

Instructions:

1. Heat the olive oil in a large pot over medium heat. Add the diced onion, minced garlic, carrots, and celery. Sauté until the vegetables are tender, about 5 minutes.

2. Add the shredded chicken to the pot and stir well to combine with the vegetables.

3. Pour the chicken broth and add the frozen green peas, chopped green beans, and dried thyme. Stir to combine all the ingredients.

4. Bring the soup to a boil, then reduce the heat and let it simmer for 20-25 minutes or until the vegetables are cooked and tender.

5. Season the chicken and vegetable soup with salt and pepper to taste. Adjust the seasoning if needed.

6. Remove the pot from heat and ladle the soup into bowls. Garnish with fresh parsley, if desired.

Nutritional Value (Per Serving):

Calories: 200 Protein: 20g Fat: 6g Salt: 500mg

Mexican Chicken Soup

Total Servings: 4 servings
Preparation Time: 15 minutes
Time to Cook: 30 minutes

Ingredients:

- 1 tablespoon olive oil
- 1 small onion, diced
- 2 cloves garlic, minced
- 2 boneless, skinless chicken breasts, diced
- 1 can (14 oz) diced tomatoes
- 4 cups low-sodium chicken broth
- 1 cup frozen corn kernels
- 1 can (14 oz) black beans, drained and rinsed
- 1 teaspoon ground cumin
- 1/2 teaspoon chili powder
- Salt and pepper to taste
- Fresh cilantro, chopped, for garnish (optional)
- Avocado slices for garnish (optional)

Instructions:

1. Heat the olive oil in a large pot over medium heat. Add the diced onion and minced garlic. Sauté until the onion becomes translucent and fragrant, about 3-4 minutes.

2. Add the diced chicken breasts to the pot and cook until they are browned on all sides, about 5 minutes.

3. Pour in the diced tomatoes (with their juice) and chicken broth. Stir in the frozen corn kernels, black beans, ground cumin, and chili powder.

4. Bring the mixture to a boil, then reduce the heat and let it simmer for 20 minutes or until the chicken is cooked through and tender.

5. Season the Mexican chicken soup with salt and pepper to taste. Adjust the seasoning if needed.

6. Remove the pot from heat and ladle the soup into bowls. Garnish with fresh cilantro and avocado slices, if desired.

Nutritional Value (Per Serving):

Calories: 250 Protein: 25g Fat: 5g Salt: 600mg

Spicy Pumpkin Soup

Total Servings: 4 servings
Preparation Time: 10 minutes
Time to Cook: 25 minutes

Ingredients:

- 1 tablespoon olive oil
- 1 small onion, diced
- 2 cloves garlic, minced
- 2 cups canned pumpkin puree
- 4 cups low-sodium vegetable broth
- 1 teaspoon ground cumin
- 1/2 teaspoon ground cinnamon
- 1/4 teaspoon cayenne pepper (adjust to taste)
- Salt and pepper to taste
- Plain Greek yogurt, for garnish (optional)
- Pumpkin seeds, for garnish (optional)

Instructions:

1. Heat the olive oil in a large pot over medium heat. Add the diced onion and minced garlic. Sauté until the onion becomes translucent and fragrant, about 3-4 minutes.

2. Add the canned pumpkin puree to the pot. Stir well to combine with the onions and garlic.

3. Pour the vegetable broth and stir in the ground cumin, cinnamon, and cayenne pepper.

4. Bring the mixture to a boil, then reduce the heat and let it simmer for 15-20 minutes, allowing the flavors to blend.

5. Season the spicy pumpkin soup with salt and pepper to taste. Adjust the seasoning if needed.

6. Remove the pot from heat and ladle the soup into bowls. Garnish with a dollop of plain Greek yogurt and sprinkle pumpkin seeds on top, if desired.

Nutritional Value (Per Serving):

Calories: 150 Protein: 5g Fat: 5g Salt: 400mg

Broccoli Potato Soup

Total Servings: 4 servings
Preparation Time: 15 minutes
Time to Cook: 30 minutes

Ingredients:

- 1 tablespoon olive oil
- 1 small onion, diced
- 2 cloves garlic, minced
- 2 medium potatoes, peeled and diced
- 4 cups low-sodium vegetable broth
- 2 cups broccoli florets
- 1/2 cup low-fat milk or unsweetened plant-based milk

- Salt and pepper to taste
- Grated Parmesan cheese, for garnish (optional)
- Fresh chives, chopped, for garnish (optional)

Instructions:

1. Heat the olive oil in a large pot over medium heat. Add the diced onion and minced garlic. Sauté until the onion becomes translucent and fragrant, about 3-4 minutes.

2. Add the diced potatoes to the pot and cook for 5 minutes, stirring occasionally.

3. Pour in the vegetable broth and bring the mixture to a boil. Reduce the heat and let it simmer for 15 minutes or until the potatoes are tender.

4. Add the broccoli florets to the pot and cook for another 5 minutes or until the broccoli is tender but still vibrant green.

5. Using an immersion or regular blender, puree the soup until smooth and creamy. If using a regular blender, allow the soup to cool slightly before blending and then reheat before serving.

6. Stir in low-fat or unsweetened plant-based milk to achieve a creamy consistency—season with salt and pepper to taste.

7. Remove the pot from heat and ladle the broccoli potato soup into bowls. Garnish with grated Parmesan cheese and fresh chives, if desired.

Nutritional Value (Per Serving):

Calories: 150 Protein: 5g Fat: 4g Salt: 400mg

Chickpea Soup

Total Servings: 4 servings
Preparation Time: 10 minutes
Time to Cook: 25 minutes

Ingredients:

- 1 tablespoon olive oil
- 1 small onion, diced
- 2 cloves garlic, minced
- 2 carrots, peeled and diced
- 2 celery stalks, diced
- 2 cups cooked chickpeas
- 4 cups low-sodium vegetable broth
- 1 teaspoon ground cumin
- 1/2 teaspoon smoked paprika
- Salt and pepper to taste
- Fresh parsley, chopped, for garnish (optional)

Instructions:

1. Heat the olive oil in a large pot over medium heat. Add the diced onion, minced garlic, carrots, and celery. Sauté until the vegetables are tender, about 5 minutes.

2. Add the cooked chickpeas to the pot and stir well to combine with the vegetables.

3. Pour the vegetable broth and stir in the ground cumin and smoked paprika.

4. Bring the soup to a boil, then reduce the heat and let it simmer for 15-20 minutes, allowing the flavors to meld together.

5. Season the chickpea soup with salt and pepper to taste. Adjust the seasoning if needed.

6. Remove the pot from heat and ladle the soup into bowls. Garnish with fresh parsley, if desired.

Nutritional Value (Per Serving):

Calories: 200 Protein: 8g Fat: 5g Salt: 400mg

Creamy Mushroom Soup

Total Servings: 4 servings
Preparation Time: 10 minutes
Time to Cook: 30 minutes

Ingredients:

- 1 tablespoon olive oil
- 1 small onion, diced
- 2 cloves garlic, minced
- 8 ounces of mushrooms, sliced
- 4 cups low-sodium vegetable broth
- 1 cup low-fat milk or unsweetened plant-based milk
- 2 tablespoons all-purpose flour
- Salt and pepper to taste
- Fresh thyme leaves, for garnish (optional)

Instructions:

1. Heat the olive oil in a large pot over medium heat. Add the diced onion and minced garlic. Sauté until the onion becomes translucent and fragrant, about 3-4 minutes.

2. Add the sliced mushrooms to the pot and cook until they release moisture and brown, about 5-7 minutes.

3. Whisk together the low-fat milk and all-purpose flour in a separate bowl until smooth.

4. Pour the vegetable broth into the pot with the mushrooms and simmer. Slowly whisk in the milk-flour mixture, stirring continuously to avoid any lumps.

5. Continue cooking the soup for 10 minutes or until it thickens slightly—season with salt and pepper to taste.

6. Remove the pot from heat and ladle the creamy

mushroom soup into bowls. Garnish with fresh thyme leaves, if desired.

Nutritional Value (Per Serving):

Calories: 120 Protein: 5g Fat: 4g Salt: 400mg

Lemon Chicken Orzo Soup

Total Servings: 4 servings
Preparation Time: 15 minutes
Time to Cook: 30 minutes

Ingredients:

- 1 tablespoon olive oil
- 1 small onion, diced
- 2 cloves garlic, minced
- 2 carrots, peeled and diced
- 2 celery stalks, diced
- 4 cups low-sodium chicken broth
- 1 cup cooked chicken breast, shredded
- 1/2 cup uncooked orzo pasta
- Juice of 1 lemon
- Salt and pepper to taste
- Fresh parsley, chopped, for garnish (optional)

Instructions:

1. Heat the olive oil in a large pot over medium heat. Add the diced onion, minced garlic, carrots, and celery. Sauté until the vegetables are tender, about 5 minutes.

2. Pour the chicken broth into the pot and bring to a boil. Add the shredded chicken and orzo pasta. Reduce the heat and let it simmer for 15 minutes or until the orzo is cooked.

3. Stir in the lemon juice and season the soup with salt and pepper to taste.

4. Remove the pot from heat and ladle the lemon chicken orzo soup into bowls. Garnish with fresh parsley, if desired.

Nutritional Value (Per Serving):

Calories: 180 Protein: 15g Fat: 4g Salt: 500mg

Creamy Zucchini Soup

Total Servings: 4 servings
Preparation Time: 10 minutes
Time to Cook: 25 minutes

Ingredients:

- 1 tablespoon olive oil
- 1 small onion, diced
- 2 cloves garlic, minced
- 3 medium zucchini, sliced
- 4 cups low-sodium vegetable broth
- 1/2 cup low-fat milk or unsweetened plant-based milk
- Salt and pepper to taste
- Fresh basil leaves for garnish (optional)

Instructions:

1. Heat the olive oil in a large pot over medium heat. Add the diced onion and minced garlic. Sauté until the onion becomes translucent and fragrant, about 3-4 minutes.

2. Add the sliced zucchini to the pot and cook for 5 minutes until they soften.

3. Pour the vegetable broth into the pot and bring it to a simmer. Cook for 15 minutes or until the zucchini is tender.

4. Using an immersion or regular blender, puree the soup until smooth and creamy. Using a regular blender, allow the soup to cool slightly before blending and reheat before serving.

5. Stir in low-fat or unsweetened plant-based milk to achieve a creamy consistency—season with salt and pepper to taste.

6. Remove the pot from heat and ladle the creamy zucchini soup into bowls. Garnish with fresh basil leaves, if desired.

Nutritional Value (Per Serving):

Calories: 90 Protein: 4g Fat: 3g Salt: 400mg

Italian Sausage Soup

Total Servings: 4 servings
Preparation Time: 10 minutes
Time to Cook: 25 minutes

Ingredients:

- 1 tablespoon olive oil
- 1 small onion, diced
- 2 cloves garlic, minced
- 2 Italian sausage links, casings removed
- 2 carrots, peeled and diced
- 2 celery stalks, diced
- 4 cups low-sodium chicken broth
- 1 cup canned diced tomatoes
- 1 cup chopped kale or spinach

- 1 teaspoon dried basil
- Salt and pepper to taste
- Grated Parmesan cheese, for garnish (optional)

Instructions:

1. Heat the olive oil in a large pot over medium heat. Add the diced onion and minced garlic. Sauté until the onion becomes translucent and fragrant, about 3-4 minutes.

2. Add the Italian sausage to the pot and cook, breaking it into small pieces, until it is browned and cooked.

3. Stir in the diced carrots and diced celery. Cook for 5 minutes or until the vegetables start to soften.

4. Pour the chicken broth and diced tomatoes into the pot. Add the dried basil. Bring the soup to a boil, then reduce the heat and let it simmer for 15 minutes.

5. Stir in the chopped kale or spinach and cook for 5 minutes or until the greens are wilted.

6. Season the Italian sausage soup with salt and pepper to taste.

7. Remove the pot from heat and ladle the soup into bowls. Garnish with grated Parmesan cheese, if desired.

Nutritional Value (Per Serving):

Calories: 220 Protein: 12g Fat: 11g Salt: 600mg

Creamy Cauliflower Soup

Total Servings: 4 servings
Preparation Time: 10 minutes
Time to Cook: 25 minutes

Ingredients:

- 1 tablespoon olive oil
- 1 small onion, diced
- 2 cloves garlic, minced
- 1 medium head cauliflower, chopped into florets
- 4 cups low-sodium vegetable broth
- 1 cup low-fat milk or unsweetened plant-based milk
- Salt and pepper to taste
- Fresh chives for garnish (optional)

Instructions:

1. Heat the olive oil in a large pot over medium heat. Add the diced onion and minced garlic. Sauté until the onion becomes translucent and fragrant, about 3-4 minutes.

2. Add the cauliflower florets to the pot and cook for 5 minutes until they soften.

3. Pour the vegetable broth into the pot and bring it to a simmer. Cook for 15 minutes or until the cauliflower is tender.

4. Using an immersion or regular blender, puree the soup until smooth and creamy. Using a regular blender, allow the soup to cool slightly before blending and reheat before serving.

5. Stir in low-fat or unsweetened plant-based milk to achieve a creamy consistency—season with salt and pepper to taste.

6. Remove the pot from heat and ladle the creamy cauliflower soup into bowls. Garnish with fresh chives, if desired.

Nutritional Value (Per Serving):

Calories: 100 Protein: 4g Fat: 3g Salt: 400mg

pepper to taste.

7. Remove the pot from heat and ladle the soup into bowls. Garnish with fresh dill, if desired.

Nutritional Value (Per Serving):

Calories: 250 Protein: 20g Fat: 8g Salt: 600mg

Greek Lemon Chicken Soup

Total Servings: 4 servings
Preparation Time: 10 minutes
Time to Cook: 25 minutes

Ingredients:

- 1 tablespoon olive oil
- 1 small onion, diced
- 2 cloves garlic, minced
- 2 chicken breasts, boneless and skinless, cut into small pieces
- 4 cups low-sodium chicken broth
- 1/2 cup orzo pasta
- Juice of 1 lemon
- 2 eggs
- Salt and pepper to taste
- Fresh dill, for garnish (optional)

Instructions:

1. Heat the olive oil in a large pot over medium heat. Add the diced onion and minced garlic. Sauté until the onion becomes translucent and fragrant, about 3-4 minutes.

2. Add the chicken breast pieces to the pot and cook until they are no longer pink in the center, about 5-7 minutes.

3. Pour the chicken broth into the pot and bring it to a boil. Add the orzo pasta and cook according to package instructions until it is al dente.

4. Whisk together the lemon juice and eggs in a small bowl until well combined.

5. Slowly pour the lemon and egg mixture into the soup while stirring continuously. This will create a creamy texture. Cook for an additional 2 minutes to thicken the soup.

6. Season the Greek Lemon Chicken Soup with salt and

Chapter 11: Smoothie and juice

Berry Blast Smoothies

Total Servings: 1 serving
Preparation Time: 5 minutes
Time to Cook: N/A (No cooking required)

Ingredients:

- 1 cup mixed berries (such as strawberries, blueberries, and raspberries)
- 1 ripe banana
- 1/2 cup low-fat yogurt or unsweetened plant-based yogurt
- 1/2 cup unsweetened almond milk or other low-fat milk alternatives
- 1 tablespoon honey or maple syrup (optional)
- Ice cubes (optional)

Instructions:

1. Combine the mixed berries, ripe banana, low-fat yogurt, unsweetened almond milk, and honey or maple syrup (if desired) in a blender.

2. Blend all the ingredients until smooth and creamy. If you prefer a thicker smoothie, add a handful of ice cubes and blend again.

3. Pour the Berry Blast Smoothie into a glass or a portable container.

4. Serve immediately and enjoy the refreshing and nutritious smoothie!

Nutritional Value (Per Serving):

Calories: 200   Protein: 8g   Fat: 2g   Salt:100mg

Green Detox Juice

Total Servings: 1 serving
Preparation Time: 10 minutes
Time to Cook: N/A (No cooking required)

Ingredients:

- 1 green apple, cored and chopped
- 1 cucumber, peeled and chopped
- 2 celery stalks, chopped
- 1/2 lemon, juiced
- 1 handful of spinach or kale
- 1-inch piece of ginger, peeled
- 1 cup cold water
- Ice cubes (optional)

Instructions:

1. Add green apple, cucumber, celery, lemon juice, spinach or kale, or ginger in a juicer or a high-speed blender.

2. Blend or juice the ingredients until smooth. Using a blender, strain the mixture through a fine-mesh sieve to remove any fibrous bits.

3. Add cold water to the juice and stir well to combine.

4. Add a few ice cubes to chill the Green Detox Juice if desired.

5. Pour the juice into a glass and serve immediately to enjoy the refreshing and detoxifying benefits.

Nutritional Value (Per Serving):

Calories: 80 Protein: 2g Fat: 1g Salt: 50mg

Tropical Paradise Smoothies

Total Servings: 1 serving
Preparation Time: 5 minutes
Time to Cook: N/A (No cooking required)

Ingredients:

- 1 ripe banana
- 1/2 cup pineapple chunks (fresh or frozen)
- 1/2 cup mango chunks (fresh or frozen)
- 1/2 cup unsweetened coconut milk
- 1/2 cup unsweetened orange juice
- 1 tablespoon chia seeds (optional)
- Ice cubes (optional)

Instructions:

1. Combine the ripe banana, pineapple chunks, mango chunks, unsweetened coconut milk, and unsweetened orange juice in a blender.

2. Blend all the ingredients until smooth and creamy. If you prefer a thicker smoothie, add a handful of ice cubes and blend again.

3. If desired, add chia seeds to the blender and pulse a few times to mix them into the smoothie.

4. Pour the Tropical Paradise Smoothie into a glass or a portable container.

5. Serve immediately and savor the tropical flavors of this delicious and nutritious smoothie!

Citrus Sunshine Juice

Total Servings: 1 serving
Preparation Time: 10 minutes
Time to Cook: N/A (No cooking required)

Ingredients:

- 2 oranges, peeled and segmented
- 1 grapefruit, peeled and segmented
- 1 lemon, juiced
- 1 lime, juiced
- 1 tablespoon honey or maple syrup (optional)
- 1 cup cold water
- Ice cubes (optional)

Instructions:

1. Add the orange, grapefruit, lemon, and lime juice in a juicer or a high-speed blender.

2. Blend or juice the ingredients until smooth. Using a blender, strain the mixture through a fine-mesh sieve to remove any fibrous bits.

3. Add honey or maple syrup (if desired) to sweeten the juice, and stir well to combine.

4. Add cold water to the juice and mix again.

5. Add a few ice cubes to chill the Citrus Sunshine Juice if desired.

6. Pour the juice into a glass and serve immediately to enjoy the refreshing and invigorating flavors.

Nutritional Value (Per Serving):

Calories: 120 Protein: 2g Fat: 0g Salt: 0mg

Strawberry Banana Smoothie

Total Servings: 1 serving
Preparation Time: 5 minutes
Time to Cook: N/A (No cooking required)

Ingredients:

- 1 ripe banana
- 1 cup fresh or frozen strawberries
- 1/2 cup low-fat yogurt
- 1/2 cup unsweetened almond milk (or any preferred milk)
- 1 tablespoon honey or maple syrup (optional)
- Ice cubes (optional)

Instructions:

1. Combine the ripe banana, strawberries, low-fat yogurt, and unsweetened almond milk in a blender.

2. Blend all the ingredients until smooth and creamy. If you prefer a thicker smoothie, add a handful of ice cubes and blend again.

3. If desired, add honey or maple syrup to sweeten the smoothie, and blend for a few more seconds to incorporate.

4. Pour the Strawberry Banana Smoothie into a glass or a portable container.

5. Serve immediately and enjoy this refreshing and nutritious smoothie!

Nutritional Value (Per Serving):

Calories: 180 Protein: 7g Fat: 2g Salt: 80mg

Antioxidant Power Juice

Total Servings: 1 serving
Preparation Time: 10 minutes
Time to Cook: N/A (No cooking required)

Ingredients:

- 1 cup fresh blueberries
- 1 cup fresh spinach leaves
- 1/2 cup chopped carrots
- 1/2 cup unsweetened cranberry juice
- 1/2 cup water
- 1 tablespoon lemon juice
- 1 tablespoon honey or maple syrup (optional)
- Ice cubes (optional)

Instructions:

1. Combine the fresh blueberries, spinach leaves, chopped carrots, unsweetened cranberry juice, water, and lemon juice in a blender or juicer.

2. Blend or juice the ingredients until smooth. Using a blender, strain the mixture through a fine-mesh sieve to remove any fibrous bits.

3. Add honey or maple syrup (if desired) to sweeten the juice, and stir well to combine.

4. Add a few ice cubes to chill the Antioxidant Power Juice if desired.

5. Pour the juice into a glass and serve immediately to enjoy the nourishing and antioxidant-rich flavors.

Nutritional Value (Per Serving):

Calories: 110 Protein: 3g Fat: 1g Salt: 40mg

Blueberry Bliss Smoothie

Total Servings: 1 serving
Preparation Time: 5 minutes
Time to Cook: N/A (No cooking required)

Ingredients:

- 1 cup frozen blueberries
- 1 ripe banana
- 1/2 cup low-fat Greek yogurt
- 1/2 cup unsweetened almond milk (or any preferred milk)
- 1 tablespoon honey or maple syrup (optional)
- 1 tablespoon chia seeds (optional)
- Ice cubes (optional)

Instructions:

1. Combine the frozen blueberries, ripe bananas, low-fat Greek yogurt, and unsweetened almond milk in a blender.

2. Blend all the ingredients until smooth and creamy. If you prefer a thicker smoothie, add a handful of ice cubes and blend again.

3. Add honey or maple syrup to sweeten the smoothie and chia seeds for added nutrition and texture if desired. Blend for a few more seconds to incorporate.

4. Pour the Blueberry Bliss Smoothie into a glass or a portable container.

5. Serve immediately and enjoy this delicious and heart-healthy smoothie!

Nutritional Value (Per Serving):

Calories: 220 Protein: 10g Fat: 3g Salt: 90mg

Green Goddess Juice

Total Servings: 1 serving
Preparation Time: 10 minutes
Time to Cook: N/A (No cooking required)

Ingredients:

- 1 cup fresh spinach leaves
- 1/2 cucumber, peeled and chopped
- 1 green apple, cored and chopped
- 1/2 lemon, juiced

- 1/2 inch ginger root, peeled
- 1/2 cup water
- Ice cubes (optional)

Instructions:

1. Combine the fresh spinach leaves, cucumber, green apple, lemon juice, ginger root, and water in a blender or juicer.

2. Blend or juice the ingredients until smooth. Using a blender, strain the mixture through a fine-mesh sieve to remove any fibrous bits.

3. Add a few ice cubes to chill the Green Goddess Juice if desired.

4. Pour the juice into a glass and serve immediately to enjoy the refreshing and nutrient-packed flavors.

Nutritional Value (Per Serving):

Calories: 100 Protein: 3g Fat: 1g Salt: 50mg

Mango Tango Smoothie

Total Servings: 1 serving
Preparation Time: 5 minutes
Time to Cook: N/A

Ingredients:

- 1 ripe mango, peeled and pitted
- 1/2 cup plain low-fat yogurt
- 1/2 cup unsweetened almond milk (or any preferred milk)
- 1 tablespoon honey or maple syrup (optional)
- 1 tablespoon flaxseeds or chia seeds (optional)
- Ice cubes (optional)

Instructions:

1. Cut the ripe mango into chunks, discard the pit, and peel.

2. Combine the mango chunks, plain low-fat yogurt, and unsweetened almond milk in a blender.

3. Blend all the ingredients until smooth and creamy. Add a handful of ice cubes and blend again for a colder smoothie if desired.

4. If you prefer a sweeter taste, add honey or maple syrup to the smoothie and blend for a few more seconds.

5. Optionally, add flaxseeds or chia seeds for fiber and omega-3 fatty acids. Blend briefly to incorporate.

6. Pour the Mango Tango Smoothie into a glass or a portable container.

7. Serve immediately and savor the tropical flavors of this heart-healthy smoothie!

Nutritional Value (Per Serving):

Calories: 230 Protein: 6g Fat: 4g Salt: 80mg

Beetroot Booster Juice

Total Servings: 1 serving
Preparation Time: 10 minutes
Time to Cook: N/A (No cooking required)

Ingredients:

- 1 small beetroot, peeled and chopped
- 1 medium carrot, peeled and chopped
- 1 red apple, cored and chopped
- 1/2 lemon, juiced
- 1-inch ginger root, peeled
- 1/2 cup water
- Ice cubes (optional)

Instructions:

1. Combine the chopped beetroot, carrot, red apple, lemon juice, ginger root, and water in a blender or juicer.

2. Blend or juice the ingredients until smooth. Using a blender, strain the mixture through a fine-mesh sieve to remove any fibrous bits.

3. Add a few ice cubes to chill the Beetroot Booster Juice if desired.

4. Pour the juice into a glass and serve immediately to enjoy beetroot's vibrant flavors and potential health benefits.

Nutritional Value (Per Serving):

Calories: 120 Protein: 2g Fat: 1g Salt: 60mg

Pineapple Passion Smoothie

Total Servings: 1 serving
Preparation Time: 5 minutes
Time to Cook: N/A (No cooking required)

Ingredients:

- 1 cup fresh pineapple chunks
- 1/2 cup spinach leaves
- 1/2 ripe banana
- 1/2 cup unsweetened coconut milk
- 1/2 cup plain Greek yogurt
- 1 tablespoon honey or maple syrup (optional)

- Ice cubes (optional)

Instructions:

1. Combine the fresh pineapple chunks, spinach leaves, ripe banana, unsweetened coconut milk, and plain Greek yogurt in a blender.

2. Blend all the ingredients until smooth and creamy. Add a handful of ice cubes and blend again for a colder smoothie if desired.

3. Taste the smoothie and add honey or maple syrup if you prefer a sweeter taste. Blend for a few more seconds to incorporate the sweetener.

4. Pour the Pineapple Passion Smoothie into a glass or a portable container.

5. Enjoy the refreshing and tropical flavors of this heart-healthy smoothie!

Nutritional Value (Per Serving):

Calories: 180 Protein: 9g Fat: 3g Salt: 100mg

Immune Boosting Juice

Total Servings: 1 serving
Preparation Time: 10 minutes
Time to Cook: N/A (No cooking required)

Ingredients:

- 1 large orange, peeled and segmented
- 1 medium carrot, peeled and chopped
- 1/2 medium lemon, juiced
- 1-inch piece of fresh ginger root, peeled
- 1/2 cup water
- Ice cubes (optional)

Instructions:

1. Combine the peeled and segmented orange, chopped carrot, lemon juice, fresh ginger root, and water in a blender or juicer.

2. Blend or juice the ingredients until smooth. Using a blender, strain the mixture through a fine-mesh sieve to remove any pulp or fiber.

3. Add a few ice cubes to chill the Immune Boosting Juice if desired.

4. Pour the juice into a glass and serve immediately to enjoy the refreshing flavors and potential immune-boosting properties.

Nutritional Value (Per Serving):

Calories: 90 Protein: 2g Fat: 1g Salt: 30mg

Creamy Avocado Smoothie

Total Servings: 1 serving
Preparation Time: 5 minutes
Time to Cook: N/A (No cooking required)

Ingredients:

- 1 ripe avocado
- 1 cup unsweetened almond milk
- 1 small ripe banana
- 1 tablespoon honey or maple syrup
- 1 tablespoon chia seeds
- Ice cubes (optional)

Instructions:

1. Cut the ripe avocado in half, remove the pit, and scoop the flesh into a blender.

2. Add the unsweetened almond milk, ripe banana, honey or maple syrup, and chia seeds to the blender.

3. Blend all the ingredients until smooth and creamy. Add a handful of ice cubes and blend again for a colder smoothie if desired.

4. Pour the Creamy Avocado Smoothie into a glass or a portable container.

5. Savor the rich and creamy taste of this heart-healthy smoothie!

Nutritional Value (Per Serving):

Calories: 320 Protein: 5g Fat: 20g Salt: 30mg

Energizing Green Juice

Total Servings: 1 serving
Preparation Time: 10 minutes
Time to Cook: N/A (No cooking required)

Ingredients:

- 1 cup fresh spinach leaves
- 1 cucumber
- 1 green apple, cored and chopped
- 1 stalk of celery
- 1/2 lemon, juiced
- 1-inch piece of fresh ginger root, peeled
- Ice cubes (optional)

Instructions:

1. Rinse the fresh spinach leaves, cucumber, green apple, and celery under cold water to clean them thoroughly.

2. Cut the cucumber and celery into smaller pieces to fit in the juicer or blender.

3. Combine the spinach leaves, cucumber, green apple, celery, lemon juice, and fresh ginger root in a juicer or blender.

4. Juice or blend the ingredients until smooth. Using a blender, strain the mixture through a fine-mesh sieve to remove any pulp or fiber.

5. Add a few ice cubes to chill the Energizing Green Juice if desired.

6. Pour the juice into a glass and enjoy this heart-healthy beverage's revitalizing and nutrient-rich flavors!

Nutritional Value (Per Serving):

Calories: 80 Protein: 2g Fat: 0g Salt: 50mg

Raspberry Delight Smoothie

Total Servings: 1 serving
Preparation Time: 5 minutes
Time to Cook: N/A (No cooking required)

Ingredients:

- 1 cup frozen raspberries
- 1 ripe banana
- 1/2 cup plain Greek yogurt
- 1 tablespoon honey or maple syrup
- 1/2 cup unsweetened almond milk
- Ice cubes (optional)

Instructions:

1. Combine the frozen raspberries, ripe bananas, plain Greek yogurt, honey or maple syrup, and unsweetened almond milk in a blender.

2. Blend the ingredients until smooth and well combined. Add a handful of ice cubes and blend again for a chilled smoothie if desired.

3. Pour the Raspberry Delight Smoothie into a glass or a portable container.

4. Enjoy the refreshing and tangy flavors of this heart-healthy smoothie!

Nutritional Value (Per Serving):

Calories: 240 Protein: 10g Fat: 3g Salt: 80mg

Watermelon Refresher Juice

Total Servings: 1 serving
Preparation Time: 10 minutes
Time to Cook: N/A (No cooking required)

Ingredients:

- 2 cups cubed watermelon
- 1/2 cucumber
- 1/2 lime, juiced
- Fresh mint leaves (optional)
- Ice cubes (optional)

Instructions:

1. Rinse the watermelon, cucumber, and lime under cold water to clean them thoroughly.

2. Cut the watermelon into small cubes and remove the skin. Cut the cucumber into smaller pieces.

3. In a juicer or blender, combine the cubed watermelon, cucumber, lime juice, and a few fresh mint leaves (if desired).

4. Juice or blend the ingredients until smooth and well combined. Using a blender, strain the mixture through a fine-mesh sieve to remove any pulp or fiber.

5. Add a few ice cubes to the Watermelon Refresher Juice to chill it further.

6. Pour the juice into a glass and relish this heart-healthy beverage's hydrating and revitalizing flavors!

Nutritional Value (Per Serving):

Calories: 70 Protein: 1g Fat: 0g Salt: 5mg

Creamy Peanut Butter Smoothie

Total Servings: 1 serving
Preparation Time: 5 minutes
Time to Cook: N/A (No cooking required)

Ingredients:

- 1 ripe banana
- 1 tablespoon creamy peanut butter (unsalted and no added sugar)
- 1/2 cup plain Greek yogurt
- 1/2 cup unsweetened almond milk
- 1 tablespoon honey or maple syrup
- Ice cubes (optional)

Instructions:

1. Peel the ripe banana and break it into smaller pieces.

2. Combine the banana, creamy peanut butter, plain Greek yogurt, unsweetened almond milk, and honey or maple syrup in a blender.

3. Blend the ingredients until smooth and creamy. Add a few ice cubes and blend again for a chilled smoothie if desired.

4. Pour the Creamy Peanut Butter Smoothie into a glass or a portable container.

5. Savor the rich and nutty flavors of this heart-healthy smoothie!

Nutritional Value (Per Serving):

Calories: 290 Protein: 18g Fat: 11g Salt: 180mg

Berry Beet Juice

Total Servings: 1 serving
Preparation Time: 10 minutes
Time to Cook: N/A (No cooking required)

Ingredients:

- 1 small beet, peeled and chopped
- 1 cup mixed berries (such as strawberries, blueberries, and raspberries)
- 1/2 cup water
- 1/2 lemon, juiced
- Fresh mint leaves (optional)
- Ice cubes (optional)

Instructions:

1. Clean the beet and berries by rinsing them under cold water. Peel and chop the beet into smaller pieces.

2. Combine the chopped beet, mixed berries, water, and freshly squeezed lemon juice in a juicer or blender.

3. Juice or blend the ingredients until smooth and well combined. Using a blender, strain the mixture through a fine-mesh sieve to remove any pulp or fiber.

4. Add a few fresh mint leaves to enhance the flavor of the Berry Beet Juice (optional).

5. Add a handful of ice cubes for a cooler beverage and blend again.

6. Pour the juice into a glass and enjoy this heart-healthy drink's vibrant colors and healthful benefits!

Nutritional Value (Per Serving):

Calories: 120 Protein: 2g Fat: 0.5g Salt: 90mg

Peachy Keen Smoothie

Total Servings: 1 serving
Preparation Time: 5 minutes
Time to Cook: N/A (No cooking required)

Ingredients:

- 1 ripe peach, pitted and sliced
- 1/2 cup plain low-fat yogurt
- 1/2 cup unsweetened almond milk
- 1 tablespoon honey or maple syrup
- 1/2 teaspoon vanilla extract
- Ice cubes (optional)

Instructions:

1. Wash and pit the ripe peach. Slice it into smaller pieces.

2. Combine the sliced peach, plain low-fat yogurt, unsweetened almond milk, honey or maple syrup, and vanilla extract in a blender.

3. Blend the ingredients until smooth and creamy. Add a few ice cubes and blend again for a chilled smoothie if desired.

4. Pour the Peachy Keen Smoothie into a glass or a portable container.

5. Sip and enjoy the refreshing and fruity flavors of this heart-healthy smoothie!

Nutritional Value (Per Serving):

Calories: 180 Protein: 6g Fat: 3g Salt: 100mg

Carrot Orange Juice

Total Servings: 1 serving
Preparation Time: 10 minutes
Time to Cook: N/A (No cooking required)

Ingredients:

- 2 medium carrots, peeled and chopped
- 2 oranges, peeled and segmented
- 1/2 lemon, juiced
- Fresh mint leaves (optional)
- Ice cubes (optional)

Instructions:

1. Peel and chop the carrots into smaller pieces.

2. Peel and segment the oranges, removing any seeds.

3. Combine the chopped carrots, orange segments, and freshly squeezed lemon juice in a juicer or blender.

4. Juice or blend the ingredients until well combined and smooth. Using a blender, strain the mixture through a fine-mesh sieve to remove any pulp or fiber.

5. Add a few fresh mint leaves to enhance the flavor of the Carrot Orange Juice (optional).

6. Add a handful of ice cubes and blend again for a chilled beverage.

7. Pour the juice into a glass and savor this heart-healthy drink's natural sweetness and nutritional benefits!

Nutritional Value (Per Serving):

Calories: 130 Protein: 2g Fat: 0.5g Salt: 50mg

Chocolate Protein Smoothie

Total Servings: 1 serving
Preparation Time: 5 minutes
Time to Cook: N/A (No cooking required)

Ingredients:

- 1 ripe banana
- 1 cup unsweetened almond milk
- 1 tablespoon unsweetened cocoa powder
- 1 tablespoon almond butter or peanut butter
- 1 scoop of chocolate protein powder
- 1/2 teaspoon vanilla extract
- Ice cubes (optional)

Instructions:

1. Peel the ripe banana and break it into smaller pieces.

2. Combine the banana, unsweetened almond milk, unsweetened cocoa powder, almond butter or peanut butter, chocolate protein powder, and vanilla extract in a blender.

3. Blend the ingredients until smooth and creamy. Add a few ice cubes and blend again for a chilled smoothie if desired.

4. Pour the Chocolate Protein Smoothie into a glass or a portable container.

5. Enjoy this delicious and protein-packed smoothie as a satisfying snack or post-workout drink!

Nutritional Value (Per Serving):

Calories: 300 Protein: 25g Fat: 10g Salt: 200mg

Green Apple Zest Juice

Total Servings: 1 serving
Preparation Time: 10 minutes

Time to Cook: N/A (No cooking required)

Ingredients:

- 2 green apples, cored and chopped
- 1 stalk celery, chopped
- 1/2 cucumber, chopped
- 1/2 lemon, juiced
- 1 handful of spinach or kale leaves
- Fresh mint leaves (optional)
- Ice cubes (optional)

Instructions:

1. Core and chop the green apples, ensuring to remove any seeds.

2. Chop the celery and cucumber into smaller pieces.

3. Combine the chopped green apples, celery, cucumber, freshly squeezed lemon juice, and spinach or kale leaves in a juicer or blender.

4. Juice or blend the ingredients until well combined and smooth. Using a blender, strain the mixture through a fine-mesh sieve to remove any pulp or fiber.

5. Add a few fresh mint leaves for freshness and flavor (optional).

6. Add a handful of ice cubes and blend again for a chilled beverage.

7. Pour the Green Apple Zest Juice into a glass and enjoy this heart-healthy drink's refreshing and nutritious qualities!

Nutritional Value (Per Serving):

Calories: 120 Protein: 2g Fat: 0.5g Salt: 50mg

Creamy Coconut Smoothie

Total Servings: 1 serving
Preparation Time: 5 minutes
Time to Cook: N/A (No cooking required)

Ingredients:

- 1 ripe banana
- 1/2 cup coconut milk
- 1/2 cup unsweetened almond milk
- 1 tablespoon unsweetened shredded coconut
- 1 tablespoon chia seeds
- 1/2 teaspoon vanilla extract
- Ice cubes (optional)

Instructions:

1. Peel the ripe banana and break it into smaller pieces.

2. Combine the banana, coconut milk, unsweetened almond milk, unsweetened shredded coconut, chia seeds, and vanilla extract in a blender.

3. Blend the ingredients until smooth and creamy. Add a few ice cubes and blend again for a chilled smoothie if desired.

4. Pour the Creamy Coconut Smoothie into a glass or a portable container.

5. Enjoy this refreshing and creamy smoothie as a nutritious breakfast or snack!

Nutritional Value (Per Serving):

Calories: 280 Protein: 4g Fat: 18g Salt: 40mg

Pineapple Ginger Juice

Total Servings: 1 serving
Preparation Time: 10 minutes
Time to Cook: N/A (No cooking required)

Ingredients:

- 1 cup fresh pineapple chunks
- 1-inch piece of fresh ginger, peeled
- 1/2 lemon, juiced
- 1/2 teaspoon honey or agave syrup (optional)
- Ice cubes (optional)

Instructions:

1. Cut the fresh pineapple into chunks, removing the skin and core.

2. Peel the fresh ginger using a vegetable peeler or the edge of a spoon.

3. In a juicer or blender, combine the pineapple chunks, peeled ginger, freshly squeezed lemon juice, and honey or agave syrup (optional).

4. Juice or blend the ingredients until well combined and smooth. Using a blender, strain the mixture through a fine-mesh sieve to remove any pulp or fiber.

5. Add a handful of ice cubes and blend again for a chilled beverage.

6. Pour the Pineapple Ginger Juice into a glass and savor this refreshing drink's tropical flavors and health benefits!

Nutritional Value (Per Serving):

Calories: 90 Protein: 1g Fat: 0g Salt: 5mg

Mixed Berry Medley Smoothie

Total Servings: 1 serving
Preparation Time: 5 minutes
Time to Cook: N/A (No cooking required)

Ingredients:

- 1 cup mixed berries (strawberries, blueberries, raspberries)
- 1/2 ripe banana
- 1/2 cup plain Greek yogurt
- 1/2 cup unsweetened almond milk
- 1 tablespoon honey or maple syrup (optional)
- Ice cubes (optional)

Instructions:

1. Wash the mixed berries and remove any stems or leaves.

2. Peel the ripe banana and break it into smaller pieces.

3. In a blender, combine the mixed berries, banana, plain Greek yogurt, unsweetened almond milk, and honey or maple syrup (if desired).

4. Blend the ingredients until smooth and creamy. Add a few ice cubes and blend again if you prefer a thicker consistency.

5. Pour the Mixed Berry Medley Smoothie into a glass or a portable container.

6. Enjoy this vibrant and antioxidant-rich smoothie as a nutritious breakfast or snack!

Nutritional Value (Per Serving):

Calories: 200 Protein: 12g Fat: 4g Salt: 100mg

Cucumber Mint Juice

Total Servings: 1 serving
Preparation Time: 10 minutes
Time to Cook: N/A (No cooking required)

Ingredients:

- 1 medium cucumber
- Handful of fresh mint leaves
- 1/2 lime, juiced
- 1/2 teaspoon honey or agave syrup (optional)
- Ice cubes (optional)

Instructions:

1. Wash the cucumber and mint leaves thoroughly.

2. Cut the cucumber into smaller pieces, leaving the skin intact if desired.

3. In a juicer or blender, combine the cucumber pieces, fresh mint leaves, freshly squeezed lime juice, and honey or agave syrup (if desired).

4. Juice or blend the ingredients until well combined and smooth. Using a blender, strain the mixture through a fine-mesh sieve to remove any pulp or fiber.

5. Add a handful of ice cubes and blend again for a chilled beverage.

6. Pour the Cucumber Mint Juice into a glass and enjoy this revitalizing drink's refreshing and hydrating flavors!

Nutritional Value (Per Serving):

Calories: 30 Protein: 1g Fat: 0g Salt: 5mg

PB&J Smoothie

Total Servings: 1 serving
Preparation Time: 5 minutes
Time to Cook: N/A (No cooking required)

Ingredients:

- 1 cup frozen mixed berries (strawberries, blueberries, raspberries)
- 1 ripe banana
- 2 tablespoons peanut butter (natural, unsweetened)
- 1 cup unsweetened almond milk (or any milk of your choice)
- 1 tablespoon chia seeds (optional)
- Ice cubes (optional)

Instructions:

1. In a blender, combine the frozen mixed berries, ripe banana, peanut butter, unsweetened almond milk, and chia seeds (if using).

2. Blend the ingredients until smooth and creamy. Add a few ice cubes and blend again if you prefer a thicker consistency.

3. Pour the PB&J Smoothie into a glass or a portable container.

4. Enjoy this delicious and satisfying smoothie that tastes like a classic PB&J sandwich but in liquid form!

Nutritional Value (Per Serving):

Calories: 350 Protein: 12g Fat: 16g Salt: 150mg

Refreshing Watermelon Juice

Total Servings: 1 serving
Preparation Time: 10 minutes

Ingredients:

- 2 cups fresh watermelon cubes
- 1/2 lime, juiced
- Handful of fresh mint leaves
- Ice cubes (optional)

Instructions:

1. Cut a fresh watermelon into cubes, removing any seeds or rind.

2. Combine the watermelon cubes, freshly squeezed lime juice, and fresh mint leaves in a blender or juicer.

3. Blend or juice the ingredients until well combined and smooth.

4. Add a handful of ice cubes and blend again for a chilled beverage.

5. Pour the Refreshing Watermelon Juice into a glass and savor this revitalizing drink's cooling and hydrating flavors!

Nutritional Value (Per Serving):

Calories: 80 Protein: 2g Fat: 0g Salt: 5mg

Tropical Green Smoothie

Total Servings: 1 serving
Preparation Time: 5 minutes
Time to Cook: N/A (No cooking required)

Ingredients:

- 1 cup fresh spinach leaves
- 1 ripe banana
- 1/2 cup pineapple chunks (fresh or frozen)
- 1/2 cup mango chunks (fresh or frozen)
- 1/2 cup coconut water
- 1 tablespoon chia seeds (optional)
- Ice cubes (optional)

Instructions:

1. In a blender, combine the fresh spinach leaves, ripe banana, pineapple chunks, mango chunks, coconut water, and chia seeds (if using).

2. Blend the ingredients until smooth and creamy. If you prefer a colder and thicker consistency, add a few ice cubes and blend again.

3. Pour the Tropical Green Smoothie into a glass or a portable container.

4. Sip on this refreshing and nutrient-packed smoothie to

start your day with a taste of the tropics!

Nutritional Value (Per Serving):

Calories: 250 Protein: 5g Fat: 3g Salt: 50mg

Carrot Ginger Detox Juice

Total Servings: 1 serving
Preparation Time: 10 minutes
Time to Cook: N/A (No cooking required)

Ingredients:

- 3 medium carrots
- 1 small apple
- 1/2-inch piece of fresh ginger
- 1/2 lemon, juiced
- 1 cup filtered water
- Ice cubes (optional)

Instructions:

1. Wash and peel the carrots, apple, and ginger. Cut them into small pieces for easier blending or juicing.

2. Add the carrot pieces, apple pieces, fresh ginger, lemon juice, and filtered water in a blender or juicer.

3. Blend or juice the ingredients until smooth and well combined.

4. Add a few ice cubes and blend or stir again for chilled juice.

5. Pour the Carrot Ginger Detox Juice into a glass and enjoy this cleansing drink's refreshing flavors and health benefits!

Nutritional Value (Per Serving):

Calories: 120 Protein: 2g Fat: 0g Salt: 20mg

Chapter 12: Snakes

Crunchy Veggie Sticks

Total servings: 1 serving.
Preparation time: 10 minutes
Time to cook: 0 minutes

Ingredients:

- 1 carrot
- 1 cucumber
- 1 bell pepper (any color)
- 2 celery stalks

Instructions:

1. Wash all the vegetables thoroughly under cold running water.

2. Peel the carrot and trim off the ends. Cut it into long, thin sticks.

3. Cut the cucumber into sticks of similar size as the carrot.

4. Remove the seeds from the bell pepper and cut them into strips.

5. Trim the ends of the celery stalks and cut them into sticks.

6. Arrange the vegetable sticks on a serving plate or tray.

Nutritional value (1 serving):

Calories: 60 Protein: 2g Fat: 0g Salt: 100mg

Greek Yogurt Dip

Total servings: 1 serving.
Preparation time: 5 minutes
Time to cook: 0 minutes

Ingredients:

- 1/2 cup plain Greek yogurt (low-fat or non-fat)
- 1 tablespoon fresh dill, finely chopped
- 1/2 tablespoon fresh lemon juice
- 1/4 teaspoon garlic powder
- Salt and pepper to taste

Instructions:

1. In a small bowl, combine the Greek yogurt, fresh dill, lemon juice, garlic powder, salt, and pepper.

2. Mix well until all the ingredients are evenly incorporated.

3. Taste the dip and adjust the seasonings according to your preference. You can add more salt, pepper, or lemon juice as desired.

4. Once the flavors are well combined, transfer the dip to a serving bowl.

Nutritional value (1 serving):

Calories: 60 Protein: 10g Fat: 0.5g Salt: 120mg

Baked Sweet Potato Fries

Total servings: 1 serving.
Preparation time: 10 minutes.
Time to cook: 25 minutes.

Ingredients:

- 1 medium sweet potato
- 1 tablespoon olive oil
- 1/2 teaspoon paprika
- 1/4 teaspoon garlic powder
- 1/4 teaspoon sea salt
- Freshly ground black pepper to taste

Instructions:

1. Preheat the oven to 425°F (220°C).

2. Wash the sweet potato thoroughly and peel if desired.

3. Cut the sweet potato into thin, even strips resembling fries.

4. Combine the olive oil, paprika, garlic powder, sea salt, and black pepper in a bowl.

5. Add the sweet potato fries to the bowl and toss them gently to coat them evenly with the seasoning mixture.

6. Place the seasoned sweet potato fries on a baking sheet lined with parchment paper, ensuring they are arranged in a single layer without overcrowding.

7. Bake in the oven for approximately 20-25 minutes or until the fries are golden brown and crispy. Flip them once halfway through the cooking time to ensure even browning.

8. Once the fries are cooked, remove them from the oven and let them cool for a few minutes before serving.

Nutritional value (1 serving):

Calories: 180 Protein: 2g Fat: 7g Salt: 230mg

Roasted Chickpeas

Total servings: 1 serving.
Preparation time: 5 minutes.
Time to cook: 30 minutes.

Ingredients:

- 1 cup cooked chickpeas (garbanzo beans)
- 1 tablespoon olive oil
- 1/2 teaspoon ground cumin
- 1/2 teaspoon paprika
- 1/4 teaspoon garlic powder
- 1/4 teaspoon sea salt
- Freshly ground black pepper to taste

Instructions:

1. Preheat the oven to 400°F (200°C).

2. Rinse and drain the cooked chickpeas, then pat them dry with a clean kitchen towel.

3. Combine the olive oil, ground cumin, paprika, garlic powder, sea salt, and black pepper in a bowl.

4. Add the chickpeas to the bowl and toss them gently to coat them evenly with the seasoning mixture.

5. Place the seasoned chickpeas on a baking sheet lined with parchment paper, spreading them out in a single layer.

6. Roast in the oven for approximately 25-30 minutes or until the chickpeas become golden brown and crispy. Shake the baking sheet gently or stir the chickpeas halfway through the cooking time for even browning.

7. Once roasted, remove the chickpeas from the oven and let them cool for a few minutes before serving.

Nutritional value (1 serving):

Calories: 180 Protein: 6g Fat: 7g Salt: 240mg

Fruit Kabobs

Total servings: 1 serving.
Preparation time: 15 minutes.
Time to cook: None (no cooking required).

Ingredients:

- 1 cup assorted fresh fruits (such as strawberries, pineapple chunks, grapes, and melon)
- Wooden skewers

Instructions:

1. Wash and prepare the fresh fruits. Hull the strawberries, peel and chop the pineapple into chunks, and cut the melon into bite-sized pieces.

2. Thread the fruits onto wooden skewers in a desired pattern, alternating the different fruits.

3. Repeat the process until all the fruits are used or until you reach your desired number of kabobs.

4. Serve the fruit kabobs immediately or refrigerate until ready to serve.

Nutritional value (1 serving):

Calories: 100 Protein: 1g Fat: 0g Salt: 0mg

Almond Energy Bites

Total servings: 12 servings.
Preparation time: 15 minutes.
Time to cook: None (no cooking required).

Ingredients:

- 1 cup rolled oats
- 1/2 cup almond butter
- 1/4 cup honey or maple syrup
- 1/4 cup chopped almonds
- 2 tablespoons chia seeds
- 1/4 teaspoon vanilla extract
- Pinch of sea salt

Instructions:

1. Combine the rolled oats, almond butter, honey or maple syrup, chopped almonds, chia seeds, vanilla extract, and sea salt in a large mixing bowl.

2. Stir all the ingredients together until well combined. The mixture should hold together when squeezed.

3. Add a tablespoon of water or more almond butter to achieve the desired consistency if the mixture seems too dry.

4. Once the mixture is ready, roll small portions into bite-sized balls using your hands.

5. Place the energy bites on a baking sheet lined with parchment paper and refrigerate for at least 30 minutes to allow them to firm up.

6. Once chilled, the almond energy bites are ready to be enjoyed. Store any leftovers in an airtight container in the refrigerator for up to a week.

Nutritional value (1 serving - 2 energy bites):

Calories: 160 Protein: 5g Fat: 9g Salt: 50mg

Guacamole Stuffed Cucumbers

Total servings: 1 serving.
Preparation time: 15 minutes.

Time to cook: None (no cooking required).

Ingredients:

- 1 small cucumber
- 1 ripe avocado
- 1/4 small red onion, finely diced
- 1 small tomato, diced
- 1 tablespoon freshly squeezed lime juice
- 1 tablespoon chopped fresh cilantro
- Salt and pepper to taste

Instructions:

1. Cut the cucumber into halves lengthwise. Scoop out the seeds using a spoon, creating a hollow space for the guacamole filling.

2. In a bowl, mash the avocado until creamy.

3. Add the finely diced red onion, diced tomato, lime juice, chopped cilantro, salt, and pepper to the mashed avocado. Stir well to combine.

4. Taste the guacamole and adjust the seasonings if needed.

5. Spoon the guacamole mixture into the hollowed-out cucumber halves, pressing it down gently.

6. Serve the guacamole stuffed cucumbers immediately, or refrigerate until ready to serve.

Nutritional value (1 serving):

Calories: 210 Protein: 4g Fat: 17g Salt: 120mg

Quinoa Trail Mix

Total servings: 4 servings.
Preparation time: 10 minutes.
Time to cook: 15 minutes.

Ingredients:

- 1 cup cooked quinoa
- 1/4 cup unsalted almonds, chopped
- 1/4 cup unsalted cashews, chopped
- 1/4 cup dried cranberries
- 2 tablespoons pumpkin seeds
- 2 tablespoons unsweetened shredded coconut
- 1 tablespoon honey or maple syrup
- 1/4 teaspoon ground cinnamon
- Pinch of sea salt

Instructions:

1. Combine the cooked quinoa, chopped almonds, chopped

cashews, dried cranberries, pumpkin seeds, shredded coconut, honey or maple syrup, ground cinnamon, and sea salt in a large bowl.

2. Mix all the ingredients until well combined and evenly coated.

3. Taste the trail mix and adjust the sweetness or seasoning if desired.

4. Transfer the quinoa trail mix to an airtight container or individual snack-sized bags for easy portioning.

5. The trail mix can be enjoyed immediately or stored in a cool, dry place for up to two weeks.

Nutritional value (1 serving - 1/4 of the recipe):

Calories: 220 Protein: 8g Fat: 12g Salt: 50mg

Caprese Skewers

Total servings: 1 serving.
Preparation time: 10 minutes.
Time to cook: None (no cooking required).

Ingredients:

- 4 cherry tomatoes
- 4 small fresh mozzarella balls
- 4 fresh basil leaves
- Balsamic glaze for drizzling
- Salt and pepper to taste
- Wooden skewers

Instructions:

1. Wash and dry the cherry tomatoes and basil leaves.

2. Thread a cherry tomato onto the wooden skewer, then a fresh basil leaf and mozzarella ball.

3. Repeat the process until all the ingredients are used or until you reach your desired number of skewers.

4. Sprinkle the skewers with salt and pepper to taste.

5. Drizzle the Caprese skewers with balsamic glaze just before serving.

6. Serve the caprese skewers immediately or refrigerate until ready to serve.

Nutritional value (1 serving):

Calories: 120 Protein: 8g Fat: 8g Salt: 160mg

Apple Slices with Nut Butter

Total servings: 1 serving.
Preparation time: 5 minutes.
Time to cook: None (no cooking required).

Ingredients:

- 1 medium apple (such as Granny Smith or Gala)
- 1 tablespoon of nut butter of your choice (such as almond butter or peanut butter)
- Optional toppings: sliced almonds, chia seeds, or cinnamon

Instructions:

1. Wash the apple thoroughly and dry it with a clean kitchen towel.

2. Core the apple and cut it into thin slices.

3. Spread the nut butter of your choice evenly on each apple slice.

4. Sprinkle optional toppings such as sliced almonds, chia seeds, or cinnamon over the nut butter if desired.

5. Arrange the apple slices on a serving plate.

6. Serve the apple slices with nut butter immediately or refrigerate until served.

Nutritional value (1 serving):

Calories: 180 Protein: 4g Fat: 8g Salt: 70mg

Mediterranean Hummus Plate

Total servings: 1 serving.
Preparation time: 10 minutes.
Time to cook: None (no cooking required).

Ingredients:

- 1/4 cup hummus (store-bought or homemade)
- 1/4 cup cherry tomatoes, halved
- 1/4 cup cucumber slices
- 1/4 cup Kalamata olives
- 1/4 cup feta cheese, crumbled
- Fresh parsley leaves for garnish
- Whole wheat pita bread or whole grain crackers for serving

Instructions:

1. Arrange a small plate or serving dish.

2. Spread the hummus evenly on the scale, creating a base for the other ingredients.

3. Place the cherry tomato halves, cucumber slices, and Kalamata olives on the hummus.

4. Sprinkle crumbled feta cheese over the vegetables.

5. Garnish the Mediterranean hummus plate with fresh parsley leaves.

6. Serve the hummus plate with whole wheat pita bread or

whole grain crackers.

Nutritional value (1 serving):

Calories: 250 Protein: 10g Fat: 15g Salt: 700mg

Greek Yogurt Parfait

Total servings: 1 serving.
Preparation time: 5 minutes.
Time to cook: None (no cooking required).

Ingredients:

- 1/2 cup Greek yogurt (plain or flavored)
- 1/4 cup granola
- 1/4 cup mixed berries (such as strawberries, blueberries, or raspberries)
- 1 tablespoon honey or maple syrup (optional)
- Fresh mint leaves for garnish (optional)

Instructions:

1. Choose a glass or bowl for serving the parfait.

2. Start by layering half of the Greek yogurt at the bottom of the glass.

3. Sprinkle half of the granola over the yogurt layer.

4. Add half of the mixed berries on top of the granola.

5. Repeat the layering process with the remaining Greek yogurt, granola, and mixed berries.

6. Drizzle honey or maple syrup over the top if desired.

7. Garnish the Greek yogurt parfait with fresh mint leaves.

8. Serve the parfait immediately or refrigerate until ready to serve.

Nutritional value (1 serving):

Calories: 250 Protein: 15g Fat: 7g Salt: 60mg

Roasted Edamame

Total servings: 1 serving.
Preparation time: 5 minutes.
Time to cook: 15 minutes.

Ingredients:

- 1 cup frozen edamame, thawed
- 1 teaspoon olive oil
- 1/2 teaspoon garlic powder
- 1/4 teaspoon sea salt
- Optional seasoning: chili powder or paprika for added flavor

Instructions:

1. Preheat the oven to 400°F (200°C) and line a baking sheet with parchment paper.

2. In a bowl, toss the thawed edamame with olive oil, garlic powder, sea salt, and any optional seasoning you choose. Mix well to coat the edamame evenly.

3. Spread the seasoned edamame in a single layer on the prepared baking sheet.

4. Roast in the oven for 15 minutes or until the edamame turns slightly golden and crispy.

5. Remove from the oven and let it cool slightly before serving.

6. Serve the roasted edamame as a snack or a side dish.

Nutritional value (1 serving):

Calories: 160 Protein: 16g Fat: 6g Salt: 240mg

Avocado Toast Bites

Total servings: 1 serving.
Preparation time: 5 minutes.
Time to cook: None (no cooking required).

Ingredients:

- 1 small ripe avocado
- 2 slices whole wheat bread
- Lemon juice (from half a lemon)
- Salt and pepper to taste
- Optional toppings: cherry tomatoes, sliced cucumbers, microgreens, or red pepper flakes

Instructions:

1. Cut the avocado, remove the pit, and scoop the flesh into a bowl.

2. Mash the avocado with a fork until smooth, adding a squeeze of lemon juice to prevent browning.

3. Toast the slices of whole wheat bread until golden and crisp.

4. Spread the mashed avocado evenly on the toasted bread slices.

5. Season with salt and pepper to taste.

6. Cut the avocado toast into bite-sized squares or rectangles.

7. If desired, top with optional toppings such as cherry tomatoes, sliced cucumbers, microgreens, or a sprinkle of red pepper flakes.

8. Serve the avocado toast bites as a nutritious snack or a light meal.

Nutritional value (1 serving):

Calories: 250 Protein: 8g Fat: 12g Salt: 400mg

Veggie Spring Rolls

Total servings: 1 serving.
Preparation time: 20 minutes.
Time to cook: None (no cooking required).

Ingredients:

- 2 rice paper wrappers
- 1/4 cup shredded carrots
- 1/4 cup thinly sliced cucumber
- 1/4 cup thinly sliced bell peppers
- 1/4 cup julienned lettuce
- 2 tablespoons chopped fresh cilantro
- 2 tablespoons chopped fresh mint
- 2 tablespoons low-sodium soy sauce or tamari for dipping

Instructions:

1. Fill a shallow dish with warm water.

2. Dip one rice paper wrapper into the warm water for 10-15 seconds until it becomes soft and pliable.

3. Place the softened rice paper wrapper on a clean or damp kitchen towel.

4. Arrange half of the shredded carrots, cucumber slices, bell peppers, lettuce, cilantro, and mint in a horizontal line on the lower third of the rice paper wrapper.

5. Fold the bottom edge of the rice paper wrapper over the filling, then fold the sides inward and roll tightly to form a spring roll.

6. Repeat steps 2-5 with the second rice paper wrapper and the remaining ingredients.

7. Slice the veggie spring rolls in half diagonally.

8. Serve the veggie spring rolls with low-sodium soy sauce or tamari for dipping.

Nutritional value (1 serving):

Calories: 180 Protein: 4g Fat: 1g Salt: 800mg

Nutty Granola Bars

Total servings: 6 bars.
Preparation time: 15 minutes.
Time to cook: 25 minutes.

Ingredients:

- 1 cup of old-fashioned oats
- 1/2 cup mixed nuts (such as almonds, walnuts, and cashews), chopped
- 1/4 cup unsweetened shredded coconut

- 1/4 cup honey or maple syrup

- 2 tablespoons almond butter or peanut butter

- 1/2 teaspoon vanilla extract

- Pinch of salt

Instructions:

1. Preheat the oven to 325°F (165°C) and line a baking dish with parchment paper.

2. Combine the oats, mixed nuts, shredded coconut, honey or maple syrup, almond butter or peanut butter, vanilla extract, and a pinch of salt in a large bowl. Mix well to combine.

3. Transfer the mixture to the prepared baking dish and press it firmly to create an even layer.

4. Bake in the oven for about 20-25 minutes or until golden brown.

5. Remove from the oven and let it cool completely before cutting into bars.

6. Once cooled, slice the mixture into 6 bars.

7. Store the nutty granola bars in an airtight container for up to one week.

Nutritional value (1 serving - 1 bar):

Calories: 200 Protein: 5g Fat: 12g Salt: 30mg

Beet Chips

Total servings: 1 serving.
Preparation time: 10 minutes.
Time to cook: 25-30 minutes.

Ingredients:

- 1 medium-sized beet

- 1 teaspoon olive oil

- Salt and pepper to taste

- Optional seasoning: garlic powder or paprika for added flavor

Instructions:

1. Preheat the oven to 325°F (165°C) and line a baking sheet with parchment paper.

2. Peel the beet and thinly slice it into rounds using a mandoline slicer or a sharp knife.

3. In a bowl, toss the beet slices with olive oil, salt, pepper, and any optional seasoning you choose. Mix well to coat the beet slices evenly.

4. Arrange the seasoned beet slices on the prepared baking sheet in a single layer.

5. Bake in the oven for 25-30 minutes or until the beet chips become crispy and slightly curled at the edges.

6. Remove from the oven and let them cool completely

before serving.

7. Serve the beet chips as a healthy and colorful snack.

Nutritional value (1 serving):

Calories: 100 Protein: 2g Fat: 5g Salt: 150mg

Smoked Salmon Cucumber Roll-Ups

Total servings: 1 serving.
Preparation time: 10 minutes.
Time to cook: None (no cooking required).

Ingredients:

- 4 cucumber slices (about 1/4 inch thick)

- 2 ounces of smoked salmon

- 2 tablespoons cream cheese (low-fat or Greek yogurt-based for a healthier option)

- Fresh dill or chives for garnish

Instructions:

1. Place the cucumber slices on a clean surface or a serving plate.

2. Spread a thin layer of cream cheese onto each cucumber slice.

3. Place a small piece of smoked salmon on top of the cream cheese on each cucumber slice.

4. Roll up the cucumber slices tightly, starting from one end.

5. Secure the roll-ups with toothpicks if necessary.

6. Garnish the smoked salmon cucumber roll-ups with fresh dill or chives.

7. Serve the roll-ups as a light and flavorful appetizer or snack.

Nutritional value (1 serving):

Calories: 150 Protein: 12g Fat: 8g Salt: 400mg

Berry Yogurt Bark

Total servings: 1 serving.
Preparation time: 10 minutes.
Time to freeze: 3 hours.

Ingredients:

- 1/2 cup Greek yogurt (low-fat or non-fat)

- 1 tablespoon honey or maple syrup

- 1/4 cup mixed berries (such as strawberries, blueberries, and raspberries), chopped

- 1 tablespoon unsweetened shredded coconut

- 1 tablespoon chopped almonds or walnuts

Instructions:

1. Mix the Greek yogurt and honey or maple syrup in a bowl until well combined.

2. Line a baking sheet with parchment paper.

3. Pour the Greek yogurt mixture onto the prepared baking sheet and spread it evenly to form a thin layer.

4. Sprinkle the chopped mixed berries, shredded coconut, and chopped almonds or walnuts over the yogurt layer.

5. Place the baking sheet in the freezer for about 3 hours or until the yogurt bark is completely frozen.

6. Once frozen, remove the yogurt bark from the freezer and break it into small pieces.

7. Serve the berry yogurt bark as a refreshing and nutritious dessert or snack.

Nutritional value (1 serving):

Calories: 180 Protein: 12g Fat: 6g Salt: 50mg

Sweet and Spicy Nuts

Total servings: 1 serving.
Preparation time: 5 minutes.
Time to cook: 10 minutes.

Ingredients:

- 1/2 cup mixed nuts (such as almonds, cashews, and pecans)
- 1 tablespoon honey
- 1/2 teaspoon ground cinnamon
- 1/4 teaspoon cayenne pepper (adjust to taste)
- Pinch of salt

Instructions:

1. Preheat the oven to 350°F (175°C) and line a baking sheet with parchment paper.

2. Combine the mixed nuts, honey, ground cinnamon, cayenne pepper, and a pinch of salt in a bowl. Mix well to coat the nuts evenly.

3. Spread the coated nuts in a single layer on the prepared baking sheet.

4. Bake in the oven for about 10 minutes, stirring once halfway through, until the nuts are golden and fragrant.

5. Remove from the oven and let them cool completely before serving.

6. Serve the sweet and spicy nuts as a tasty and satisfying snack.

Nutritional value (1 serving):

Calories: 200 Protein: 6g Fat: 15g Salt: 100mg

Chapter 13: Desserts

Berry Chia Pudding

Total servings: 1 serving.
Preparation time: 5 minutes.
Time to set: 4 hours or overnight.

Ingredients:

- 2 tablespoons chia seeds
- 1/2 cup unsweetened almond milk or any other plant-based milk
- 1/2 teaspoon vanilla extract
- 1 tablespoon honey or maple syrup
- 1/4 cup mixed berries (such as strawberries, blueberries, and raspberries)
- Optional toppings: additional berries, sliced almonds, or shredded coconut

Instructions:

1. Combine the chia seeds, almond milk, vanilla extract, and honey or maple syrup in a bowl. Mix well to ensure the chia seeds are evenly distributed.

2. Let the mixture sit for 5 minutes, and then give it another stir to prevent clumping.

3. Cover the bowl and refrigerate for at least 4 hours or overnight to allow the chia seeds to absorb the liquid and form a pudding-like consistency.

4. Once the chia pudding has been set, please stir it to break up any clumps.

5. Layer the mixed berries in a glass or jar, alternating with spoonfuls of the chia pudding.

6. Top with additional berries, sliced almonds, or shredded coconut if desired.

7. Enjoy the berry chia pudding as a healthy and filling breakfast or snack.

Nutritional value (1 serving):

Calories: 200 Protein: 7g Fat: 9g Salt: 50mg

Dark Chocolate Bites

Total servings: 1 serving.
Preparation time: 10 minutes.
Time to set: 1 hour.

Ingredients:

- 1 ounce dark chocolate (at least 70% cocoa), chopped
- 1 tablespoon unsalted almonds, chopped
- 1 tablespoon unsweetened dried cranberries or goji berries
- Pinch of sea salt

Instructions:

1. Line a small plate or baking sheet with parchment paper.

2. In a microwave-safe bowl, melt the dark chocolate in 30-second intervals, stirring in between, until smooth and fully softened. Alternatively, melt the chocolate using a double boiler.

3. Pour the melted chocolate onto the prepared plate or baking sheet and spread it to form a thin layer.

4. Sprinkle the chopped almonds, dried cranberries or goji berries, and a pinch of sea salt evenly over the melted chocolate.

5. Place the plate or baking sheet in the refrigerator for about 1 hour or until the chocolate has hardened.

6. Once the chocolate is firm, break it into bite-sized pieces.

7. Serve the dark chocolate bites as a satisfying and indulgent treat.

Nutritional value (1 serving):

Calories: 150 Protein: 3g Fat: 10g Salt: 50mg

Frozen Yogurt Bark

Total servings: 1 serving.
Preparation time: 5 minutes.
Time to freeze: 4 hours or overnight.

Ingredients:

- 1/2 cup Greek yogurt (low-fat or non-fat)
- 1 tablespoon honey or maple syrup
- 1/4 cup mixed berries (such as strawberries, blueberries, and raspberries)
- 1 tablespoon unsweetened shredded coconut
- 1 tablespoon chopped almonds or walnuts

Instructions:

1. Mix the Greek yogurt and honey or maple syrup in a bowl until well combined.

2. Line a baking sheet with parchment paper.

3. Pour the Greek yogurt mixture onto the prepared baking sheet and spread it evenly to form a thin layer.

4. Sprinkle the mixed berries, shredded coconut, and chopped almonds or walnuts over the yogurt layer.

5. Place the baking sheet in the freezer for about 4 hours or overnight until the yogurt bark is completely frozen.

6. Once frozen, remove the yogurt bark from the freezer and break it into small pieces.

7. Serve the frozen yogurt bark as a refreshing and nutritious dessert or snack.

Nutritional value (1 serving):

Calories: 160 Protein: 10g Fat: 6g Salt: 50mg

Almond Butter Cookies

Total servings: 1 serving.
Preparation time: 10 minutes.
Time to bake: 10–12 minutes.

Ingredients:

- 1/4 cup almond flour
- 1 tablespoon almond butter (unsweetened and unsalted)
- 1 tablespoon honey or maple syrup
- 1/4 teaspoon vanilla extract
- Pinch of salt

Instructions:

1. Preheat the oven to 350°F (175°C) and line a baking sheet with parchment paper.

2. Combine the almond flour, almond butter, honey or maple syrup, vanilla extract, and a pinch of salt in a bowl. Mix well until a dough forms.

3. Roll the dough into small balls about 1 inch in diameter, and place them on the prepared baking sheet.

4. Use a fork to press down on each ball, creating a crisscross pattern on top of the cookies.

5. Bake in the oven for 10-12 minutes or until the cookies are lightly golden around the edges.

6. Remove from the oven and let them cool completely on a wire rack before serving.

7. Enjoy the almond butter cookies as a delicious and nutritious treat.

Nutritional value (1 serving):

Calories: 180 Protein: 6g Fat: 12g Salt: 100mg

Fruit Salad Parfait

Total servings: 1 serving.
Preparation time: 10 minutes.

Ingredients:

- 1 cup mixed fresh fruits (such as berries, sliced bananas, chopped mangoes, and diced melons)
- 1/4 cup Greek yogurt (low-fat or non-fat)
- 1 tablespoon honey or maple syrup
- 2 tablespoons granola or chopped nuts for topping

Instructions:

1. Wash and prepare the fresh fruits by cutting them into bite-sized pieces.

2. In a glass or bowl, layer half of the mixed fruits.

3. Mix the Greek yogurt and honey or maple syrup in a separate bowl until well combined.

4. Spoon half the yogurt mixture over the fruits in a glass or bowl.

5. Repeat the layering process with the remaining fruits and yogurt mixture.

6. Sprinkle granola or chopped nuts on top for added crunch and texture.

7. Serve the fruit salad parfait immediately as a nutritious, refreshing breakfast or snack.

Nutritional value (1 serving):

Calories: 200 Protein: 10g Fat: 3g Salt: 50mg

Banana Nice Cream

Total servings: 1 serving.
Preparation time: 5 minutes.
Time to freeze: 2–3 hours.

Ingredients:

- 1 large ripe banana, peeled and sliced
- 1/4 cup unsweetened almond milk or any other plant-based milk
- 1/2 teaspoon vanilla extract
- Optional toppings: sliced fresh fruits, chopped nuts, or shredded coconut

Instructions:

1. Place the sliced banana in a ziplock bag and freeze for 2-3 hours until firm.

2. Once the banana slices are frozen, transfer them to a blender or food processor.

3. Add the almond milk and vanilla extract to the blender or food processor.

4. Blend the mixture until smooth and creamy, scraping down the sides as needed.

5. Transfer the nice banana cream to a bowl.

6. If desired, top with sliced fresh fruits, chopped nuts, or shredded coconut for added flavor and texture.

7. Serve the nice banana cream immediately as a healthy, guilt-free dessert or snack.

Nutritional value (1 serving):

Calories: 150 Protein: 3g Fat: 2g Salt: 0mg

Coconut Energy Balls

Total servings: 8 energy balls.
Preparation time: 15 minutes.

Ingredients:

- 1 cup dates, pitted
- 1 cup unsweetened shredded coconut
- 1/2 cup almonds
- 2 tablespoons chia seeds
- 1 tablespoon coconut oil
- 1/2 teaspoon vanilla extract
- Pinch of salt
- Additional shredded coconut for rolling (optional)

Instructions:

1. Place the dates in a bowl and cover them with warm water. Let them soak for about 5 minutes to soften.

2. Add the soaked dates, shredded coconut, almonds, chia seeds, coconut oil, vanilla extract, and a pinch of salt in a food processor.

3. Process the mixture until well combined and the ingredients start to stick together.

4. Use your hands to take small portions of the mixture and roll them into balls.

5. Roll the energy balls in additional shredded coconut for added flavor and texture if desired.

6. Place the energy balls on a plate or baking sheet and refrigerate for 1 hour to firm up.

7. Serve the coconut energy balls as a healthy and energizing snack.

Nutritional value (1 serving, 1 energy ball):

Calories: 140 Protein: 2g Fat: 9g Salt: 10mg

Chocolate Avocado Mousse

Total servings: 1 serving.
Preparation time: 10 minutes.

Ingredients:

- 1 ripe avocado, pitted and peeled
- 2 tablespoons unsweetened cocoa powder
- 2 tablespoons maple syrup or honey
- 1/4 teaspoon vanilla extract
- Pinch of salt
- Optional toppings: sliced strawberries, shredded coconut, or dark chocolate shavings

Instructions:

1. Add the avocado, cocoa powder, maple syrup or honey, vanilla extract, and a pinch of salt in a blender or food processor.

2. Blend the ingredients until smooth and creamy, scraping down the sides as needed.

3. Transfer the chocolate avocado mousse to a bowl.

4. Top the mousse with sliced strawberries, shredded coconut, or dark chocolate shavings for added flavor and presentation.

5. Serve the chocolate avocado mousse immediately as a rich and satisfying dessert.

Nutritional value (1 serving):

Calories: 230 Protein: 4g Fat: 15g Salt: 30mg

Greek Yogurt Popsicles

Total servings: 4 popsicles.
Preparation time: 5 minutes.
Time to freeze: 4-6 hours.

Ingredients:

- 1 cup Greek yogurt (low-fat or non-fat)
- 2 tablespoons honey or maple syrup
- 1/2 teaspoon vanilla extract
- 1 cup mixed fresh fruits (such as sliced strawberries, blueberries, and diced peaches)

Instructions:

1. Mix the Greek yogurt, honey or maple syrup, and vanilla extract in a bowl until well combined.

2. Prepare the popsicle molds or small paper cups.

3. Spoon a small amount of the yogurt mixture into each mold, filling them about one-third full.

4. Add a layer of mixed fresh fruits to each mold.

5. Repeat the layering process with the remaining yogurt mixture and fruits, filling the molds to the top.

6. Insert popsicle sticks into each mold.

7. Place the popsicles in the freezer and let them freeze for 4-6 hours or until firm.

8. Once frozen, remove the popsicles from the molds by running them under warm water for a few seconds.

9. Serve the Greek yogurt popsicles as a delicious and

refreshing treat.

Raspberry Sorbet Cups

Total servings: 2 cups.
Preparation time: 10 minutes.
Time to freeze: 4-6 hours.

Ingredients:

- 2 cups frozen raspberries
- 2 tablespoons honey or maple syrup
- 1 tablespoon lemon juice
- Fresh mint leaves for garnish (optional)

Instructions:

1. Combine the frozen raspberries, honey or maple syrup, and lemon juice in a blender or food processor.

2. Blend the mixture until smooth and creamy.

3. Transfer the raspberry sorbet mixture to small dessert cups.

4. Place the cups in the freezer and let them freeze for 4-6 hours or until firm.

5. Once frozen, remove the sorbet cups from the freezer and let them sit at room temperature for a few minutes to soften slightly.

6. Garnish with fresh mint leaves, if desired.

7. Serve the raspberry sorbet cups as a refreshing and naturally sweet dessert.

Nutritional value (1 serving, 1 cup):

Calories: 100 Protein: 2g Fat: 0.5g Salt: 0mg

Baked Apples with Cinnamon

Total servings: 1 serving.
Preparation time: 10 minutes.
Time to cook: 25-30 minutes.

Ingredients:

- 1 medium-sized apple
- 1 teaspoon cinnamon
- 1 teaspoon honey or maple syrup (optional)
- 1 tablespoon chopped nuts (such as walnuts or almonds)

- Greek yogurt or low-fat vanilla ice cream for serving (optional)

Instructions:

1. Preheat the oven to 350°F (175°C).

2. Wash the apple and slice it in half horizontally. Remove the core and seeds.

3. Place the apple halves on a baking sheet or in a small baking dish, cut side up.

4. Sprinkle the cinnamon evenly over the apple halves. If desired, drizzle with honey or maple syrup for added sweetness.

5. Bake the apples in the oven for 25-30 minutes or until tender.

6. Remove the baked apples from the oven and let them cool for a few minutes.

7. Sprinkle the chopped nuts over the apples for added crunch and texture.

8. Serve the baked apples warm, optionally accompanied by a dollop of Greek yogurt or a scoop of low-fat vanilla ice cream.

Nutritional value (1 serving):

Calories: 120 Protein: 2g Fat: 2g Salt: 0mg

Peanut Butter Banana Bites

Total servings: 1 serving.
Preparation time: 5 minutes.

Ingredients:

- 1 medium-sized banana
- 1 tablespoon natural peanut butter (unsweetened, with no added oils)
- 1 tablespoon unsalted peanuts, chopped

Instructions:

1. Peel the banana and slice it into bite-sized rounds.

2. Spread a thin layer of peanut butter onto each banana round.

3. Sprinkle the chopped peanuts over the peanut butter layer.

4. Serve the peanut butter banana bites immediately as a healthy and satisfying snack.

Nutritional value (1 serving):

Calories: 160 Protein: 4g Fat: 9g Salt: 0mg

Strawberry Shortcake Cups

Total servings: 1 serving.
Preparation time: 10 minutes.
Time to cook: 15 minutes.

Ingredients:

- 1 whole wheat pita bread
- 1 tablespoon unsalted butter, melted
- 1 teaspoon honey or maple syrup
- 1/2 cup sliced fresh strawberries
- 1/4 cup Greek yogurt (low-fat or non-fat)
- Fresh mint leaves for garnish (optional)

Instructions:

1. Preheat the oven to 350°F (175°C).

2. Cut the pita bread into small triangles or squares.

3. In a bowl, mix the melted butter and honey or maple syrup.

4. Brush the butter mixture onto both sides of each pita bread piece.

5. Place the pita bread pieces on a baking sheet and bake in the oven for about 15 minutes or until crispy and golden brown.

6. Remove the baked pita bread from the oven and let it cool.

7. Layer the sliced strawberries and Greek yogurt in a serving cup or bowl.

8. Break the baked pita bread into small pieces and sprinkle them over the strawberry and yogurt layers.

9. Garnish with fresh mint leaves, if desired.

10. Enjoy the strawberry shortcake cups as a delicious and heart-healthy dessert.

Nutritional value (1 serving):

Calories: 220 Protein: 7g Fat: 7g Salt: 160mg

Watermelon Fruit Pizza

Total servings: 1 serving.
Preparation time: 10 minutes.

Ingredients:

- 1 thick slice of watermelon (approximately 1 inch thick)
- 2 tablespoons Greek yogurt (low-fat or non-fat)
- Assorted fresh fruits (such as berries, sliced kiwi, and grapes)
- 1 tablespoon unsalted nuts (such as almonds or walnuts), chopped

Instructions:

1. Cut the watermelon slice into a circular shape to resemble a pizza crust.

2. Pat the watermelon slice dry with a paper towel to remove excess moisture.

3. Spread a thin layer of Greek yogurt evenly over the watermelon slice, leaving a small border around the edges.

4. Arrange the assorted fresh fruits on top of the yogurt layer.

5. Sprinkle the chopped nuts over the fruit toppings.

6. Slice the watermelon fruit pizza into smaller slices, similar to pizza slices.

7. Serve the watermelon fruit pizza immediately as a refreshing and nutritious dessert.

Nutritional value (1 serving):

Calories: 160 Protein: 7g Fat: 5g Salt: 30mg

Mixed Berry Crumble

Total servings: 1 serving.
Preparation time: 10 minutes.
Time to cook: 25-30 minutes.

Ingredients:

- 1/2 cup mixed berries (such as strawberries, blueberries, and raspberries)
- 1 tablespoon honey or maple syrup
- 2 tablespoons rolled oats
- 1 tablespoon almond flour
- 1 tablespoon unsalted nuts (such as walnuts or almonds), chopped
- 1/2 tablespoon unsalted butter, melted
- 1/4 teaspoon cinnamon

Instructions:

1. Preheat the oven to 350°F (175°C).

2. Mix the mixed berries with half of the honey or maple syrup in a small baking dish.

3. Combine the rolled oats, almond flour, chopped nuts, melted butter, remaining honey or maple syrup, and cinnamon in a separate bowl. Mix well until the ingredients are evenly incorporated.

4. Spread the oat mixture over the mixed berries in the baking dish, covering them completely.

5. Bake in the preheated oven for 25-30 minutes or until the topping is golden brown and the berries are bubbling.

6. Remove from the oven and let it cool for a few minutes.

7. Serve the mixed berry crumble warm as a delicious and heart-healthy dessert.

Mango Coconut Chia Pudding

Total servings: 1 serving.
Preparation time: 10 minutes
(plus overnight chilling time).

Ingredients:

- 1/4 cup chia seeds
- 3/4 cup unsweetened coconut milk
- 1/2 ripe mango, diced
- 1 tablespoon unsweetened shredded coconut
- Fresh mint leaves for garnish (optional)

Instructions:

1. In a jar or bowl, mix the chia seeds and coconut milk. Stir well to ensure the chia seeds are evenly distributed.

2. Cover the jar or bowl and refrigerate overnight or for at least 4 hours to allow the chia seeds to absorb the liquid and form a pudding-like consistency.

3. Before serving, give the chia pudding a good stir to break up any clumps.

4. Top the chia pudding with diced mango and sprinkle the shredded coconut.

5. Garnish with fresh mint leaves, if desired.

6. Enjoy the mango coconut chia pudding as a nutritious and satisfying breakfast or snack.

Frozen Grapes

Total servings: 1 serving.
Preparation time: 5 minutes.
Time to freeze: 2 hours or until solid.

Ingredients:

- 1 cup seedless grapes (red or green)

Instructions:

1. Wash the grapes under cold running water and pat them dry with a paper towel.

2. Place the grapes in a single layer on a baking sheet lined with parchment paper.

3. Place the baking sheet with the grapes in the freezer.

4. Freeze the grapes for at least 2 hours or until they are solid and firm.

5. Once frozen, transfer the grapes to an airtight container or a zip-top bag for storage in the freezer.

6. Enjoy the frozen grapes as a refreshing and healthy snack straight from the freezer.

Pistachio Date Balls

Total servings: 1 serving.
Preparation time: 15 minutes.
Time to set: 1 hour.

Ingredients:

- 6 Medjool dates, pitted
- 1/4 cup shelled pistachios
- 1 tablespoon unsweetened cocoa powder
- 1/2 teaspoon vanilla extract
- Pinch of salt

Instructions:

1. Place the pitted dates, shelled pistachios, cocoa powder, vanilla extract, and salt in a food processor.

2. Process the ingredients until they are well combined, forming a sticky dough-like consistency.

3. Scoop out small portions of the mixture and roll them into bite-sized balls using your hands.

4. Place the pistachio date balls on a plate or baking sheet lined with parchment paper.

5. Refrigerate the date balls for at least 1 hour or until firm.

6. Once set, the pistachio date balls are ready to enjoy as a nutritious, energy-boosting snack.

Pineapple Sorbet Cups

Total Servings: 4 servings.
Preparation Time: 10 minutes.
Time to Freeze: 4-6 hours.

Ingredients:

- 2 cups frozen pineapple chunks
- 1 ripe banana
- 1 tablespoon honey (optional)

- Fresh mint leaves for garnish (optional)

Instructions:

1. a. Place the frozen pineapple chunks, ripe banana, and honey (if desired) in a blender or food processor.

2. b. Blend the ingredients on high speed until smooth and creamy. Stop occasionally to scrape down the sides if needed.

3. c. Taste the mixture and adjust the sweetness by adding more honey if desired.

4. d. Once the sorbet mixture is smooth and well combined, transfer it to an airtight container and freeze for 4-6 hours or until firm.

5. e. Before serving, remove the sorbet from the freezer and let it sit at room temperature for a few minutes to soften slightly.

6. f. Scoop the pineapple sorbet into individual serving cups or bowls.

7. g. Garnish with fresh mint leaves if desired.

8. h. Serve immediately and enjoy!

Nutritional value (per serving):

Calories: 90 Protein: 1g Fat: 0g Sodium: 0mg

Lemon Poppy Seed Muffins

Total Servings: 12 muffins.
Preparation Time: 15 minutes.
Time to Bake: 20-25 minutes.

Ingredients:

- 2 cups whole wheat flour
- 1/2 cup granulated sugar
- 2 teaspoons baking powder
- 1/2 teaspoon baking soda
- 1/4 teaspoon salt
- Zest of 2 lemons
- 1/4 cup fresh lemon juice
- 1/2 cup unsweetened applesauce
- 1/4 cup olive oil
- 1/2 cup unsweetened almond milk (or any plant-based milk)
- 2 tablespoons poppy seeds

Instructions:

1. a. Preheat the oven to 375°F (190°C) and line a muffin tin with paper liners.

2. b. In a large mixing bowl, combine the whole wheat flour,

granulated sugar, baking powder, baking soda, salt, and lemon zest.

3. c. whisk together the fresh lemon juice, unsweetened applesauce, olive oil, and almond milk in a separate bowl.

4. d. Pour the wet ingredients into the dry ingredients and mix until combined. Be careful not to overmix; a few lumps are fine.

5. e. Gently fold in the poppy seeds.

6. f. Divide the batter equally among the prepared muffin cups, filling each about 2/3 full.

7. g. Bake in the preheated oven for 20-25 minutes or until a toothpick inserted into the center of a muffin comes out clean.

8. h. Remove the muffins from the oven and let them cool in the pan for a few minutes before transferring them to a wire rack to cool completely.

9. i. Once cooled, serve the lemon poppy seed muffins and enjoy!

Nutritional value (per serving - 1 muffin):

Calories: 160 Protein: 3g Fat: 5g Sodium: 150mg

Chocolate-Dipped Strawberries

Total Servings: 4 servings.
Preparation Time: 10 minutes.
Time to Cook: 0 minutes.

Ingredients:

- 8 large strawberries
- 2 ounces dark chocolate (at least 70% cocoa)
- 1 teaspoon coconut oil (optional)
- Assorted toppings: chopped nuts, shredded coconut, chia seeds, etc. (optional)

Instructions:

1. a. Rinse the strawberries under cold water and pat them dry with a paper towel.

2. b. In a microwave-safe bowl, break the dark chocolate into small pieces and add the coconut oil (if using).

3. c. Microwave the chocolate in 30-second intervals, stirring in between, until melted and smooth. Be careful not to overheat the chocolate.

4. d. Holding a strawberry by the stem, dip it into the melted chocolate, allowing any excess chocolate to drip off.

5. e. If desired, roll the chocolate-dipped strawberry in your preferred toppings while the chocolate is still wet.

6. f. Place the chocolate-dipped strawberries on a parchment-lined tray or plate and repeat the process with the remaining strawberries.

7. g. Once all the strawberries are dipped and decorated, transfer the tray or plate to the refrigerator to allow the chocolate to set, approximately 15-20 minutes.

8. h. Once the chocolate is firm, remove the strawberries from the refrigerator and serve immediately.

Nutritional value (per serving - 2 strawberries):

Calories: 100 Protein: 2g Fat: 6g Sodium: 0mg

Blueberry Oatmeal Cookies

Total Servings: 12 cookies.
Preparation Time: 15 minutes.
Time to Cook: 12-15 minutes.

Ingredients:

- 1 cup of old-fashioned oats
- 1 cup whole wheat flour
- 1/2 teaspoon baking soda
- 1/4 teaspoon salt
- 1/4 cup unsweetened applesauce
- 1/4 cup coconut oil, melted
- 1/4 cup honey or maple syrup
- 1 teaspoon vanilla extract
- 1/2 cup fresh or frozen blueberries

Instructions:

1. a. Preheat the oven to 350°F (175°C) and line a baking sheet with parchment paper.

2. b. In a large mixing bowl, combine the oats, whole wheat flour, baking soda, and salt.

3. c. whisk together the applesauce, melted coconut oil, honey or maple syrup, and vanilla extract in a separate bowl.

4. d. Pour the wet ingredients into the dry ingredients and stir until well combined.

5. e. Gently fold in the blueberries, being careful not to overmix.

6. f. Drop spoonfuls of the cookie dough onto the prepared baking sheet, spacing them a couple of inches apart.

7. g. Flatten each cookie slightly with the back of a spoon.

8. h. Bake in the oven for 12-15 minutes or until the edges are golden brown.

9. i. Remove the cookies from the oven and let them cool on the baking sheet for a few minutes before transferring them to a wire rack to cool completely.

10. j. Once cooled, serve the blueberry oatmeal cookies and enjoy!

Nutritional value (per serving - 1 cookie):

Calories: 100 Protein: 2g Fat: 4g Sodium: 75mg

Greek Yogurt Cheesecake Bites

Total Servings: 6 servings.
Preparation Time: 15 minutes.
Time to Cook: 0 minutes.

Ingredients:

- 1 cup plain Greek yogurt
- 4 ounces of reduced-fat cream cheese, softened
- 2 tablespoons honey or maple syrup
- 1 teaspoon vanilla extract
- Fresh berries or sliced fruit for topping (optional)

Instructions:

1. a. In a medium mixing bowl, combine the Greek yogurt, softened cream cheese, honey or maple syrup, and vanilla extract.

2. b. Use an electric mixer or whisk to blend the ingredients until smooth and well combined.

3. c. Spoon the mixture into small serving glasses or silicone molds, filling them about 3/4 full.

4. d. Smooth the tops of the cheesecake bites with a spatula.

5. e. top each cheesecake bite with fresh berries or sliced fruit if desired.

6. f. Place the cheesecake bites in the refrigerator and let them chill for at least 2 hours to firm up.

7. g. Once chilled, remove the cheesecake bites from the refrigerator and serve immediately.

Nutritional value (per serving - 1 cheesecake bite):

Calories: 100 Protein: 7g Fat: 5g Sodium: 80mg

Cinnamon Baked Pears

Total Servings: 4 servings.
Preparation Time: 10 minutes.
Time to Cook: 30-35 minutes.

Ingredients:

- 4 ripe pears
- 2 tablespoons honey or maple syrup
- 1 teaspoon ground cinnamon
- 1/4 teaspoon ground nutmeg

- 1/4 teaspoon vanilla extract
- 1/4 cup chopped walnuts (optional)

Instructions:

1. a. Preheat the oven to 375°F (190°C) and line a baking dish with parchment paper.

2. b. Cut each pear in half lengthwise and remove the core and seeds with a spoon.

3. c. Place the pear halves, cut side up, in the prepared baking dish.

4. d. Drizzle the honey or maple syrup evenly over the pear halves.

5. e. In a small bowl, combine the ground cinnamon, ground nutmeg, and vanilla extract.

6. f. Sprinkle the cinnamon mixture over the pears, ensuring they are evenly coated.

7. g. If desired, sprinkle the chopped walnuts over the pears for added crunch.

8. h. Bake in the oven for 30-35 minutes or until the pears are tender and caramelized.

9. i. Remove the baked pears from the oven and let them cool for a few minutes before serving.

10. j. Once cooled slightly, serve the cinnamon-baked pears and enjoy!

Nutritional value (per serving - 1 baked pear):

Calories: 120 Protein: 1g Fat: 0.5g Sodium: 0mg

Vanilla Protein Pancakes

Total Servings: 2 servings.
Preparation Time: 10 minutes.
Time to Cook: 10-15 minutes.

Ingredients:

- 1/2 cup whole wheat flour
- 1/2 cup oat flour (ground oats)
- 2 scoops vanilla protein powder
- 1 teaspoon baking powder
- 1/4 teaspoon salt
- 1 cup unsweetened almond milk (or any plant-based milk)
- 1 tablespoon honey or maple syrup
- 1 teaspoon vanilla extract
- Cooking spray or coconut oil for greasing the pan

Instructions:

1. a. In a large mixing bowl, combine the whole wheat flour, oat flour, protein powder, baking powder, and salt.

2. b. Whisk the almond milk, honey or maple syrup, and vanilla extract in a separate bowl.

3. c. Pour the wet ingredients into the dry ingredients and stir until combined. Be careful not to overmix; a few lumps are fine.

4. d. Let the batter rest for 5 minutes to allow the flour to hydrate.

5. e. Preheat a non-stick skillet or griddle over medium heat and lightly grease it with cooking spray or coconut oil.

6. f. Scoop 1/4 cup portions of the pancake batter onto the hot skillet, spreading it slightly to form circles.

7. g. Cook the pancakes for 2-3 minutes on one side until bubbles form on the surface, then flip and cook for another 2-3 minutes on the other side until golden brown.

8. h. Repeat the process with the remaining batter until all the pancakes are cooked.

9. i. Serve the vanilla protein pancakes warm with your favorite toppings, such as fresh berries, sliced bananas, or a drizzle of honey.

Nutritional value (per serving - 2 pancakes):

Calories: 250 Protein: 20g Fat: 4g Sodium: 300mg

Coconut Lime Popsicles

Total Servings: 6 popsicles.
Preparation Time: 10 minutes.
Time to Freeze: 4-6 hours.

Ingredients:

- 1 cup unsweetened coconut milk
- 1 cup plain Greek yogurt
- 1/4 cup honey or maple syrup
- Zest and juice of 2 limes
- 1/2 teaspoon vanilla extract
- Shredded coconut, for garnish (optional)

Instructions:

1. a. In a blender or food processor, combine the coconut milk, Greek yogurt, honey or maple syrup, lime zest, lime juice, and vanilla extract.

2. b. Blend the ingredients until smooth and well combined.

3. c. Taste the mixture and adjust the sweetness by adding more honey or maple syrup if desired.

4. d. Pour the mixture into popsicle molds, leaving a little space at the top for expansion during freezing.

5. e. If desired, sprinkle some shredded coconut on each popsicle for added texture.

6.f. Insert popsicle sticks into the molds and place them in the freezer.

7.g. Freeze for 4-6 hours or until completely firm.

8.h. Once the popsicles are frozen, remove them from the molds by running them under warm water for a few seconds.

9.i. Serve the coconut lime popsicles immediately or store them in an airtight container in the freezer.

Nutritional value (per serving - 1 popsicle):

Calories: 100 Protein: 6g Fat: 6g Sodium: 20mg

Orange Chocolate Truffles

Total Servings: 12 truffles.
Preparation Time: 20 minutes.
Time to Chill: 1 hour.

Ingredients:

- 1 cup pitted dates
- 1/2 cup raw almonds
- Zest of 1 orange
- 2 tablespoons unsweetened cocoa powder
- 1/2 teaspoon vanilla extract
- Pinch of salt
- Unsweetened shredded coconut for rolling (optional)

Instructions:

1. a. Cover the pitted dates in a bowl with warm water. Let them soak for 10 minutes to soften.

2.b. Drain the dates and pat them dry with a paper towel.

3.c. combine the soaked dates, raw almonds, orange zest, cocoa powder, vanilla extract, and salt in a food processor.

4.d. Process the mixture until it forms a sticky dough-like consistency.

5.e. Scoop tablespoon-sized portions of the mixture and roll them into balls using your hands.

6.f. If desired, roll the truffles in unsweetened shredded coconut for additional texture and flavor.

7.g. Place the truffles on a parchment-lined tray or plate and refrigerate them for at least 1 hour to firm up.

8.h. Once chilled, remove the truffles from the refrigerator and serve immediately, or store them in an airtight container in the fridge for up to a week.

Nutritional value (per serving - 2 truffles):

Calories: 150 Protein: 3g Fat: 6g Sodium: 20mg

Berry Frozen Yogurt

Total Servings: 4 servings.
Preparation Time: 10 minutes.
Time to Freeze: 4-6 hours.

Ingredients:

- 2 cups frozen mixed berries (such as strawberries, blueberries, and raspberries)
- 2 cups plain Greek yogurt
- 2 tablespoons honey or maple syrup
- 1 teaspoon vanilla extract

Instructions:

1. a. In a blender or food processor, combine the frozen mixed berries, Greek yogurt, honey or maple syrup, and vanilla extract.

2.b. Blend the ingredients until smooth and well combined.

3.c. Taste the mixture and adjust the sweetness by adding more honey or maple syrup if desired.

4.d. Pour the mixture into a shallow container or loaf pan.

5.e. Smooth the top with a spatula and cover the container with plastic wrap or a lid.

6.f. Place the container in the freezer and let the mixture freeze for 4-6 hours or until firm.

7.g. Every 30 minutes for the first 2 hours, remove the container from the freezer and stir the mixture with a fork to prevent ice crystals from forming.

8.h. Once the frozen yogurt is completely frozen, remove it from the freezer and let it sit at room temperature for a few minutes to soften slightly.

9.i. Scoop the berry frozen yogurt into bowls or cones and serve immediately.

Nutritional value (per serving - 1/2 cup):

Calories: 100 Protein: 8g Fat: 0g Sodium: 30mg

Apple Cinnamon Crisp

Total Servings: 4 servings.
Preparation Time: 15 minutes.
Time to Cook: 30-35 minutes.

Ingredients:

- 4 medium-sized apples, peeled, cored, and sliced
- 1 tablespoon lemon juice
- 1/2 cup rolled oats
- 1/4 cup almond flour
- 2 tablespoons honey or maple syrup

- 1 tablespoon melted coconut oil
- 1 teaspoon ground cinnamon
- 1/4 teaspoon salt

Instructions:

1. a. Preheat the oven to 350°F (175°C) and lightly grease a baking dish.

2. b. In a bowl, toss the apple slices with lemon juice to prevent browning.

3. c. Spread the apple slices evenly in the prepared baking dish.

4. d. In a separate bowl, combine the rolled oats, almond flour, honey or maple syrup, melted coconut oil, cinnamon, and salt. Mix well until the mixture forms a crumbly texture.

5. e. Sprinkle the oat mixture over the apple slices, covering them evenly.

6. f. Bake in the oven for 30-35 minutes until the apples are tender, and the topping is golden brown.

7. g. Remove from the oven and let it cool for a few minutes before serving.

8. h. Serve the apple cinnamon crisp warm or at room temperature. It pairs well with a dollop of Greek yogurt or a scoop of vanilla ice cream if desired.

Nutritional value (per serving):

Calories: 180 Protein: 2g Fat: 6g Sodium: 75mg

Almond Joy Bites

Total Servings: 10 bites.
Preparation Time: 15 minutes.
Time to Chill: 30 minutes.

Ingredients:

- 1 cup unsweetened shredded coconut
- 1/4 cup almond butter
- 2 tablespoons honey or maple syrup
- 2 tablespoons unsweetened cocoa powder
- 1/2 teaspoon vanilla extract
- Pinch of salt
- 10 whole almonds for garnish (optional)

Instructions:

1. a. In a mixing bowl, combine the shredded coconut, almond butter, honey or maple syrup, cocoa powder, vanilla extract, and salt. Mix well until the mixture is evenly combined.

2. b. Roll tablespoon portions of the mixture into small balls using your hands.

3. c. If desired, press a whole almond into the center of each bite.

4. d. Place the almond joy bites on a baking sheet or plate lined with parchment paper.

5. e. Refrigerate the bites for at least 30 minutes to allow them to firm up.

6. f. Once chilled, remove the almond joy bites from the refrigerator and serve immediately.

7. g. Store any leftovers in an airtight container in the refrigerator for up to one week.

Nutritional value (per serving - 1 bite):

Calories: 90 Protein: 2g Fat: 7gSodium: 10mg

+

Chapter 14:

30 days meal plan

Week 1

Day	Breakfast	A.m/P.m Snack	Lunch	Dinner
Monday	Berry Yogurt Parfait	Crunchy Veggie Sticks with Greek Yogurt Dip	Tomato Basil Soup	Spicy Grilled Shrimp
Tuesday	Veggie Omelet	Baked Sweet Potato Fries	Grilled Shrimp Skewers	Herb-Roasted Chicken Breast with Vegetables
Wednesday	Overnight Chia Pudding	Roasted Chickpeas	Chicken Noodle Soup	Ginger Soy Beef
Thursday	Avocado Toast	Fruit Kabobs	Minestrone Soup	Orange Glazed Salmon
Friday	Green Smoothie Bowl	Almond Energy Bites	Butternut Squash Soup	Honey Mustard Turkey
Saturday	Quinoa Breakfast Bowl	Guacamole Stuffed Cucumbers	Black Bean Soup	Rosemary Roasted Pork
Sunday	Egg White Scramble	Quinoa Trail Mix	Broccoli Cheddar Soup	Chipotle Chicken Skewers

Week 2

Day	Breakfast	A.m/P.m Snack	Lunch	Dinner
Monday	Banana Pancakes	Apple Slices with Nut Butter	Mushroom Soup	Citrus Herb Baked Fish
Tuesday	Spinach Feta Frittata	Mediterranean Hummus Plate	Spinach Tortellini Soup	Turkey and Spinach Patties
Wednesday	Almond Butter Toast	Roasted Edamame	Corn Chowder	Mediterranean Grilled Lamb
Thursday	Greek Yogurt Bowl	Avocado Toast Bites	Grilled Salmon Fillet	Pan Seared Scallops
Friday	Sweet Potato Hash	Nutty Granola Bars	Lemon Garlic Shrimp	Garlic Butter Shrimp
Saturday	Blueberry Protein Shake	Beet Chips	Baked Cod Fish	Sesame Ginger Salmon
Sunday	Oatmeal with Berries	Smoked Salmon Cucumber Roll-Ups	Spicy Cajun Prawns	Spicy Sriracha Shrimp

Week 3

Day	Breakfast	A.m/P.m Snack	Lunch	Dinner
Monday	Smoked Salmon Wrap	Berry Yogurt Bark	Teriyaki Glazed Salmon	Grilled Halibut Fillet
Tuesday	Peanut Butter Banana Smoothie	Sweet and Spicy Nuts	Lemon Dill Trout	Herb-Roasted Sea Bass
Wednesday	Veggie Breakfast Burrito	Berry Chia Pudding	Grilled Tuna Steak	Lemon Pepper Cod
Thursday	Quinoa Fruit Salad	Dark Chocolate Bites	Citrus Herb Baked Fish	Teriyaki Shrimp Skewers
Friday	Spinach Mushroom Omelet	Frozen Yogurt Bark	Grilled Chicken Breast	Cajun Blackened Catfish
Saturday	Apple Cinnamon Overnight Oats	Almond Butter Cookies	Baked Salmon Fillet	Baked Lemon Herb Tilapia
Sunday	Mediterranean Egg Muffins	Fruit Salad Parfait	Turkey Meatballs	Garlic Herb Roasted Chicken

Week 4

Days	Breakfast	A.m/P.m Snack	Lunch	Dinner
Monday	Almond Flour Pancakes	Banana Nice Cream	Beef Stir Fry	Tomato Basil Soup
Tuesday	Walnut Banana Bread	Greek Yogurt Popsicles	Tomato Basil Soup	Lemon Garlic Shrimp
Wednesday	Quinoa Breakfast Cookies	Veggie Spring Rolls	Lentil Vegetable Soup	Sesame Ginger Salmon
Thursday	Spinach and Tomato Wrap	Almond Butter Cookies	Black Bean Soup	Spicy Sriracha Shrimp
Friday	Raspberry Chia Pudding	Caprese Skewers	Mushroom Soup	Grilled Halibut Fillet
Saturday	Greek Yogurt Parfait	Avocado Toast Bites	Spinach Tortellini Soup	Herb-Roasted Sea Bass
Sunday	Veggie Frittata Muffins	Roasted Edamame	Broccoli Cheddar Soup	Lemon Pepper Cod

Week 5

Days	Breakfast	A.m/P.m Snack	Lunch	Dinner
Monday	Berry Yogurt Parfait	Fruit Salad Parfait	Chicken and Rice Soup	Teriyaki Shrimp Skewers
Tuesday	Greek Yogurt Bowl	Greek Yogurt Dip with Crunchy Veggie Sticks	Italian Wedding Soup	Baked Lemon Herb Tilapia

Chapter 15:

Conclusion

Remember, your heart is the epicenter of vitality, the rhythm that fuels your every beat. Through the pages of this cookbook, you've discovered the keys to nurturing and protecting this invaluable organ. From deliciously wholesome meals to refreshing snacks and indulgent desserts, you've unlocked a treasure trove of heart-healthy options that are as delectable as they are beneficial.

As you savor each bite, know you're consciously prioritizing your heart health. Feel the surge of energy, the clarity of mind, and the inner radiance that stems from nourishing your body with love and care. Every ingredient graces your plate is a testament to your commitment to a vibrant life.

Let this cookbook be your steadfast companion on your journey towards heart-healthy living. Share its wisdom with loved ones, spreading the joy of wholesome eating and its profound impact on our lives. Together, we can create a world where vibrant hearts beat in harmony and lives are enriched with vitality.

So, as you close this book, remember that the power to nurture your heart and transform your life lies within your hands. Embrace the delicious flavors, the vibrant colors, and the nutritional choices that will elevate your well-being. Let your heart lead the way, and may your journey be filled with joy, abundance, and an unyielding commitment to heart health.

Go forth, dear reader, and let your heart soar, for a healthier, happier life awaits.

Made in United States
Orlando, FL
07 October 2023